Career De Interventions for Social Justice

Career Development Interventions for Social Justice

Addressing Needs across the Lifespan in Educational, Community, and Employment Contexts

Edited by
Margo A. Jackson
Allyson K. Regis
Kourtney Bennett

ROWMAN & LITTLEFIELD
Lanham • Boulder • New York • London

Associate Editor: Katie O'Brien
Production Editor: Jessica McCleary

Published by Rowman & Littlefield
An imprint of The Rowman & Littlefield Publishing Group, Inc.
4501 Forbes Boulevard, Suite 200, Lanham, Maryland 20706
www.rowman.com

6 Tinworth Street, London SE11 5AL

British Library Cataloguing in Publication Information Available

Library of Congress Cataloging-in-Publication Data

Names: Jackson, Margo A., editor. | Regis, Allyson K., 1989– editor. | Bennett, Kourtney, 1985– editor.
Title: Career development interventions for social justice : addressing needs across the lifespan in educational, community, and employment contexts / edited by Margo A. Jackson, Allyson K. Regis, Kourtney Bennett.
Description: Lanham, Maryland : Rowman & Littlefield, [2019] | Includes bibliographical references and index.
Identifiers: LCCN 2018038199 (print) | LCCN 2018048797 (ebook) | ISBN 9781538124901 (electronic) | ISBN 9781538124888 (cloth : alk. paper) | ISBN 9781538124895 (pbk. : alk. paper)
Subjects: LCSH: Vocational guidance—Social aspects. | Career development—Social aspects. | Social justice.
Classification: LCC HF5381 (ebook) | LCC HF5381 .C26557 2019 (print) | DDC 331.702—dc23
LC record available at https://lccn.loc.gov/2018038199

Printed in the United States of America

Contents

Part III: Career Development Interventions for Social Justice Needs in Educational Contexts with Underserved Adolescents (High School Ages)

Part IV: Career Development Interventions for Social Justice Needs in Educational Contexts with Underserved College Students

Part V: Career Development Interventions for Social Justice Needs in Educational Contexts in Diversity Training with Colleges and Universities

Part VI: Career Development Interventions for Social Justice Needs in Community and Employment Contexts with Underserved Adolescents

Part VII: Career Development Interventions for Social Justice Needs in Community and Employment Contexts with Underserved Adults

Part VIII: Career Development Interventions for Social Justice Needs in Community and Employment Contexts with Underserved Older Adults

Preface

PURPOSE OF THE BOOK AND INTENDED AUDIENCE

Social justice has been defined as action focused on promoting equitable access to resources, human rights, and fairness in policies and practices (Toporek, Sapigao, & Rojas-Arauz, 2017). Social justice action and advocacy by counselors and psychologists are needed because social injustices persist as barriers to empathic understanding, effective communication, and healthy human development. Career development interventions can serve as one means to constructively address the problems of inequitable access to educational and occupational options and achievement that promote health and well-being (Jackson, Leon, & Zaharopoulos, 2010).

Career development entails the lifelong process of managing one's learning and work in order to move toward one's preferred future (Canadian Council for Career Development, 2018). A counseling intervention is a professional response to a problem or need (Campbell & Bragg, 2007). This edited book provides practical examples of career development interventions that address social justice needs in a range of contexts across the lifespan. *Career Development Interventions for Social Justice: Addressing Needs across the Lifespan in Educational, Community, and Employment Contexts* is grounded in theoretical perspectives, scientific evidence, and professional competencies for best practices in multicultural career counseling and social justice advocacy.

Each chapter offers a sample career development intervention that is tailored to the needs and context of a specific underserved group of individuals.

The details outlined in these samples will help readers consider how they might adapt relevant components to their own contexts and with the particular populations they serve. The presentation of each of these interventions integrates relevant career development theory, research, ethical and multicultural considerations, and elements of sound program design and evaluation. In each chapter, relevant competencies in career counseling and social justice advocacy are highlighted by two tables that outline how designing and implementing that chapter's career development intervention might help counselors develop skills in these areas.

Unique to this book are the contributions of authors, including practicing professional counselors and psychologists, who share their personal reflections of self-awareness from privileged and marginalized identities regarding potential biases and resources of relevance to their chapter's intervention. The value added in social justice advocacy and sound career counseling practice is highlighted by these authors' examples of their own engagement in this critically important and ongoing process for promoting multicultural self-awareness. In the process of designing and providing career development services for individuals from marginalized groups, it is imperative for counselors to continually reflect on and consult about their own biases and resources for empathic understanding and effectiveness with those whom we serve (Jackson & Mathew, 2017).

This book will serve as a valuable resource for counselors, psychologists, trainees, and educators for selecting, adapting, and implementing career development interventions to serve underserved needs of diverse students and clients across the lifespan in a range of contexts. As a primary market, graduate courses in career development and counseling are required by the national accreditation or state licensing standards for most programs in U.S. colleges and universities that train master's-level counselors in the human services helping professions, for example, in mental health, school, rehabilitation, community, and marriage/relationship and family counseling (Jackson & Scheel, 2013). Also, core competency components of doctoral training in counseling psychology include scientist-practitioner approaches to promote culturally relevant career development (Fouad & Jackson, 2013). Thus, this book may be of interest as a primary or supplementary textbook to many graduate programs in counseling and counseling psychology that require foundational courses in career counseling and in the psychology of career development theory, research, and practice.

As a secondary market, practicing professional counselors, psychologists, and other social service providers (e.g., social workers) and educators (e.g., teachers, human resource trainers, student development specialists) may be interested in this book. Practitioners may use the book as a professional resource for selecting, adapting, and implementing career development activities and programs to better address the needs of those whom they serve.

Finally, this book may serve as a resource to researchers in career counseling and vocational psychology. In particular, researchers might select career development interventions presented in this book to empirically investigate, better understand, and evaluate explanations for what works for whom and under what conditions.

HOW THE BOOK CAME TO BE

The first coeditor of this book, Margo A. Jackson, is a professor of counseling psychology who has practiced for many years as a career counselor. She has also taught master's and doctoral courses in theory, research, assessment, and practice of career development in accredited programs in counseling psychology, mental health counseling, and bilingual school counseling. In her experience, Dr. Jackson had found books that well covered many foundational aspects of career counseling practice. She found no books, however, that well integrated these aspects to provide (a) practical examples of career development interventions at points along the lifespan that specifically addressed social justice needs, and (b) methods for counselors and trainees to apply relevant competencies to specific interventions they might develop of personal interest and professional value. Thus, she designed a rubric for a final paper assignment to help students integrate key foundational elements of culturally relevant theory, research, and practice in career counseling into a career development intervention proposal of relevance to their own professional practice interests. Dr. Jackson selected exemplary final papers and invited their authors, most of whom are now practicing counselors and psychologists, to develop these proposals into chapter manuscripts for this book. Two of these former students, Dr. Allyson K. Regis and Dr. Kourtney Bennett, took the initiative to serve as coeditors in developing this book. These three coeditors have not only provided their own chapter contributions, but they have also closely mentored all the contributors through the process of updating and developing their exemplary final papers or conceptualizations into chapters designed for this book.

CHAPTER-BY-CHAPTER ORGANIZATION AND CONTENT DESCRIPTIONS

Each chapter begins with the title of the career development intervention and an abstract. Thereafter, adapting a template for effective program design and evaluation, the subheadings of each chapter generally include (in roughly the following order or in some combination):

- Social Justice Needs and Rationale for the Career Development Intervention
- Measurable Objectives and Expected Outcomes
- Plan for Promoting Services
- Plan for Delivering Services
- Intervention Program Content
- Resources Needed
- Methods of Evaluation
- Plan for Revision
- Reflections on Counselor Self-Awareness of Potential Resources and Biases from Privileged and Marginalized Identities

All the chapters integrate career development theoretical frameworks (e.g., in the rationale for the intervention and program content). Most chapters integrate ethical and multicultural considerations at various points in the career development interventions outlined; however, some chapters include a separate subheading for "Ethical Considerations." Several chapters include a "Conclusion" subheading. Within each chapter, relevant competencies in career counseling and social justice advocacy are highlighted by two tables (titled, respectively, "Relevance to Career Counseling Competencies" and "Relevance to Advocacy Competencies"). These chapter tables correspond to the competencies outlined in the two appendices of the book, appendix A, "Career Counseling Competencies" and appendix B, "Advocacy Competencies." Most chapters include appendix supplements with, for example, program outlines, worksheets, or additional resources.

The fifteen chapters of the book are organized developmentally across the lifespan, ranging from underserved elementary school–aged children to underserved older adults. Furthermore, the chapters are organized into eight parts. Parts I–V are on career development intervention in educational contexts," and parts VI–VIII deal with career development intervention in community and employment contexts.

Chapter 1 is titled "Antibias Career Development for Evolving Identities in Elementary School Children." The authors, Broems and Jackson, propose a program to enhance the effectiveness of antibias education with young children by incorporating activities to help them expand their learning about themselves, each other, and potential career interests and abilities that challenge stereotypes. With young adolescents of middle school age, chapter 2 presents a career development intervention for "Identifying Strength-Based Transferable Skills from Personal Accomplishment Narratives to Expand Educational/Career Pathways with Marginalized Youth." The authors (Jackson, Dillon, Bennett, and Regis) describe how the intervention was developed with youth from members of groups underrepresented in STEM (science, technology, engineering, and math) professions.

Chapters 3, 4, and 5 offer career development interventions to address social justice needs with underserved adolescents of high school age. In chapter 3, Bennett presents an intervention for "Crossing Sociopolitical Barriers: Promoting Critical Consciousness and Career Development among High School Students." In the focus on sexual minority youth in chapter 4, Huang describes "A Program to Promote Career Development and Counseling Services in High Schools with LGBT Students." In chapter 5, Quiñones proposes a "Step-Up Career Development Program with Unaccompanied Latinx Refugee Youth in Resettlement High Schools." Designed for Latino/Latina refugee youth who fled to the United States without their parents or a previous primary caregiver, this program promotes their becoming career- or college-ready high school graduates with concrete goals for the future.

In chapter 6, designed for a group of underserved college students, Sorensen offers "Gen1 Quick-Start: Academic Major and Career Decision-Making Workshop for Latina First-Generation Freshman." The educational context chapters conclude with a career development intervention designed for diversity training with colleges and universities. In chapter 7, Jackson describes a workshop designed for a range of university community members titled "Coming to Understand and More Constructively Respond to Racial Microaggressions."

The first chapter for community and employment contexts (Part VI) begins with a career development intervention to address social justice needs with a group of underserved adolescents. In chapter 8, Sonnabend proposes a program titled "Girls in Action: Career Development with Juvenile Justice–Involved Adolescent Girls."

Chapters 9–14 offer career development interventions to address social justice needs in community and employment contexts with underserved adults (Part VII). In chapter 9, O'Neill focuses on "Addressing Employment Uncertainty of Rural Working Adults: A Telemental Health Community Workshop." In chapter 10, Hahn offers a "Life-Design Group Course for Laid-Off Workers." In chapter 11, Tucker proposes "Empowering Battered Women with BRAVER." In chapter 12, Kuang describes a "Career Progression Workshop for the Internationally Educated." In chapter 13, Regis and Dillon propose a career development intervention for "Gradually Reintegrating Ex-Offenders into the Workforce." In chapter 14, Romano proposes a program for "Developing Managers' Skills for Countering Racial Color Blindness and Constructively Addressing Racial Microaggressions in the Workplace."

Part VIII concludes with a career development intervention designed for underserved older adults who are often subjected to ageism. In chapter 15, Selkirk proposes a program titled "Booming through Retirement: Optimizing Psychosocial Resources for Retirement Success in Baby Boomers."

Finally, a range of theoretical approaches and related assessments ground the career development interventions described in this book. These include the major theories of career development: Holland's (1997) theory of vocational personality and work environment types; the theory of work adjustment (Dawis, 2005); Super's (1980, 1990) life-span, life-space theory; Gottfredson's (2005) theory of circumscription and compromise; social learning theory of career decision-making and counseling (Krumboltz, 1996); social cognitive career theory (Lent, Brown, & Hackett, 1994); Blustein's (2006) psychology of working framework; Richardson's (2012) framework of counseling for work and relationships; and Savickas's (2013) career construction theory and life design paradigm. Other theoretical frameworks incorporated in the career development interventions include self-determination cognitive career theory (Johnson, 2013; chapter 13) and resource-based dynamic theory of retirement (Wang, Henkens, & van Solinge, 2011; chapter 15).

A range of theories may serve as potential explanatory frameworks from various perspectives. We view the role of theoretical grounding as a framework from which counselors can name their assumptions and seek both confirming and disconfirming evidence in the process of gathering assessment data and tailoring interventions to effectively help those whom they serve. Grounded also in research evidence and professional competencies for best practices in multicultural career counseling and social justice advocacy, this book offers practical examples of career development interventions that may be adapted to constructively address social justice needs at various points across the lifespan in educational, community, and employment contexts.

REFERENCES

Blustein, D. L. (2006). *The psychology of working: A new perspective for career development, counseling, and public policy.* Mahwah, NJ: Erlbaum.

Campbell, M., & Bragg, N. (2007). The bigger picture: Social work educators' role in civic engagement. In M. Nadel, V. Majewski, & M. Sullivan-Cosetti (Eds.), *Social work service learning: Partnerships for social justice* (pp. 209–218). Lanham, MD: Rowman & Littlefield.

Canadian Council for Career Development. (2018). *What is career development?* Retrieved from http://cccda.org/cccda/index.php/the-career-development-profession/what-is-career-development.

Dawis, R. V. (2005). The Minnesota theory of work adjustment. In S. D. Brown & R. W. Lent (Eds.), *Career development and counseling: Putting theory and research to work* (pp. 3–23). New York, NY: Wiley.

Fouad, N. A., & Jackson, M. A. (2013). Vocational psychology: Strengths, weaknesses, threats, and opportunities. In W. B. Walsh, M. Savickas, & P. Hartung (Eds.), *Handbook of vocational psychology* (4th ed., pp. 305–320). New York, NY: Routledge.

Gottfredson, L. S. (2005). Applying Gottfredson's theory of circumscription and compromise in career guidance and counseling. In S. D. Brown & R. W. Lent (Eds.), *Career development and counseling: Putting theory and research to work* (pp. 71–100). New York, NY: Wiley.

Holland, J. L. (1997). *Making vocational choices* (3rd ed.). Odessa, FL: Psychological Assessment Resources.

Jackson, M. A., Leon, C. A., & Zaharopoulos, M. (2010). Multiculturally competent career counseling interventions with adolescents vulnerable to discrimination. In J. G. Ponterotto, J. M. Casas, L. A. Suzuki, & C. A. Alexander (Eds.), *Handbook of multicultural counseling* (3rd ed., pp. 715–730). Thousand Oaks, CA: Sage.

Jackson, M. A., & Mathew, J. T. (2017). Multicultural self-awareness challenges for trainers: Examining intersecting identities of power and oppression. In J. M. Casas, L. A. Suzuki, C. M. Alexander, & M. A. Jackson (Eds.), *Handbook of multicultural counseling* (4th ed., pp. 433–444). Thousand Oaks, CA: Sage.

Jackson, M. A., & Scheel, M. J. (2013). Quality of master's education: A concern for counseling psychology? *The Counseling Psychologist, 41*, 669–699. doi: 10.1177/0011000011434644.

Johnson, K. F. (2013). Preparing ex-offenders for work: Applying the self-determination theory to social cognitive career counseling. *Journal of Employment Counseling, 50*(2), 83–93. doi: 10.1002/j.2161-1920.2013.00027.x.

Krumboltz, J. D. (1996). A learning theory of career counseling. In M. L. Savickas & W. B. Walsh (Eds.), *Integrating career theory and practice* (pp. 233–280). Palo Alto, CA: CPP Books.

Lent, R. W., Brown, S. D., & Hackett, G. (1994). Toward a unifying social cognitive theory of career and academic interest, choice, and performance [Monograph]. *Journal of Vocational Behavior, 45*, 79–122. doi: 10.1006/jvbe.1994.1027.

Richardson, M. S. (2012). Counseling for work and relationship. *The Counseling Psychologist, 40*, 190–242. doi: 10.1177/0011000011406452.

Savickas, M. L. (2013). Career construction theory and practice. In S. D. Brown & R. W. Lent (Eds.), *Career development and counseling: Putting theory to work* (2nd ed., pp. 147–186). Hoboken, NJ: Wiley.

Super, D. E. (1980). A life-span, life-space approach to career development. *Journal of Vocational Behavior, 13*, 282–298.

———. (1990). A life-span, life-space approach to career development. In D. Brown & L. Brooks (Eds.), *Career choice and development: Applying contemporary theories to practice* (2nd ed., pp. 197–261). San Francisco, CA: Jossey-Bass.

Toporek, R. L., Sapigao, W., & Rojas-Arauz, B. O. (2017). Fostering the development of a social justice perspective and action: Finding a social justice voice. In J. M. Casas, L. A. Suzuki, C. A. Alexander, & M. A. Jackson (Eds.), *Handbook of multicultural counseling* (4th ed., pp. 17–30). Thousand Oaks, CA: Sage.

Wang, M., Henkens, K., & van Solinge, H. (2011). Retirement adjustment: A review of theoretical and empirical advancements. *American Psychologist, 66*(3), 204–213. doi:10.1037/a0022414.

Acknowledgments

We express deep gratitude to the contributing authors who worked diligently to produce these fifteen chapters, which serve as practical examples of career development interventions across the lifespan and are grounded in theoretical perspectives, scientific evidence, and professional competencies for best practices in multicultural career counseling and social justice advocacy. We appreciate how each author contributed a focus on their own professional interests and extended the development of their chapters to support our vision of this book. We are also grateful to these authors for sharing their personal reflections of self-awareness from privileged and marginalized identities regarding potential biases and resources of relevance to their chapter's intervention.

We appreciate all the researchers and writers whose works are cited throughout the text. They provide the foundation on which this book builds to propose career development interventions serving social justice needs across the lifespan in a range of contexts. We thank the practitioners who keep the researchers and educators pragmatically in touch with the reality and complexity of the problems and strengths that their clients navigate on a daily basis. Of central importance, we thank our clients and students. They serve to remind us of our ethical responsibilities—including ongoing development of critical consciousness and social justice action—to live up to the human and professional principles that give meaning and purpose to our personal and professional lives.

From our personal perspectives, we are indebted to our families for their love and support, not only throughout the development of this book but always. We thank many colleagues, as well, for their valuable encouragement and practical help.

Finally, we are deeply appreciative of the Rowman & Littlefield publications team for their adept, patient, and invaluable support throughout the development of the book and entire publication process. We especially thank associate editor Katie O'Brien and former associate editor Molly White.

I

CAREER DEVELOPMENT INTERVENTIONS FOR SOCIAL JUSTICE NEEDS IN EDUCATIONAL CONTEXTS WITH UNDERSERVED CHILDREN (ELEMENTARY SCHOOL AGES)

Antibias Career Development for Evolving Identities in Elementary School Children

Victoria Broems and Margo A. Jackson

The effectiveness of antibias education with young children may be enhanced with learning activities to explore and expand their identity development for considering potential career interests and abilities that challenge stereotypes. This career development intervention also requires that consulting school psychologists, counselors, and teachers engage in continuing education to challenge their own potential biases.

SOCIAL JUSTICE NEEDS AND RATIONALE FOR THE CAREER DEVELOPMENT INTERVENTION

Children illustrate their curiosity with and knowledge of issues in society at an early age, revealing their understanding of differences through dialogue in play, classroom discussion, and peer interaction (Kuh, LeeKeenan, Given, & Beneke, 2016). As children in elementary school begin to develop their identities in awareness of self and others, it is critically important that educators help challenge bias and stereotypes that are rooted in the history of this society, which has built unjust advantages and disadvantages into its institutions and systems. These advantages and disadvantages are enduring and affect the level of access children have to understanding and expanding equitable opportunities for careers in their future. Thus, antibias education in elementary school is essential for promoting optimal child development (Derman-Sparks & Edwards, 2010). Consulting school psychologists and counselors can play a vital role with young children in facilitating their competence development and advocating for social justice, in particular through the career development intervention proposed in this chapter.

A lack of diversity in many career fields, including segregation by gender, racial, ethnic, and other cultural group memberships, is a consequence of unjust social structures and can act as a barrier to entry for young professionals (McWhirter, 1997). These barriers are exacerbated by stereotypes and social injustices that prevail and prevent children from translating their personal and academic interests into a wider range of career options. Inequity in access to resources and the biases that justify this inequity have a pervasive influence on children's lives and shape their self-concept, understanding of others, and perception of what their future careers can be. Psychologists, counselors, and educators should work diligently to raise bias awareness and advance equity where opportunities and resources for children are distributed unjustly (Toporek, Sapigao, & Rojas-Arauz, 2017).

One promising approach is a proposed career development intervention with second graders and their teachers. The intervention plan is based on antibias education principles with young children (Derman-Sparks & Edwards, 2010), particularly in second grade (Goss, 2009), and it focuses on raising bias awareness by which stereotypes such as assumed gender roles and racial stigmas associated with careers can be constructively challenged (Jackson, Kacanski, Rust, & Beck, 2006). This intervention may not only help underserved children gain access to more equitable opportunities for their future careers but also increase bias awareness and expand career exploration with all children. Furthermore, this career development intervention includes continuing education in bias awareness for the teachers and consulting school psychologists or counselors. In order to effectively implement antibias interventions, educators and facilitators must simultaneously challenge their own biases and reflect on how they fit in and identify themselves in the world (Derman-Sparks & Edwards, 2010).

Theoretical Grounding

In *Pedagogy of the Oppressed*, Paolo Freire (1970; 2000) argued that the overriding system of social order maintains a society in which individuals inhibit the voices of and infuse negative self-images into the group it oppresses. Freire claimed that education is required to engage in a learning process to develop *critical consciousness*. This can be defined as awareness to acknowledge and take action against the oppressive aspects that exist in all societal systems. Bias and stereotypes are built into systems such as schools, and a vital role of educators is to use critical consciousness to examine their own privilege and biases as well as act to promote social justice (Jackson & Mathew, 2017).

Stereotypes are "rigid and inaccurate preconceived notions that [one holds] about all people who are members of a particular group, whether it be defined along racial, religious, sexual, or other lines" (Sue, 2003, p. 25). In their book on *Preventing Prejudice: A Guide for Counselors, Educators, and Parents*, Ponterotto, Utsey, and Pedersen (2006) noted the importance of learning activities designed to challenge one's own and others' harmfully limiting stereotypes. "Stereotypes are most powerful when they are unexamined and untested against the reality of the ethnic, racial, or cultural groups being represented" (Ponterotto et al., 2006, p. 210).

In particular, it is imperative that school psychologists, counselors, and educators understand how discrimination, stereotyping, and racism impact career decision-making by children whose access to educational and career development is systemically limited (Parris, Owens, Johnson, Grbevski, & Holbert-Quince, 2010). Restrictive social roles (e.g., by gender, race, and class) are set into place for children before they are able to comprehend and express their perspectives and preferences. With this, children begin to develop a sense of where they fit into the world with limiting biases and stereotypes embedded in their thought processes. For example, girls may think they may become capable of working as a nurse but not as a doctor. Girls and boys from racial or ethnic minority groups may have difficulty imagining themselves in any profession at all, because images in books, movies, and schools fail to depict professional individuals of color as often as they depict professional White individuals (Parris et al., 2010). Limiting stereotypes associated with careers, especially salient for youth vulnerable to discrimination, call for career development interventions that can challenge inferiority assumptions and provide equitable opportunities in future careers for all children.

Regarding the importance of career development interventions in elementary school, Magnuson and Starr (2000) emphasized that "what happens at one level of development will influence subsequent levels" (p. 98). During the elementary school years, children begin to form a sense of their identity in relation to others, and they draw conclusions that include assumptions about their current and future place in the world. It is critical that children experience success and support at this stage for developing their sense of industry or competence versus inferiority (Erikson, 1963). Thus, the elementary school years constitute a key developmental period for constructively challenging children's stereotyped assumptions about their evolving career identities.

Linda Gottfredson's (2005) theory of circumscription and compromise focuses on the cognitive development of evolving vocational self-concepts from childhood to early adolescence to explain why children's vocational expectations become constrained by gender and social class stereotypes. She proposed that as children grow in their awareness of themselves and their social place in the world, they begin to eliminate vocational options as inappropriate (through a process of *circumscription*) or as inaccessible (through a process of *compromise*) based on occupational stereotypes related to gender and prestige. From Gottfredson's theoretical perspective,

> While the process of circumscription and compromise occurs gradually and, typically, without conscious awareness, individuals may be helped to reconsider vocational options they have ruled out as unacceptable in sex-type and prestige through formative new learning experiences or changes in their social environment. . . . [Relevant career development interventions include] exploring a broader range of occupational options and constructively addressing occupational stereotypes related to gender and prestige that might unnecessarily restrict alternatives considered. (Jackson & Verdino, 2012, pp. 1165–1166)

Furthermore, beyond gender binary perspectives, antibias career-development interventions should include considerations with children of transgender identity development.

The career development intervention proposed in this chapter aims to help second-graders to explore and expand their identity development for considering potential career interests and abilities that challenge stereotypes. Its foundational pedagogy is antibias education, an approach in which educators actively seek to counter patterns of institutional bias based on social differences and proactively create classroom environments that mirror the diverse histories and cultures of all children (Chen, Nimmo, & Fraser, 2009). The four goals of antibias education with young children are: building positive social identities, welcoming human diversity, recognizing unfairness, and developing skills to act against discrimination (Derman-Sparks & Edwards, 2010). In the proposed career development intervention, these four antibias education goals are applied to challenge stereotypes that exist in careers through facilitated class discussions, visual representations in classrooms of individuals who challenge stereotypes about careers, and hosting a career day with a diverse group of speakers whose experiences challenge social biases surrounding careers. Second-graders can learn through facilitated discussions and a diverse range of role models, including those who counter stereotypes, to recognize and constructively challenge stereotypes about who can and cannot pursue various career options. This includes learning about the work tasks, conditions, interests, abilities, and values for various career options in which diversity has been limited and stereotypes abound.

MEASURABLE OBJECTIVES AND EXPECTED OUTCOMES

Class discussions, visual representations, and a career day led by a diverse group of professionals are the main components of the antibias career development intervention proposed in this chapter. Measureable objectives and outcomes can be realized through applications of the career development intervention to the four goals of antibias education to build positive social identities, welcome diversity, recognize unfairness, and develop skills to act against discrimination (Derman-Sparks & Edwards, 2010). The following general discussion of objectives and outcomes may be adapted to the specific context and relevant measures through a process of formative and summative evaluation (for resources, see citations under Methods of Evaluation).

The process of building positive social identities in children allows them to understand bias and stereotypes, what they are, and how they operate in society and their desired careers. A key task for educators (teachers, school psychologists, and counselors) is to discuss how people of all genders, races, and ethnicities are able to break prevailing social barriers. In doing this, the expected outcome is that children will build positive gender, racial, and/or ethnic identities that can enable them to feel confident about pursuing their desired career path and feel stronger about who they are in society.

Welcoming human diversity is a goal for students to learn to embrace and welcome differences in their classmates and in society. Through facilitated class discussions, visual representations, and a career day, children will be able to discuss with one another their unique stories and identities, as well as the value of diversity. This objective will be met if students begin to critically discuss diversity in healthy and positive ways, express pride in their different cultures, and are able to welcome all different types of people, both in the classroom and in a range of potential future professions.

Recognition of unfairness or injustice is a central goal of this intervention and social justice in general. The idea that teachers ought to be female and doctors should be male, for example, are unsound and unfair barriers that affect children's perceptions of what type of careers are accessible to them. In learning about stereotypes and actively working to counter them, it is the objective of the career development intervention that children begin to recognize that these socially constructed barriers are unfair and baseless. This will help students to dispute such thoughts and pursue their career interests despite gender, racial, or ethnic norms that prevent them from doing so. It is expected that through this intervention, students will be better able to recognize stereotypes and injustice when they encounter them.

The development of skills to act against discrimination is a goal to build children's capacity to act as change agents in society and constructively confront stereotypes in careers. In implementing the career intervention posited in this chapter, it is expected that it will help students develop skills for how to participate in open dialogue discussions about challenging biases in specific fields and speaking up for others when they are faced with injustice.

The expected outcome for educators who engage in professional development and continuing education to challenge their own biases is that they become more critically conscious and able to recognize internal biases and why they harbor them. It is hoped that educators will become more self-aware and work diligently to address their biases when they arise. It is expected that they will also analyze their privilege and how it shapes the way they think and act (Edwards, 2017; Jackson & Mathew, 2017). In understanding the stereotypes that exist in specific careers, students and educators are expected to learn how to successfully challenge such stereotypes in class discussion, class activities, and peer engagement.

PLAN FOR PROMOTING SERVICES

In using antibias education methods as a means to promote the challenging of stereotypes in careers, it is critical that the consulting school psychologists or counselors have buy-in from administration, parents, and teachers in schools. Using antibias education is not always easy, as bias and injustice are sensitive topics for many individuals and can receive pushback from administration, parents, and teachers. In an article entitled "How to Get Started with

Anti-Bias Education in Your Classroom and Program," Julie Olsen Edwards (2017) highlighted an example from a school that successfully implemented antibias education. The author notes that implementation of this method of education can, at first, generate negative responses from parents with questions or comments like, "Why are you changing our tradition?" and "You're just being *politically correct*." In response to this negative reaction, the school sent out a detailed email explaining the full process of how staff came to the decision to implement an intervention, with examples of stereotypes found in schools and how those messages hurt and hinder children (Edwards, 2017). The school expressed its deep commitment to providing children with interventions and activities that actively represent the diverse world in which they live, rather than abiding by the stereotypes that our society perpetuates and silences. Eventually, the families not only came to welcome the changes, they also began to use antibias education at home. This case study demonstrates the initial struggles that consulting school psychologists or counselors may face when implementing these services. However, through dialogue, administration, parents, and teachers can come to appreciate these services and this approach (Edwards, 2017).

Furthermore, the benefits for young children of early career development programs should be promoted. For example, research has found that effective career development programs in elementary schools help children to not only advance their social understanding, including awareness of self and others, but also build bridges to more complex learning by expanding their understanding of occupational possibilities (Hanover Research, 2012). Consistent with these benefits, the proposed career development intervention would help second-graders to explore and expand their understanding for developing potential career interests and abilities that challenge stereotypes.

Another important step in building support for antibias education as a means to promote career development with young children may include proactively and directly eliciting any questions parents may have through PTA meetings and face-to-face interaction. Posting flyers around schools and in faculty rooms as well as hosting one-on-one meetings with faculty members can be useful in raising awareness among teachers about these services. Evidence-based literature, such as the sources cited in this chapter, can be used to justify and support how antibias education and career development are beneficial for children and society. Literature can be shared both in meetings and via email to optimize knowledge sharing and thoroughly promote these career development intervention concepts in a school.

PLAN FOR DELIVERING SERVICES

Although programs could be prepared for antibias education as a means to promote career development with young children at each developmental level in elementary school, the proposed intervention is designed for second-graders and their teachers. The facilitators who lead the intervention, while consulting and coordinating with the teachers throughout the process, should be professionally well-qualified school psychologists or counselors. The additional qualifications needed for facilitators relevant to this intervention include competencies in culturally relevant career development interventions for young children, antibias education, and demonstrated commitment to engaging in their own ongoing professional development and continuing education. This commitment includes examining their own privileged and marginalized identities as well as applying in their practices critical consciousness and social justice advocacy (Jackson & Mathew, 2017). See tables 1.1 and 1.2 for an outline of competencies in career counseling and advocacy, respectively, that highlight how designing and implementing this intervention might help facilitators develop needed relevant skills (Lewis, Arnold, House, & Toporek, 2003; National Career Development Association, 1997, 2009).

Table 1.1.   Relevance to Career Counseling Competencies

Career Counseling Competency	Addressed by Career Intervention	Relevance to Corresponding Competency
1. Career Development Theory	X	Grounded in Gottfredson's (2005) career development theory of circumscription and compromise, and incorporates psychosocial development (Erikson, 1963), critical consciousness (Freire, 2000), and antibias education (Derman-Sparks & Edwards, 2010).
2. Individual and Group Counseling Skills	X	Facilitators establish and maintain helpful relationships with children in psychoeducational group discussions to challenge career stereotypes, value diversity, and promote community.
3. Individual/Group Assessment	X	May include in program evaluation plan.
4. Information/ Resources/ Technology	X	Obtains, prepares, and uses information, resources, and multimedia to promote culturally relevant antibias career development.
5. Program Promotion, Management, and Implementation	X	Applies recommended approaches to promoting antibias education and research on effective career development interventions in elementary schools.

Career Counseling Competency	Addressed by Career Intervention	Relevance to Corresponding Competency
6. Coaching, Consultation, and Performance Improvement	X	Facilitators maintain consultative relationships with educators to answer questions and promote open dialogue throughout the course of the antibias career development intervention.
7. Diverse Populations	X	Demonstrates competencies to promote culturally relevant career development and antibias education goals to value and support diverse identities.
8. Supervision	X	Facilitators should seek ongoing consultation or supervision to helpfully challenge their own biases and constructively address influences in their roles to ethically and effectively support the intervention.
9. Ethical/Legal Issues	X	Ethical considerations are to be addressed throughout the program in planning, implementation, and evaluation.
10. Research/ Evaluation	X	Considers adapting evidence-based evaluation methods to determine effectiveness of the intervention and to inform revisions.

Source: NCDA, 1997, 2009.

Table 1.2. Relevance to Advocacy Competencies

Advocacy Competency	Addressed by Career Intervention	Relevance to Corresponding Competency
1. Client/Student Empowerment	X	Helps identify students' evolving career identity strengths and resources as well as social, political, economic, and cultural influences that may limit or expand their learning; develops students' self-advocacy skills for considering potential career interests and abilities that challenge stereotypes.
2. Client/Student Advocacy	X	Negotiates antibias career development services and educational activities on behalf of the students.
3. Community Collaboration	X	Develops alliances with the teachers and broader school community to collaborate.
4. Systems Advocacy	X	Evaluation outcomes may inform relevant recommendations to leaders for systemic change at the school.
5. Public Information	X	Information about the program might be ethically communicated and disseminated to the public through a variety of media.
6. Social/Political Advocacy	X	If evidence supports effectiveness of the intervention, facilitators and educators might join with allies to lobby legislators and other policy makers for further support.

Source: Lewis et al., 2003.

The format for delivering the intervention will include facilitated discussions of learning experiences with readings, visual images, interactions with role models who challenge stereotypes about careers, and building advocacy skills for diversity and social justice. The primary setting for the intervention will be the classroom. Yet visual representations of individuals in careers that challenge stereotypes might be extended to the entire school. Also, the antibias career day with community volunteers might be extended in participation (e.g., including parents) and in space at a larger location at the school.

RESOURCES NEEDED

Every successful career development intervention requires adequate resources in order to accomplish its objectives. First and foremost, support from administration, parents, and teachers is necessary. Facilitators might seek funding for literature about antibias education to distribute to faculty and school personnel. Other resources needed are posters, graphics, books, video clips, and other media that portray the value of diversity, particularly with people from social and cultural groups that challenge stereotypes in a wide range of careers. Time commitments from teachers and facilitators will also be needed in order to engage in initial training and ongoing consultation for the intervention and to work together to codevelop and coordinate associated activities, including career-day recruitment and preparation of community volunteers who challenge stereotypes in their careers. Throughout the intervention, time commitments are needed to maintain active communication with teachers to collect and share evaluation data.

INTERVENTION PROGRAM CONTENT

The first step in delivering the antibias career development intervention is to continue dialogue with administration, parents, and teachers that began in the promotion phase. This continued communication helps build relationships needed to plan logistics for service delivery (Edwards, 2017). With this foundation, the facilitators provide training with teachers about antibias education, how it may work in the classroom, and how it may impact the students as well as the teachers. Facilitators might begin the discussion by asking teachers if they have ever noticed if children are choosing to play more exclusively with children of their own racial identity or gender. They might also ask if teachers have apprehension about the news of fatal shootings of unarmed Black people by police, or the persistence of school failure for children of families with low incomes, or any of the insensitive "isms" that society struggles with and allows to impact a child's learning (Edwards, 2017). Opening up the conversation with this discussion can be used to demonstrate how bias plays out in the classroom and affects students. This gives facilitators an opening to explain what antibias education is and how it can be applied to career interventions with young children that may serve as social justice action in both the short and long term. Facilitators should provide the teachers with a list of the resources with relevant literature that helps them to understand the rationale with their students for the antibias career development intervention (see appendix 1.1).

Furthermore, by facilitating teachers in examining their own privileges and biases, this process can help them to better serve their students and realize their success (Derman-Sparks & Edwards, 2010; Edwards, 2017; Jackson & Mathew, 2017). This process of analysis begins with self-refection by using a teachable moment to consider how bias and stereotypes influence our thinking about careers. This can take shape as a series of prompt questions, such as "Who fits the stereotypes about nurses?" and "Who fits the stereotypes about police officers?" and "Why or why not?" With this facilitated exercise, teachers can begin to realize their own biases about potential career options for their own students' evolving interests, abilities, values, and identities. Teachers can make mistakes when implementing antibias education, as it is also a learning experience for them. Although mistakes will be made, this is part of the process; teachers can "learn as they go" and begin practicing in their classrooms as soon as training and literature are reviewed with the facilitators (Edwards, 2017). To enhance self-reflection with the teachers throughout the course of the antibias career development intervention for their students, the facilitators might ask the teachers to keep journals about their students' and their own progress, including challenges and triumphs. The facilitators could collect these self-reflective journals from the teachers at regular intervals in order to review, provide feedback, and helpfully collaborate. Facilitators will provide ongoing support for and consultation with the teachers throughout the intervention.

The next step is to facilitate similar, yet age-appropriate, classroom discussions with the second-graders about stereotypes they perceive as related to a range of careers. Consistent with antibias education, facilitators should promote a learning environment in which the children and adults can freely ask questions, share thoughts and feelings, and engage in dialogues open to diverse perspectives for analysis (Derman-Sparks & Edwards, 2010). Facilitators will begin by engaging students in a discussion about common and popular careers and how they might describe the people in these professions. Children may, for example, describe nurses, teachers, and hairstylists as careers for women in contrast to doctors, police officers, and firefighters as careers for men. Facilitators should nonjudgmentally explore with the children their reasons for more and less stereotyped beliefs about careers. Then, they can help the children learn how to identify stereotypes about careers, which are defined as untrue assumptions (or jumping to conclusions) about who can and cannot do the work of certain careers based on what group they belong to; for example, by gender, race, religion, income, or disability. Facilitators can further explain how career stereotypes, if not identified and challenged, may keep them from learning more about their own and others' developing interests and abilities for what work they may want to do when they grow up. Through further discussions with the students, facilitators can help them deconstruct myths and learn more about various careers, challenge their stereotypes about who is and is not capable of developing skills for different careers, and rethink for themselves and others about potential career options that may counter stereotyped expectations. Continuing discussions will include presentations of images, stories, and experiences of individuals who challenge career stereotypes. (See appendix 1.2, "Examples of Prompt Questions to Facilitate an Elementary School Antibias Career Development Intervention").

In order to reinforce as well as prompt further relevant discussions in the classroom and in other school environments, children will be exposed to pictures posted throughout the classroom of individuals of various ethnicities, races, and cultures, as well as curriculum books, movies, and activities that include diverse group members. Not only will these images depict a wide range of career options in everyday life, but they will also have a specific focus in challenging stereotypes in careers. For example, images might include Latino male teachers, Black female doctors, White female firefighters, male nurses of color, Asian male hairstylists, and Native female police officers. In addition to discussions with the facilitators, teachers can use daily opportunities to promote learning activities in the classroom that help children challenge career stereotypes and realize the four goals of antibias education.

A culminating aspect of the antibias career development intervention will be to demonstrate how in reality, stereotypes that are thought to be true can be challenged and deconstructed in people's everyday lives. By hosting a career day in which individuals who challenge stereotypes come to class to discuss their career and their experiences, students will be able to visualize real-world examples of their classroom discussions. These community adult volunteers will serve as role models for a wide range of careers representing diverse identity groups. They will be asked to share their experiences with challenging biases in their fields, promoting diversity and embracing differences among their peers, and speaking up for others when they are faced with injustice.

With these young children and through the process of challenging career stereotypes that arise inside and outside the classroom, educators will foster an open environment for discussion of social justice that helps realize the four goals of anti-bias education. Children will likely begin to embrace diversity and differences between individuals, while simultaneously developing their own identities and their career interests. Antibias classrooms are vital for children from dominant social groups, such as White males, in order for their members to feel assured about who they are without the need to feel superior to others. For nondominant social or cultural group members, the goal is to enable them to participate fully in the broader society as well as their home culture or social identity group. With a confident identity, children of a nondominant group can learn to negotiate issues that may arise from the differences between their home culture or social group and the dominant culture, and they can learn to advocate for themselves when they encounter injustice (Chen et al., 2009).

METHODS OF EVALUATION

Throughout the program, facilitators and educators should reflect on, consult about, and document all ethical considerations in planning, implementation, and evaluation. For example, in discussions about valuing diverse identities and challenging stereotypes about who can succeed in various careers, a common professional ethical responsibility is to strive to promote the welfare and treatment of others and avoid doing harm (American Psychological Association, 2002).

At the end of the antibias career development intervention program, facilitators should reengage teachers and students for evaluation of the program. To consider the effectiveness of the program, including strengths and limitations, evaluation should analyze the degree to which the intervention helped students and teachers to constructively challenge their own stereotypes about careers as well as met the four goals of antibias education. Evaluation methods may include review of self-reflective journal entries, surveys, and observations.

We recommend considering the evaluation approaches of Goss (2009) and Chen et al. (2009). Relevant evaluation methods might be adapted to the specific school where the antibias career development intervention program is applied. In an article published by the National Association for the Education of Young Children, first- and second-grade teacher Elizabeth Goss (2009), in a low-income urban school with predominantly African American students, demonstrated "how 6- and 7-year-olds can eagerly engage with difficult issues of social justice" (p. 1). Goss described how she developed, implemented, and evaluated her antibias curriculum and teaching in her class focused on the ethics of social justice. Her evaluation data included observations from classroom discussions and meetings, writings from class projects, journal entries by students and herself as the teacher, and surveys of students' parents. For teachers embarking on the antibias journey to become culturally responsive early childhood educators, Chen et al. (2009) developed a self-study tool to support reflection and evaluation of four aspects of relevance to promoting antibias education: self-awareness, including one's own cultural self-identities, personal views of difference, and readiness to respond to bias; physical environment; pedagogical environment; and relationships with the classroom, families, and community.

PLAN FOR REVISION

For every intervention, there is always room for improvement. In evaluating the antibias career development intervention discussed in this chapter, targeted areas of strengths and limitations will surface and will provide insights on specific revisions to plan for the future.

REFLECTIONS ON COUNSELOR SELF-AWARENESS OF POTENTIAL RESOURCES AND BIASES FROM PRIVILEGED AND MARGINALIZED IDENTITIES

Victoria Broems

As first author, I am a student studying to earn my doctoral degree in school psychology while living and working on Long Island, New York. I am a

White, heterosexual woman of European descent (Italian, German, and Irish), middle-class socioeconomic status, and U.S. citizenship. I was born and raised on Long Island in a home in which diversity is not always accepted and White privilege is often denied or not a topic of conversation. During my undergraduate studies, I sought ways to gain more multicultural competence and, in the process, I began to understand more about White privilege and forms of oppression related to racial and gender identities.

In a course on foundations of education taught by a mentor of mine, we analyzed the history of racial and gender privilege in the United States and how they impact and create biases against social groups, especially those that have been historically marginalized. Inspired by this class, I worked with another professor and mentor to identify ways of addressing racial and gender bias in my professional career as a White woman. She recommended I read the book *Waking up White* by Debby Irving (2014). This text began an ongoing journey of recognizing my identity and privilege, and how I may develop and use this awareness to positively impact my practice in the school psychology field. Antibias education has become a primary interest of mine, and I hope to continue to further research the topic in the future.

As an undergraduate, I worked as an intern with school psychologists at two different schools in the Hudson Valley region of New York. In these roles I was often awed by the pervasive influence of racial and gender stereotypes in play, class discussion, and classroom decorations. An incident that struck me most occurred during a classroom observation I conducted during free playtime in a first-grade classroom. I noticed that the classroom became segregated by gender, with boys choosing play stations with blocks and trains and the girls choosing to play at a station with a kitchen set and another with dolls. When a boy walked over to the kitchen station and picked up a doll, the girls at first said, "no boys allowed" but later included him to play. Seeing this, the teacher approached me and said, "Isn't it funny that he's playing with all the girls. He always gravitates toward the girly toys. He's a sweet boy." This comment, which was the most striking aspect of my observation, displays the pervasive effect stereotypes have not only on children, but also on adult educators. It is also important to note that the classroom was decorated and color-coded by gender. Girls were provided pink nametags for their desks, and boys were given blue.

The above example is just one of many stereotypes I have observed in schools. Such stereotypes and displays of implicit biases are also perpetuated outside of schools. I did not say anything to the teacher or student at the time of this incident, as I was unsure how to address the situation in my role as an intern. A discussion about stereotypes, their negative impacts, and ways to counter them, could have been a corrective course of action. Teachable moments like these can be helpful career development interventions. This case speaks to the impact of stereotypes in schools and society, and the importance of antibias education in overcoming them.

Margo A. Jackson

As second author, I am a professor of counseling psychology and a White, middle-aged, heterosexual woman of European descent (English, Scottish, and Irish), Presbyterian religious affiliation, middle-class socioeconomic status, and U.S. citizenship. I was born in New York City and raised in rural upstate New York. I am married to my life partner, a Black man of African and Native American descent, and we have raised two biracial daughters in California and New York. My research, teaching, and service focus on methods to assess and constructively address hidden biases and strengths of helping professionals, educators, and other leaders; career development and social justice advocacy across the lifespan; and training and supervision in multicultural counseling and psychology. I continually strive to develop and use my own awareness of my intersecting identities of privilege and marginalization as resources to promote antibias education goals across the lifespan.

In my experience as a parent of our biracial daughters, when they were young children I was sometimes struck by the pervasive influence of gender and racial stereotypes in limiting their own perceptions and others' expectation of them. For example, at age four one of our daughters commented on a mural painted on a fence at their preschool of four life-size children representing four different racial/ethnic characteristics. She pointed to the White child's image, saying she liked that child best, and she pointed to the Black child's image, saying she did not like that child. Although heartbroken, I tried to nonjudgmentally ask her to explain her reasons; she did not know. Then, we talked about who she knew among her own family and friends who resembled these children's images and what she liked or disliked about each of them from her own experience. I pointed out how sometimes people may think that "White = good" and "Black = bad," but we know from our own experience that the truth is different.

Thankfully, our daughters and family benefited from many more opportunities for experiences that constructively challenged stereotypes in the context of the antibias education provided at their preschool. At the preschool, their teachers ranged in age and included men, women, and people of color. Throughout the preschool environment, activities, and parent cooperative arrangements, the teachers explicitly promoted antibias education goals and outcomes supported by the National Association for the Education of Young Children. These included posters throughout the center showing people in career activities that countered gender and racial/ethnic stereotypes, play stations and activities that encouraged inclusion and exploration beyond stereotypes, and parents and other community members representing diversity coming to share their vocational and avocation passions with the children. Building on this foundation, our chapter proposes an antibias career development intervention with children and educators in elementary school.

APPENDIX 1.1

Antibias Career Identity Development
Sample Resources for Elementary Educators

Articles

Chen, Nimmo, & Fraser (2009). "Becoming a culturally responsive early childhood educator: A tool to support reflection by teachers embarking on the anti-bias journey."

Edwards (2017). "How to get started with anti-bias education in your classroom and program."

Gottfredson (2005). "Applying Gottfredson's theory of circumscription and compromise in career guidance and counseling."

Hanover Research (2012). "Effective career awareness and development programs for K–8 students."

Books

Derman-Sparks, L., & Edwards, J. O. (2010). *Anti-bias education for young children and ourselves*. NAEYC.

Derman-Sparks, L., LeeKeenan, D., & Nimmo, J. (2014). *Leading anti-bias early childhood programs: A guide for change*. Teachers College Press.

Derman-Sparks, L., & Ramsey, P. G. (2011). *What if all the kids are white? Anti-bias multicultural education with young children and families*. Teachers College Press.

Sykes, M. (2014). *Doing the right thing for children: Eight qualities of leadership*. Redleaf Press.

Wolpert, E. (2005). *Start seeing diversity: The basic guide to an anti-bias classroom*. Redleaf Press.

Websites

Exploring Bias and Discrimination in Hiring Practices. (n.d.). Retrieved from https://www
.tolerance.org/classroom-resources/tolerance-lessons/exploring-bias-and-discrimination-in
-hiring-practices.

"Hang Out" with Anti-Bias Education Experts. (n.d.). Retrieved from https://www.tolerance
.org/magazine/hang-out-with-antibias-education-experts.

Minimizing the Impact of Biases. (n.d.). Retrieved from https://www.tolerance.org/classroom
resources/tolerance-lessons/minimizing-the-impact-of-biases.

Professional Development Resources for "Let's Talk! Discussing Race, Racism and Other
Difficult Topics with Students." (n.d.). Retrieved from http://www.tolerance.org/sites/
default/files/general/Lets_Talk_Resources.pdf.

Children's Book Lists Links for Anti-Bias Classrooms

Early Childhood: Learning about Culture & Language. (n.d.). Retrieved from https://social
justicebooks.org/booklists/early-childhood/culture/.

Early Childhood: Learning about Gender Identity. (n.d.). Retrieved from https://socialjustice
books.org/booklists/early-childhood/gender/.

Early Childhood: Learning about Racial Identity. (n.d.). Retrieved from https://socialjustice
books.org/booklists/early-childhood/racial-identity/.

APPENDIX 1.2

Examples of Prompt Questions to Facilitate an Elementary School Antibias Career Development Intervention (adapted from Derman-Sparks & Edwards, 2010; Edwards, 2017)

Questions to Ask Teachers

- Have you ever noticed if children are choosing to play more exclusively with children of their own racial identity or gender?
- In addition to male and female sex role stereotypes, what bias and stereotypes might nonbinary and transgender individuals experience?
- Do you have apprehension about the news of fatal shootings of unarmed Black people by police?
- Do you have apprehension about the persistence of school failure for children of families with low incomes, or any of the insensitive "isms" that society struggles with and allows to impact a child's learning?
- Can you think of a time in which your bias or privilege has impacted your life or identity?

- Who fits the stereotypes about nurses? Why or why not?
- Who fits the stereotypes about police officers? Why or why not?

Questions to Ask Students

- What are some examples of jobs or careers that you have seen adults have?
- How do you describe the people in these jobs or careers?
- Have you ever thought that some careers are only for women or that some careers are only for men? Why or why not?
- What careers are you interested in when you grow up?

REFERENCES

American Psychological Association. (2002). Ethical principles of psychologists and code of conduct. *American Psychologist, 57*(12), 1060–1073. doi: 10.1037/0003-066X.57.12.1060.

Chen, D. W., Nimmo, J., & Fraser, H. (2009). Becoming a culturally responsive early childhood educator: A tool to support reflection by teachers embarking on the anti-bias journey. *Multicultural Perspectives, 11*(2), 101–106. doi: 10.1080/15210960903028784.

Derman-Sparks, L., & Edwards, J. O. (2010). *Anti-bias education for young children and ourselves.* Washington, DC: NAEYC.

Edwards, J. O. (2017). How to get started with anti-bias education in your classroom and program. *Child Care Exchange*, January/February 2017. Retrieved from http://www.anti biasleadersece.com/childcare-exchange/.

Erikson, E. H. (Ed.). (1963). *Youth: Change and challenge.* New York, NY: Basic Books.

Freire, P. (1970; 2000). *Pedagogy of the oppressed.* New York, NY: The Continuum International Publishing Group.

Goss, E. (2009). If I were president: Teaching social justice in the primary classroom. *Voices of practitioners: Teacher research in early childhood education, 4*(2), 1–14. Retrieved from http://www.naeyc.org/files/naeyc/file/vop/Voices_GossFINAL.pdf.

Gottfredson, L. S. (2005). Applying Gottfredson's theory of circumscription and compromise in career guidance and counseling. In S. D. Brown & R. W. Lent (Eds.), *Career development and counseling: Putting theory to work* (pp. 71–100). Hoboken, NJ: Wiley.

Hanover Research. (2012). *Effective career awareness and development programs for K–8 students.* Author: Washington, DC. Retrieved from https://isminc.com/pdf/research-free/school-head/3376.

Irving, D. (2014). *Waking up White and finding myself in the story of race.* Cambridge, MA: Elephant Room Press.

Jackson, M. A., Kacanski, J. M., Rust, J. P., & Beck, S. E. (2006). Constructively challenging diverse inner-city youth's beliefs about educational/career barriers and supports. *Journal of Career Development, 32*, 203–218. doi: 10.1177/0894845305279161.

Jackson, M. A., & Mathew, J. T. (2017). Multicultural self-awareness challenges for trainers: Examining intersecting identities of power and oppression. In J. M. Casas, L. A. Suzuki, C. A. Alexander, & M. A. Jackson (Eds.), *Handbook of multicultural counseling* (4th ed., pp. 433–444). Thousand Oaks, CA: Sage.

Jackson, M. A., & Verdino, J. (2012). Vocational psychology. In R. W. Rieber (Ed.), *Encyclopedia of the history of psychological theories* (pp. 1157–1170). New York, NY: Springer. doi: 10.1007/978-1-4419-0463-8.

Kuh, L., LeeKeenan, D., Given, H., & Beneke, M. (2016). Moving beyond anti-bias activities: Supporting the development of anti-bias practices. *Young Children, 71*(1), 58–65. Retrieved from http://www.naeyc.org/yc/.

Lewis, J., Arnold, M. S., House, R., & Toporek, R. L. (2003). *Advocacy competencies.* Endorsed by the American Counseling Association Governing Council. Retrieved from https://www.counseling.org/Resources/Competencies/Advocacy_Competencies.pdf.

Magnuson, C. S., & Starr, M. F. (2000). How early is too early to begin life career planning? The importance of the elementary school years. *Journal of Career Development, 27*, 89–101. doi: 10.1023/A:1007844500034.

McWhirter, E. H. (1997). Perceived barriers to education and career: Ethnic and gender differences. *Journal of Vocational Behavior, 50*(1), 124–140. doi:10.1006/jvbe.1995.1536.

National Career Development Association. (1997). *Career counseling competencies.* Broken Arrow, OK: Author.

———. (2009). *Minimum competencies for multicultural career counseling and development.* Broken Arrow, OK: Author. Retrieved from https://www.ncda.org/aws/NCDA/pt/fli/12508/false.

Parris, G. P., Owens, D., Johnson, T., Grbevski, S., & Holbert-Quince, J. (2010). Addressing the career development needs of high-achieving African American high school students: Implications for counselors. *Journal for the Education of the Gifted, 33*(3), 417–436. doi:10.1177/016235321003300306.

Ponterotto, J. G., Utsey, S. O., & Petersen, P. B. (2006). *Preventing prejudice: A guide for counselors, educators, and parents* (2nd ed.). Thousand Oaks, CA: Sage.

Sue, D. W. (2003). *Overcoming our racism: The journey to liberation.* Hoboken, NJ: Wiley.

Toporek, R. L., Sapigao, W., & Rojas-Arauz, B. O. (2017). Fostering the development of a social justice perspective and action: Finding a social justice voice. In J. M. Casas, L. A. Suzuki, C. M. Alexander, & M. A. Jackson (Eds.), *Handbook of multicultural counseling* (4th ed., pp. 17–30). Thousand Oaks, CA: Sage.

II

CAREER DEVELOPMENT INTERVENTIONS FOR SOCIAL JUSTICE NEEDS IN EDUCATIONAL CONTEXTS WITH UNDERSERVED YOUNG ADOLESCENTS (MIDDLE SCHOOL AGES)

2

Identifying Strength-Based Transferable Skills from Personal Accomplishment Narratives to Expand Educational/Career Pathways with Marginalized Youth

Margo A. Jackson, Gary L. Dillon Jr., Kourtney Bennett, and Allyson K. Regis

Adolescents in low-income environments, members of racial/ethnic minority groups, and recent U.S. immigrants continue to be subject to limited access to educational attainment and future career options, including those in higher-paying professions in STEM fields (science, technology, engineering, and math). The middle school years are a key developmental period for interventions to expand access to vocational options with marginalized youth. Using a method that integrates science and culturally relevant practice with middle school youth from groups underrepresented in STEM, this chapter presents a career development learning activity. In collaborative large and small groups, trained facilitators help participants identify strength-based sources of self-efficacy through examining their personal accomplishment stories and linking potential transferable skills to consider expanded educational/career pathways.

SOCIAL JUSTICE NEEDS AND RATIONALE FOR THE CAREER DEVELOPMENT INTERVENTION

A significant educational/career achievement gap persists in higher-paying professions, particularly in STEM fields, for women and members of racial-ethnic minority groups, particularly for Black, Hispanic, and American Indians (Fouad & Santana, 2017). Although interventions have been developed to increase STEM interests among youth of color, research evidence suggests these youth report high interest in STEM fields but low self-efficacy or confidence in their ability to succeed (Jackson, Fietzer, Altschuler, & Woerner, 2010). In general, and particularly with vocationally marginalized youth, much feedback in education is focused on errors or failures and less on specific learning from success experiences (Jackson et al., 2011). As a learning activity and career development intervention with a strength-based focus, the PATS (Personal Accomplishments/Transferable Skills) exercise was developed by the first author and her research teams (adapted from Bolles, 2005) to identify evidence for building constructive self-efficacy and expanding access to educational/career pathways in STEM and other professions (Jackson et al., 2014).

Following is a brief chronology and further rationale for the development of the PATS as a strength-based method to use with middle school youth to help address STEM educational/career disparities. The middle school years are a key developmental period for interventions to expand access to vocational options with marginalized youth. Students in middle school are evolving in the development of their potential vocational identities. This process (from a perspective in social cognitive career theory; Lent, Brown, & Hackett, 1994) includes learning experiences that might facilitate or hinder their taking courses in high school in math, science, and college preparation that serve as gateways to access STEM and other professional pathways. As one effort to help address the educational/career achievement gap with middle school youth from groups underrepresented in STEM, the first author has led a series of research-service projects to develop a strength-based, theoretically grounded, culturally relevant, and psychometrically supported survey instrument (the Success Learning Experiences Questionnaire; SLEQ;[1] Jackson et al., 2010, 2011, 2012, 2014). One service component of these projects included providing career assessment and counseling with participants who were middle school youth from low-income and culturally diverse school districts. This included facilitating an experiential career development learning activity, the PATS exercise, designed to help participants identify potential transferable skills by analyzing their accomplishment experiences in life story narratives (essentially, applying a career construction approach to life design; Savickas, 2013). Transferable skills can be defined as abilities to do something well that is learned in one context (e.g., through education or other life contexts) that can be transferred to or applied in another context (e.g., in careers). Transferable skills include those considered central to occupational competence in a range of careers and at many levels in the work-place; for example, communication, problem solving, organization management, leadership, and teamwork (Bennett, 2002; Scherer, 2016).

MEASURABLE OBJECTIVES AND EXPECTED OUTCOMES

While the PATS exercise may be adapted for use with individuals and groups from a wide range of ages and diverse needs in career development, it was designed as one tool for career assessment and intervention with low-income and culturally diverse middle school students to help increase their access to educational/career opportunities in STEM and other higher-paying professions. The objectives of the PATS career development exercise are to help participants (a) consider potentially relevant career-related interests, abilities, and learning experiences for building self-efficacy strengths; (b) share personally valued accomplishment stories; (c) analyze these narratives to identify themes of strength-based transferable skills; and (d) connect to resources for expanding their access to relevant educational and career pathways including STEM opportunities.

PLAN FOR PROMOTING SERVICES

Career development intervention services with the PATS exercise may be promoted in schools, after-school programs, community settings, or summer youth programs that serve middle school students who are members of groups underrepresented in STEM fields. Whether conducted as part of a school's curriculum or an organization's program, qualified PATS service providers should meet with stakeholders to explain the purpose of the PATS learning activity, assess and adapt to relevant needs of potential youth participants, and together develop a plan for implementation and promotion. A range of communication methods for promotion might include orientation meetings with students and families, mailings, posters, flyers, and newsletters and social media postings. It is important to highlight not only the career development focus of the PATS learning activity for expanding access to educational and vocational knowledge and resources, but also its emphasis on nurturing self-efficacy by building on evidence for students' evolving strengths.

PLAN FOR DELIVERING SERVICES

Because the PATS career development exercise is a psychoeducational activity conducted with vocationally marginalized youth, qualified PATS providers should be licensed professional counselors, psychologists, or social workers who have competence in career counseling assessment and intervention that is ethically grounded, developmentally tailored, and culturally relevant (see tables 2.1 and 2.2 for relevant competencies in career counseling and social justice advocacy; Lewis, Arnold, House, & Toporek, 2003; National Career Development Association, 1997, 2009). These qualifications should also include (a) career counseling skills to facilitate constructive group process with adolescents; (b) ongoing development of their own self-awareness in multicultural counseling practice whereby they challenge potential biases and attend to strengths (Jackson & Mathew, 2017); and (c) supervision skills to effectively train and support paraprofessionals and other PATS facilitators.

Table 2.1.   Relevance to Career Counseling Competencies

Career Counseling Competency	Addressed by Career Intervention	Relevance to Corresponding Competency
1. Career Development Theory	X	The PATS psychoeducational exercise is grounded in social cognitive career theory (Lent et al., 1994); sources of self-efficacy beliefs (Bandura, 1986); Holland's (1997) theory of vocational types; and the theory of career construction (Savickas, 2013).
2. Individual and Group Counseling Skills	X	PATS facilitators use individual and group career counseling skills with participants.
3. Individual/Group Assessment	X	Facilitators help participants assess valued vocational interests and abilities then identify potentially related sources of self-efficacy strengths in their accomplishment stories.
4. Information/ Resources/ Technology	X	Facilitators provide participants with take-home resources to find educational and career information (e.g., from trustworthy online sources) related to their PATS results that expands their vocational development.
5. Program Promotion, Management, and Implementation	X	PATS providers use skills to develop, plan, implement, and manage this career development learning activity with facilitators and stakeholders at the school or program site.

Career Counseling Competency	Addressed by Career Intervention	Relevance to Corresponding Competency
6. Coaching, Consultation, and Performance Improvement	X	Qualified PATS providers train and coach facilitators to engage in expanding culturally relevant and strength-based career development services with vocationally marginalized youth.
7. Diverse Populations	X	Facilitators demonstrate an understanding of achievement gaps in STEM fields, particularly among women and people of color, as a social justice rationale for PATS services.
8. Supervision	X	Qualified PATS providers provide career counseling supervision to facilitators in implementing PATS services during the process of training.
9. Ethical/Legal Issues	X	PATS providers, with participants and facilitators whom they train and supervise, demonstrate the knowledge and awareness essential for ethical and legal practice in career development assessment and intervention with vocationally marginalized middle school youth.
10. Research/ Evaluation	X	The PATS exercise is empirically grounded, and providers, facilitators, and stakeholders review program evaluation to make improvements.

Source: NCDA, 1997, 2009.

Table 2.2.   Relevance to Advocacy Competencies

Advocacy Competency	Addressed by Career Intervention	Relevance to Corresponding Competency
1. Client/Student Empowerment	X	The PATS exercise fosters skills that empower students in identifying career development resources relevant to expanding their self-awareness of valued strengths.
2. Client/Student Advocacy	X	PATS providers negotiate services on behalf of vocationally marginalized youth with school or community program stakeholders, helping youth gain access to expanded career development resources.
3. Community Collaboration	X	PATS providers and facilitators are positioned to act as allies to schools and community programs that serve youth from groups underrepresented in STEM.

(*continued*)

Table 2.2. *Continued*

Advocacy Competency	Addressed by Career Intervention	Relevance to Corresponding Competency
4. Systems Advocacy	X	The PATS is an early intervention (in middle school) and strength-based method aimed to address gender, racial, ethnic, and socioeconomic disparities in STEM fields.
5. Public Information	X	PATS providers and facilitators share relevant knowledge and resources tailored to using career assessments and accomplishment narratives to expand career development with vocationally marginalized youth.
6. Social/Political Advocacy	X	If evaluation data and future research support the efficacy of the PATS exercise, then results might be used to address how laws and public policies might be improved to expand career development and access, particularly to STEM opportunities, with vocationally marginalized youth.

Source: Lewis et al., 2003.

INTERVENTION PROGRAM CONTENT

Part 1: Introduction

Following is an introductory script about the PATS exercise for facilitators to relay with participants. PATS stands for Personal Accomplishments/ Transferable Skills. Many of us may not be aware of, or tend to take for granted, what we are good at (our abilities). Also, we may not have thought about how our abilities intersect with or relate to our interests (what we like) and our values (what is important to us). By analyzing a few of our own personally important accomplishments, we can use the PATS to help us identify some of our most valued abilities that may be developed into transferable skills and applied in a wide range of careers and educational pathways—that is, to find career pathways that may not only build on your own strengths but also give you joy in how *you* may make a difference in the world. We will start with handouts developed for the PATS exercise.

Part 2: Interests and Abilities

Facilitators display and distribute the handout titled "Vocational Interests and Abilities Valued" (figure 2.1; adapted from "The Party" exercise in

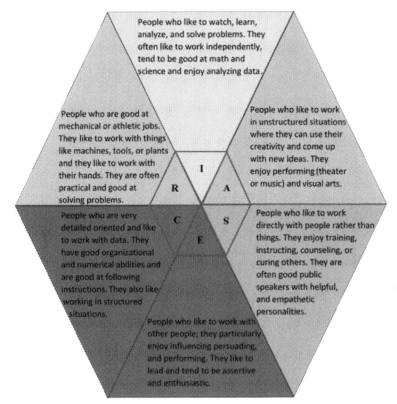

People who like to watch, learn, analyze, and solve problems. They often like to work independently, tend to be good at math and science and enjoy analyzing data.

People who are good at mechanical or athletic jobs. They like to work with things like machines, tools, or plants and they like to work with their hands. They are often practical and good at solving problems.

People who like to work in unstructured situations where they can use their creativity and come up with new ideas. They enjoy performing (theater or music) and visual arts.

People who are very detailed oriented and like to work with data. They have good organizational and numerical abilities and are good at following instructions. They also like working in structured situations.

People who like to work directly with people rather than things. They enjoy training, instructing, counseling, or curing others. They are often good public speakers with helpful, and empathetic personalities.

People who like to work with other people; they particularly enjoy influencing persuading, and performing. They like to lead and tend to be assertive and enthusiastic.

Figure 2.1. Vocational interests and abilities valued. *Adapted from* What Color Is Your Parachute? Workbook, *revised (p. 35), by R. N. Bolles, 2005, Berkeley, CA: Ten Speed Press. Adapted with permission.*

Bolles, 2005, p. 35). They then playfully engage participants by prompting them to progressively select (and record on the handout) to which of the six corners of the hexagonal room they might gravitate, first based on their shared interests at this imaginary party and then based on their shared abilities. Thereafter, facilitators lead a brief discussion of participants' experience of the exercise so far.

Next, facilitators explain the basis of the hexagon model. Scientific research has generally supported Holland's (1997) theory of how individuals' career-related personality types may relate to similar types of work environments. Holland's hexagon model has six basic vocational types of interests and abilities: Realistic, Investigative, Artistic, Social, Enterprising, and Conventional domains. Types closer to each other in the model are more similar, and types farther from each other are less similar. Many people may be described by a combination of two or three of the six types. According to

Holland's theory, if people find a work environment that is compatible with their vocational personality, then they may be more likely to be satisfied and productive. Next, facilitators have participants explore and discuss their strongest interests and abilities based on these six career-related domains, to date. Facilitators note how the "predictions" they made through the "party" exercise might be clues to potential educational and career pathways for them.

Part 3: Sources of Self-Efficacy Strengths and Transferable Skills

Facilitators display and distribute the handout titled "Self-Efficacy Strength Sources Model" (figure 2.2; a strength-based adaptation of Bandura's (1986) theory by Jackson et al., 2011). They review the definition of self-efficacy beliefs that is focused on our learning experiences with success (the center circle of the handout). They explain how research has shown that even beyond our abilities, our self-efficacy beliefs are more powerful predictors of performance. Facilitators further explain how this model shows four types of learning experiences that may lead to, or are sources for, developing self-efficacy strength: performance accomplish-

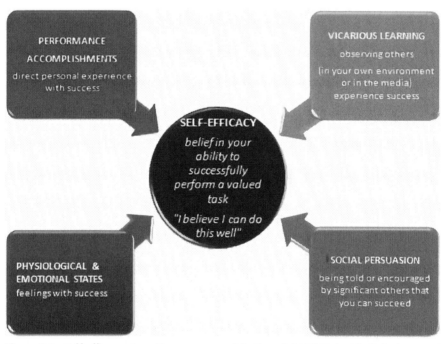

Figure 2.2   Self-efficacy strengths sources model. *Copyright 2013 by M. A. Jackson and G. L. Dillon Jr. Reprinted with permission.*

ments, vicarious learning, social persuasion, and physiological and emotional states (as illustrated and described in the handout, figure 2.2). Then, facilitators lead a brief discussion by soliciting from participants some examples of their own learning experiences with success from these four potential sources of self-efficacy strengths.

Finally, in preparation for part 4, facilitators distribute a list of examples of transferable skills (e.g., Hansen, n.d.). This list can be used to help participants identify in their accomplishment stories some of their most valued abilities and strength-based sources of self-efficacy that may be developed as transferable skills to apply in several potential careers and educational pathways.

Part 4: Sharing and Analyzing Personal Accomplishment Stories

To begin this key part of the PATS exercise (adapted from "My Seven Life Stories" in Bolles, 2005, p. 9), facilitators instruct participants to individually jot down a sentence on a separate sheet of paper for each of three specific times in their life when they did something about which they felt especially proud or happy (something they did that felt like an accomplishment, big or small, that made them feel good or proud or glad). Using a fishbowl group discussion format, the facilitator asks a volunteer participant to tell a story about each of the three personal accomplishments the participant wrote down. The facilitator serves as the interviewer and note-taker (notes to be returned to the participant when done), and the other participants serve as observers and consultants. Interview prompt questions may include: (a) What did you do? (b) Where were you? (c) Who were you with, and what did they say or do? (d) How did you feel? (e) What was important about this to you? (f) What made you most proud?

Next, the facilitator reads aloud the notes to summarize and check understanding in naming the participant's personal accomplishment experiences. Thereafter, the process is to analyze the participant's accomplishment stories to identify what themes and valued transferable skills the participant notices, first by asking the participant to share some observations. The facilitator's own observations follow, then the observing consultation group gives feedback on what themes and transferable skills they notice in the participant's accomplishment stories.

The next step in the process is to have the participant briefly review valued types of vocational interests, abilities, and learning experiences with self-efficacy strengths that the participant had identified (using the handouts, figure 2.1 and 2.2, respectively), and then consider how the themes and valued transferable skills of the participant's personal accomplishment stories might connect or help in discovering new connections. As noted by one middle school participant of color who later served as a co-facilitator of the PATS, "Then they can see that they were more than they thought they were. . . . We all have different abilities than we thought we had" (Jabari Cox, February 8, 2014).

The facilitator concludes the fishbowl part of the PATS by (a) highlighting themes of the participant's valued transferable skills; (b) noting how the participant might find information and helpful resources to explore next steps in their career development and educational pathways (e.g., PATS facilitators may provide take-home informational resources and follow-up career assessment and counseling services); (c) returning to the participant the notes taken; and (d) thanking and applauding all participants. Once the PATS has been demonstrated with the fishbowl method, participants may be directed to assemble in pairs or small groups to take turns completing the PATS, either by alternating in the interviewer and interviewee roles or, ideally, with a trained facilitator for each participant. Facilitators should conclude the PATS with a summary statement about the power of self-awareness in naming, with evidence, one's own valued assets that may be key transferable skills for exploring and pursuing educational and career development goals and pathways.

RESOURCES NEEDED

Resources needed for providing the PATS career development learning activity include (1) PATS providers and facilitators—well qualified, trained, and supervised—who are appropriately compensated (e.g., as employees, as part of their workload, or as contracted service providers); (2) time—for planning, promotion, training and supervising facilitators, conducting the PATS exercise, collecting and reviewing evaluation feedback; (3) space—adequate for the size of the larger group (e.g., a classroom to conduct the fishbowl part of the PATS) then divide into smaller groups that can work productively apart from each other (e.g., without distractions); and (4) materials and equipment—handouts, paper, pens, audiovisual projection with a computer and internet connection for large-group instruction and demonstration of sample career exploration sites for follow-up.

METHODS OF EVALUATION

Methods of evaluation may be developed specific to the needs of the participants and the learning objectives of focus for the site. Generally, a short-term evaluation might include soliciting feedback in a written survey about the degree to which the PATS exercise helped participants to realize the objectives outlined (see Measurable Objectives and Expected Outcomes) and requesting suggestions for improvement. If greater resources are available and the PATS exercise is used to promote further career development learning activities, then researchers might be engaged to design and conduct evaluation studies to investigate more short-term and longitudinal effects (e.g., measuring educational and career-related interests, abilities, self-efficacy, and achievements in STEM fields, with subsequent participation in PATS learning activities at several development points after middle school).

PLAN FOR REVISION

Evaluation feedback should be considered toward developing a plan for revisions to improve future adaptations of the PATS learning activity. If evaluations are positive, then qualified PATS providers might offer professional development training with teachers, school counselors, or other youth program staff members to integrate this learning activity in the site's broader career development curriculum or program.

REFLECTIONS ON COUNSELOR SELF-AWARENESS OF POTENTIAL RESOURCES AND BIASES FROM PRIVILEGED AND MARGINALIZED IDENTITIES

Margo A. Jackson

As a professor of counseling psychology, I embrace the values of my discipline's focus on holistic, strength-based, developmental, vocational, preventative, healthful, multiculturally competent, and socially just advocacy approaches to theory and practice. Furthermore, I endorse a scientist-practitioner approach to training and research-service integration. My own career development and professional identity over the past thirty-six years has predominantly been grounded in a quest to understand how multicultural career counseling can serve as a means to promote social justice access and human development potentials. In my early career counseling practice and teaching, I recall having first read about and adapting two career development learning activities of Richard Bolles—the *Party* exercise and his method of eliciting accomplishment stories to analyze transferable skills. Since then and over these many years, I have continually been inspired by the power and efficiency of these methods for helping me facilitate with a wide range of diverse clients and students a process to "discover" and name their valued strengths and potentially transferable skills, a process that often helps us capture core intersections of their identities, interests, and relevant goals to pursue next. In more recent years, it has been my honor and privilege to work with the coauthors of this chapter—Dr. Gary Dillon, Dr. Kourtney Bennett, and Dr. Allyson Regis—as well as many others (e.g., members of my Participatory Action Research teams, youth participants, and stakeholders) to further develop and disseminate the PATS career development learning activity as a strength-based, culturally relevant, theoretically grounded, and developmentally tailored method to address STEM disparities and expand access with vocationally marginalized youth.

As required for providing any ethical and effective counseling intervention, including the PATS exercise—whether through direct service, supervised training, research investigations, or other leadership roles—I am committed to continually monitor and consult about my potential biases and resources relevant to those with whom I work, solicit and constructively respond to feedback, and further develop my skills in multicultural awareness and social justice advocacy. My potential biases and resources for empathic understanding and effectiveness in this work may be elicited by my perspectives from intersecting social positions of more or less power in my privileged and marginalized identities, respectively. My privileged identities include my position of power as a counseling psychologist and professor, my race, and ethnicity (White and of European descent; English, Scottish, Irish), PhD education, middle-class socioeconomic status, U.S. citizenship, heterosexual orientation, married status, and Presbyterian religious affiliation. More subjugated identities include my gender and age, as a middle-aged woman. My husband and life partner is a Black man of African and Native American descent, and we have raised two resilient biracial daughters. Thus, of relevance to the development of the PATS exercise, I have a vested interest, not only professionally but also personally, in promoting my own daughters' healthy development, including expanding their vocational access and thriving in their process of being and growing their potentials.

Gary L. Dillon Jr.

As a young Black male, I grew up in a single-parent household, raised by my mother in various low-income communities. Our address changed often as we looked for a better place to live, but what didn't change was my mother's dream that I would do better than she and her mother before her did. My mother explained to me at a young age the harsh reality that as a person of color, I would have to make major strides in order to succeed, and education was my ticket out of the impoverished neighborhoods where I resided. She arranged for me to be bussed into better schools in communities where resources were abundant. Many times, I would only see another person of color once I was home, which made me very aware of my own blackness and others' understanding of my blackness in relation to them. It was then that I began to value the idea of a culturally diverse environment within academia.

I went to a local community college in the hopes of raising my grades and getting into my dream school, New York University. When I did gain acceptance into the school two years later, I was again faced with being surrounded by people who looked nothing like me. This only further fueled my awareness of and interest in topics such as academic achievement, retention, and the like, regarding students of color. I could only imagine that if I didn't see people like me in the classrooms, then I would not see them in the positions and jobs that a degree would afford either. In turn, I was motivated by this and channeled my passion for understanding the social justice plight of marginalized populations, within academia as well as other areas of life, into my doctoral research. In particular, I focused on the experiences of undocumented youth (namely Latinx) in their search for education and support, in addition to those experiences of Black men who dealt with racial/ethnic microaggressions. I now translate the observations learned through research and lived experience to identifying the coping, compensatory, and transferable skills that people of color employ to become successful in their lives and careers.

As a psychologist with a doctoral degree, my education attainment and field of study can serve as both a resource and bias. I am very adept at making and establishing connections with others in the space of limited time, and I have the tendency to view and work with people from a strength-based perspective. I also have high hopes for what other people of color can achieve and highly value education and college as a way by which to gain success. My identity as a person of color serves as a resource, perhaps allowing me to connect to other people of color in a way that may be difficult for those who do not have this shared identity. However, as a man with inherent power, I work to become more aware of the ways in which this power may be used or viewed.

Kourtney Bennett

My choice to pursue a career in counseling psychology drew attention to what had often been lacking in my previous attempts to authentically name my personal and professional values. I more explicitly realized the ways in which my intersecting identities shaped my professional journey. As a Black woman, raised in a household where education and professional development were highlighted as core values, I quickly learned, in working with youth of color in career development settings, that while my skin color may have, in some cases, served as a point of connection, my education status and that of my parents sometimes marked a line of privilege and difference. While implementing the PATS program through participatory action research with the chapter's authors, I learned from middle school participants who challenged my assumptions about notions of "achievement" and access to STEM field resources. I was positioned to more honestly process how I, as a clinician, might tailor career development theory in a way that is more grounded in the experiences of the individuals I hoped to serve. Most importantly, I learned that to authentically and competently implement any career development or counseling intervention, I would need to more honestly assess my potential biases, sociopolitical identities, assumptions about career choice, notions of career development access, and beliefs of success.

Allyson K. Regis

As a Black woman who grew up in a diverse New York City neighborhood, I was surrounded by people who shared many of my identities and others who did not. Most of my direct experiences as a child had been with adults in my neighborhood and spending time with the same children at school for many years. While I was exposed to people from various walks of life, I did not understand the effect that our differences could have on our ways of viewing and experiencing the world until I was older.

I did not realize that I had the privilege of growing up in environments—both personally and academically—in which adults strived to foster my self-efficacy. Attending private school and being in academically high-performing ("gifted") classes in public school, I can remember my parents and teachers encouraging me to do my best. They provided me with the physical resources that I needed (e.g., textbooks) and helped me to find my own internal resources that I would need in order to succeed. Being surrounded by classmates who (as far as I knew) also received similar messages from their environment led me to believe that this was the standard by which most people lived. It wasn't until I was in college that it became most evident that others had not been given the same preparation and support.

It's been many years since then, and this is an area in which I am still growing. Through my self-reflection and professional experience as a counseling psychologist, I've thought more about the effects that our interactions with others can have on our sense of self. Importantly, I've learned that it can be hard to see greatness in yourself when it's not reflected in your surroundings. Additionally, many times others are in a better position to see what we cannot about our own abilities. This perspective has affected and been affected by my commitment to strength-based approaches to wellness.

NOTE

1. Research is ongoing in developing the SLEQ. If interested in further information, please contact Dr. Margo A. Jackson: mjackson@fordham.edu.

REFERENCES

Bandura, A. (1986). *Social foundations of thought and action: A social cognitive approach.* Englewood Cliffs, NJ: Prentice Hall.

Bennett, R. (2002). Employers' demands for personal transferable skills in graduates: A content analysis of 1000 job advertisements and an associated empirical study. *Journal of Vocational Education & Training, 54*(4), 457–476. doi: 10.1080/13636820200200209.

Bolles, R. N. (2005). *What color is your parachute? Workbook, revised.* Berkeley, CA: Ten Speed Press.

Fouad, N. A., & Santana, M. C. (2017). SCCT and underrepresented populations in STEM fields: Moving the needle. *Journal of Career Assessment, 25*(1), 24–39. doi: 10.1177/1069072716658324.

Hansen, R. S. (n.d.). *Transferable skill sets for job seekers.* Retrieved from Quintessential LiveCareer, https://www.livecareer.com/quintessential/transferable-skills-set.

Holland, J. L. (1997). *Making vocational choices: A theory of vocational personalities and work environments* (3rd ed.). Odessa, FL: Psychological Assessment Resources.

Jackson, M. A., Dillon Jr., G. L., Welikson, G. A., Regis, A. K., Pagnotta, J. N., Schreyer, G., Bennett, K., . . . Robles, C. (2014, February). *How to identify strength-based sources of self-efficacy and transferable skills to expanded educational/career pathways.* Workshop presentation at the 31st annual Winter Roundtable for Cultural Psychology and Education, Teachers College Columbia University, New York, NY.

Jackson, M. A., Fietzer, A. W., Altschuler, E., & Woerner, S. W. (2010, May). Career-related success learning experiences of academically at-risk adolescents. In M. Barnett (Chair), *STEM career development: Lessons learned from the NSF ITEST program.* Symposium at the annual convention of the American Educational Research Association, Denver, CO.

Jackson, M. A., Hashimoto, N., Holland, Y. J., Bennett, K., Welikson, G. A., Fingerhut, E. C., & Cole, K. (2012, August). *STEM self-efficacy sources in urban youth's career-related success learning experiences.* Poster presentation at the annual conference of the American Psychological Association, Orlando, FL.

Jackson, M. A., & Mathew, J. T. (2017). Multicultural self-awareness challenges for trainers: Examining intersecting identities of power and oppression. In J. M. Casas, L. A. Suzuki, C. A. Alexander, & M. A. Jackson (Eds.), *Handbook of multicultural counseling* (4th ed., pp. 433–444). Thousand Oaks, CA: Sage.

Jackson, M. A., Perolini, C. M., Fietzer, A. W., Altschuler, E., Woerner, S., & Hashimoto, N. (2011). Career-related success learning experiences of academically underachieving urban middle school students. *The Counseling Psychologist, 39*(7), 1024–1060. doi: 10.1177/0011000010397555.

Lent, R. W., Brown, S. D., & Hackett, G. (1994). Toward a unifying social cognitive theory of career and academic interest, choice, and performance [Monograph]. *Journal of Vocational Behavior, 45*, 79–122. doi: 10.1006/jvbe.1994.1027.

Lewis, J., Arnold, M. S., House, R., & Toporek, R. L. (2003). *Advocacy competencies.* Endorsed by the American Counseling Association Governing Council. Retrieved from https://www.counseling.org/Resources/Competencies/Advocacy_Competencies.pdf.

National Career Development Association. (1997). *Career counseling competencies.* Broken Arrow, OK: Author.

———. (2009). *Minimum competencies for multicultural career counseling and development.* Broken Arrow, OK: Author. Retrieved from https://www.ncda.org/aws/NCDA/pt/fli/12508/false.

Savickas, M. L. (2013). Career construction theory and practice. In S. D. Brown & R. W. Lent (Eds.), *Career development and counseling: Putting theory to work* (2nd ed., pp. 147–186). Hoboken, NJ: Wiley.

Scherer, R. (2016). Learning from the past: The need for empirical evidence on the transfer effects of computer programming skills. *Frontiers in Psychology, 7*, article 1390, 1–4. doi: 10.3389/fpsyg.2016.01390.

III

CAREER DEVELOPMENT INTERVENTIONS FOR SOCIAL JUSTICE NEEDS IN EDUCATIONAL CONTEXTS WITH UNDERSERVED ADOLESCENTS (HIGH SCHOOL AGES)

3

Crossing Sociopolitical Barriers

Promoting Critical Consciousness and Career Development among High School Students

Kourtney Bennett

Adolescents find themselves not only at a critical point in biological, psychological, and emotional development when they begin high school, but also at the immediate stepping-stone to their identified vocational pursuits. Developing and becoming aware of vocational identity takes time and adequate resources, a form of support that is not equitably distributed in the United States. In particular, high school students with group memberships that are subject to sociopolitical barriers in school systems and education (e.g., people of color or low income) are underserved in access to career development and counseling. The proposed intervention aims to address and counter some of the barriers high school students knowingly and unknowingly face, drawing upon the social cognitive career theory of vocational development and the Watts five-stage model of critical consciousness to identify ways to improve career outcomes among potentially underserved high school students.

SOCIAL JUSTICE NEEDS AND RATIONALE FOR THE CAREER DEVELOPMENT INTERVENTION

Theorists identify high school as a critical point at which students begin to make choices that may impact and direct career outcomes (Gushue, Clarke, Pantzer, & Scanlan, 2006). Many high school students are inundated by media depictions of success and achievement. Young people are often left striving for what the media has socialized them to believe they are capable of accomplishing (Watts, Abdul-Adil, & Pratt, 2002). In other cases, teens may feel that they are only able to do the things their parents have done (Whiston & Keller, 2004). Moreover, developing and becoming aware of one's career identity takes time and adequate resources, which are not equitably distributed. For instance, as noted by Diemer and Blustein (2006), access to career identity development resources may vary inequitably by socioeconomic status, geographic region, and school district resources. These sociopolitical barriers perpetuate social injustice (i.e., discrimination by race, gender, sexual orientation, religion, and other cultural identity factors), and it is important to address these barriers, with a focus on school-based, career development programming that nurtures appropriate internal and external resources (Diemer & Blustein, 2006). The intervention outlined below aims to challenge some of the institutional and systemic barriers that underserved high school students face in establishing career goals and expanding career exploration. Social cognitive career theory (SCCT; Lent, Brown, & Hackett, 1994) is referenced as a guide for addressing the role of one's social environment in the determination of self and career choice; critical consciousness is considered as a framework for self-empowerment.

Lent and colleagues (1994), grounded in Bandura's social cognitive theory of development (1986), presented a model that explains the way in which career interests and goals are developed and achieved. More specifically, SCCT considers the relationships between a person's cognitive process (such as self-efficacy, goal setting, and outcome expectations) and environmental factors (such as race, gender, sexual orientation, religion, parental support, economic access, and potential barriers) in the development of career interests and the career decision-making process (Lent, Brown, & Hackett, 2000; Lent & Brown, 2017). In the United States, one's social and cultural identity has sociopolitical implications that impact social, political, and economic outcomes (Diemer & Blustein, 2006). It is valuable to consider the role of critical consciousness as it complements SCCT's consideration of the environmental factors that inform vocational development.

"Critical consciousness is theorized to be one 'antidote' to oppression by serving as an internal resource to draw upon in coping with oppression and overcoming sociopolitical barriers" (Diemer & Blustein, 2006, p. 221). Social constructs such as structural racism, inequitable resources, xenophobia, homophobia, transphobia, or religious prejudice can limit the propensity for academic and career achievement for low-income students, students of color, religious minorities, or students of immigrant families (Diemer & Blustein, 2006). The Watts five-stage model (1999) aims to explain the process of developing critical consciousness regarding a person's perceived ability to change or overcome inequities in their communities and social environments; the stages include the Acritical stage, the Adaptive stage, the Pre-critical stage, the Critical stage, and Liberation (Watts, Griffith, & Abdul-Adil, 1999; Watts, Abdul-Adil, & Pratt, 2002; Diemer & Blustein, 2006). It is proposed that recognizing "oppression in one's own life could motivate youth to change inequitable social conditions for themselves" (Diemer, Wang, Moore, Gregory, Hatcher, & Voight, 2010, p. 620).

The Crossing Barriers intervention aims to support high school students with group memberships that are subject to sociopolitical barriers and are underserved in access to career development and counseling. This program can help expand opportunities for career exploration and provide a way for educators, counselors, and administrators to aid these students in understanding the relationship between their cultural identities, sociopolitical barriers, and career development. While students may be aware of differences in career prestige, they may not have been encouraged to explore the role of privilege and sociopolitical barriers in shaping their communities or perceived career options (Diemer et al., 2010). Grounded in SCCT and Watts model of critical consciousness, this intervention aims to address sociopolitical barriers to career exploration and attainment by fostering identity exploration, the development of intrinsic and extrinsic values, and career planning.

INTERVENTION PROGRAM CONTENT

The program consists of three modules: (1) exploring cultural identity; (2) cultural identity, career values, and overcoming barriers; and (3) career exploration and goal setting. Module 1 consists of four to five sessions, considering the following topics: introduction, confidentiality, ground rules, and an icebreaker activity; review of group expectations; considering cultural identity; critical consciousness: power, privilege, and oppression; and critical consciousness: considering sociopolitical barriers (appendix 3.1).

Module 2 includes four to five sessions exploring intrinsic and extrinsic values; value assessment administration such as the Career Orientation

Placement Evaluation Survey (COPES; EdITS, 2017) or the Values Sort (Mucinkas, 2015); sociopolitical barriers that inform values; and the relationship between values, culture, and career (appendix 3.2). Finally, module 3 will consist of six to eight sessions considering career exploration; speed networking preparation and implementation; career advantages and challenges; identifying and overcoming obstacles; and career action planning (appendix 3.3).

MEASURABLE OBJECTIVES AND EXPECTED OUTCOMES

The goal of this intervention is to help expand career interest and increase career self-efficacy by fostering critical consciousness among high school students. Students will be exposed to various career options, identifying the ways in which environmental factors, such as culture and perceived barriers, inform values and establish meaningful career goals. By the end of the program, students will be able to:

1. Define and identify sociopolitical barriers in their immediate and broader community; identify and explore cultural identity (see appendix 3.1)
2. Identify ways in which social and cultural identities are connected to notions of power, privilege, and oppression in the United States (see appendix 3.1)
3. Explain how privilege and oppression influence opportunity (see appendix 3.1)
4. Identify ways to overcome sociopolitical barriers (see appendix 3.1)
5. Express values related to career choice (see appendix 3.2; Niles & Harris-Bowlsbey, 2009)
6. State occupational interests and related career fields (see appendix 3.3)
7. Complete an action plan for reaching defined career goals including required postsecondary education (see appendix 3.3)
8. List possible challenges and advantages of preferred careers (see appendix 3.3)
9. Create a list of internship or volunteer opportunities that can help clarify interest in a career field (see appendix 3.3; Niles & Harris-Bowlsbey, 2009; Swanson & Fouad, 2009)

PLAN FOR DELIVERING SERVICES

Intervention services can be provided in a variety of settings and formats. The intervention includes twenty-one possible sessions and can be implemented with ninth- through twelfth-grade students. Suggested curriculum content was developed using the research of Diemer et al. (2010) and others exploring critical consciousness (Watts et al., 1999, 2002). Media resources such as film, social media posts, or news articles, can be used, at the facilitator's discretion, to highlight sociopolitical barriers in the United States; and individual reflection and group discussions will help students conceptualize structural barriers in the community. Students will be empowered to challenge such barriers through advocacy, engagement with community professionals, and goal setting.

Professionals from a variety of careers that represent the cultural communities of the school's student population will be sought out. Speakers will share their personal stories in presentation or interview format, and students will be asked to consider how the presenters have overcome structural barriers in their perspective communities. Using the career interviews or presentation as a guide, students can complete a career action plan that outlines careers of interest, required training, and internship or service opportunities that would allow for exposure to the career field. Students will have the opportunity to share what they have learned with the class at the end of module 3 (see appendix 3.3).

PROGRAM PLANNING AND PROMOTION

Program planning and promotion will encompass three main areas. First is intervention planning, student participation, and implementation. First, an intervention planning committee will be organized and should include: at least one parent from the school, two students from each grade, the principal or assistant principal, two teachers, and two school counselors. These individuals will agree upon the curriculum and approve the program schedule. Next, students will be invited to participate in a pilot version of the course for one hour after school, two days per week. Finally, upon evaluation of the pilot program, the "Crossing Sociopolitical Barriers" curriculum can be implemented two days per week during the homeroom hour or two days per week for sixty to ninety minutes after school (Niles & Harris-Bowlsbey, 2009).

RESOURCES NEEDED

The primary resources needed to implement this program include staff; training capacity; and electronic, assessment, and literature resources. This intervention can be implemented by undergraduate education students, teachers, school counselors, and school counseling or social work interns. A licensed school counselor or psychologist (see relevant competencies needed in tables 3.1 and 3.2) can train identified program facilitators in the curriculum and offer biweekly supervision of the course. It is expected that each facilitator will require three eight-hour training days prior to the beginning of the school year. Expected time for program facilitators per week, including curriculum development, implementation, speaker recruitment, and evaluation, is five hours per week. The expected time for supervision by a school counselor or psychologist is one hour per week. One to two program facilitators are recommended per program offering.

Table 3.1. Relevance to Career Counseling Competencies

Career Counseling Competency	Addressed by Career Intervention	Relevance to Corresponding Competency
1. Career Development Theory	X	This intervention plan would encourage counselors to review the Social Cognitive Career Theory (Lent, Brown, & Hackett, 1994).
2. Individual and Group Counseling Skills	X	This program requires multiculturally informed individual and group counseling skills with adolescents.
3. Individual/Group Assessment	X	An occupational values assessment is used to explore career identity development and options.
4. Information/ Resources/ Technology	X	Counselors monitor career trends, partner with potential presenters, and identify resources that would broaden access to a diversity of career and postsecondary education options. Additionally, it incorporates multiple forms of media.
5. Program Promotion, Management, and Implementation	X	Coordinating intervention tools, budget, and planning will foster competency in this area.
6. Coaching, Consultation, and Performance Improvement	X	The intervention incorporates the use of an intervention planning committee that serves a consultative role in program implementation.

Career Counseling Competency	Addressed by Career Intervention	Relevance to Corresponding Competency
7. Diverse Populations	X	This intervention serves high school students from diverse groups subject to sociopolitical barriers in access to career identity development.
8. Supervision	X	Counselors must supervise the planning committee and intervention facilitators.
9. Ethical/Legal Issues	X	Ethical boundaries and expectations should be considered in assessment and intervention with students below the age of consent and confidentiality.
10. Research/ Evaluation	X	Program evaluation is necessary.

Source: NCDA, 1997, 2009.

Table 3.2. Relevance to Advocacy Competencies

Advocacy Competency	Addressed by Career Intervention	Relevance to Corresponding Competency
1. Client/Student Empowerment	X	This intervention seeks to highlight student strengths, identify social identity factors that may impact perceptions about career choice, and train students to address internalized oppression that may impact vocational development by enhancing sociopolitical consciousness.
2. Client/Student Advocacy	X	Counselors will coordinate with and navigate the appropriate educational services to increase student access to career development resources and mentorship.
3. Community Collaboration	X	Program facilitators will partner with community members by recruiting professionals from diverse career fields to present to students or serve on the career panel.
4. Systems Advocacy	X	The intervention's grounding in Social Cognitive Career Theory and Critical Consciousness allows participants and facilitators to identify environmental factors that may impact the student's development.
5. Public Information	—	—
6. Social/Political Advocacy	X	Module 3 of this intervention challenges students and facilitators to identify community allies that can support students in career planning and attainment.

Source: Lewis et al., 2003.

Regarding technology needs, one computer for every two students in the class is preferred, in addition to copy and printing capacities. Journal articles, entertainment account access (i.e., Netflix, Hulu, or Amazon Prime), and news articles will be used. Adequate facilities are also needed; it is expected that the program will benefit from office space, a classroom large enough for participants, and a computer lab.

Finally, the COPES (EdITS, 2017) or Values sort (Mucinkas, 2015) assessments can be used to supplement the curriculum and might be useful tools in helping students and instructors understand the significance of values. Assessment administration will require the purchase of the COPES *Self-Scoring Booklets* and an equivalent number of the COPES *Self-Interpretation Profile and Guides*. Items can be purchased from EdITS (*Self-Scoring Booklet, Self-Interpretation Profile and Guides*). The Values Sort is free (Mucinkas, 2015; Niles & Harris-Bowlsbey, 2009).

METHODS OF EVALUATION

Summative and formative approaches to program evaluation are suggested to ensure comprehensive consideration of implementation strengths and challenges from both the student and administrator perspective. All students will be randomly selected and interviewed to evaluate their thoughts on the program and suggestions for improvement. Suggested interview questions include: What did you learn from the Cross Sociopolitical Barriers program; what parts of the program did you find most helpful; what parts of the program would you change; and in what ways did the program help you connect your cultural identity to career values and choice?

Facilitators will also be interviewed to evaluate curriculum training and provide suggestions for program change. Finally, the intervention planning committee will meet at the completion of program implementation to consider outcomes and to evaluate program costs based on the organizational budget and efficacy of the intervention modules (Niles & Harris-Bowlsbey, 2009).

PLAN FOR REVISION

Once evaluation has been completed, the intervention planning committee will reconvene during designated planning hours. Committee members will consider the usefulness of the program and make appropriate revisions. For instance, the committee may recommend providing the program during two homeroom classes per week rather than one so that the curriculum is not rushed. Additionally, school administrators will need to consider the cost of the program.

ETHICAL CONSIDERATIONS

It is important to consider ethical boundaries and expectations before implementing an intervention in any setting. When working with adolescents and young people below the age of eighteen, it is important to receive permission from school administrators, if housed in a school setting, and parents before implementing new curriculum or programs. Parents and students will be asked for consent and assent prospectively as the course may show films or clips that may be offensive to some. It will be important to make sure that students and parents are aware of the program's focus on the intersections between career development, cultural identity, and sociopolitical constructs. All students will be asked to participate in the intervention but may choose not to participate.

The ethical standards presented by the National Career Development Association (2009) should also be addressed in intervention implementation. It is important that confidentiality and privacy, professional responsibility, relationships with other professionals, assessment interpretation, internet use, and supervision and training be considered (Niles & Harris-Bowlsbey, 2009). Adequate training and supervision should be provided to help prevent ethical violations.

As a complement to training in the use of the COPES and Values Sort, it would be beneficial to include community-based bias awareness training for facilitators prior to teaching the course. "Values assumptions underlie all question related to ethical behavior in career development interventions" (Niles & Harris-Bowlsbey, 2009, p. 434). Also, when using assessments, it is important to ensure the validity of assessments and appropriate multicultural application. While the COPES assessment has been validated among a sixth-grade through college sample, the intervention plan committee should review the research basis, content, and reading level of any proposed assessment to ensure appropriateness for the student population served. An explanation of the assessment should be provided to help students understand its significance (Fisher, 2009; Niles & Harris-Bowlsbey, 2009).

Moreover, the sociopolitical and multicultural focus of the program warrants careful consideration of the variety of values represented in the student population. Instructors must be sensitive to the needs of the class during discussions and should aim to create an open atmosphere that prioritizes tolerance, empowerment, and acceptance of difference (Maulucci & Menshah, 2015). The American Counseling Association's Advocacy Competencies (Lewis, Arnold, House, & Toporek, 2003) and the Multicultural and Social Justice Competencies (Ratts, Singh, Nassar-McMillan, Butler, & McCullough, 2015) can serve as valuable resources to ensure that diversity issues and multicultural identity are ethically explored and validated.

REFLECTIONS ON COUNSELOR SELF-AWARENESS OF POTENTIAL RESOURCES AND BIASES FROM PRIVILEGED AND MARGINALIZED IDENTITIES

There are several moments that stand out as broad, metaphorical summations of my own vocational journey. One such moment occurred while working as a site coordinator at a nonprofit organization dedicated to providing free educational services to children and adolescents performing below grade level. I met several students there that unknowingly shaped my professional and personal path. One student stands out.

While walking through the hallway one Saturday morning, monitoring the various tutoring sessions taking place, I noticed a student-tutor pair struggling to get started. Nick, a first-grader, was fixated on his fingers while his tutor tried in vain to engage him in the material. Instead of phonetically sounding out his words, Nick insisted upon picking at his fingers. I ventured over and asked, "What's wrong, Nick?" He peered up at me and whispered, "My ears. They are dirty; I forgot to clean my ears this morning," quickly redirecting his gaze to the wax on his fingers. Although initially taken aback by his distraction, I could also understand his struggle. Nick did not finish his morning ritual before arriving. Thus, he was not ready to learn. Once his ears, and hands, were cleaned to his satisfaction, Nick was ready for tutoring. Suddenly, the reading book he previously ignored captured his interest.

As I began my journey to become a counseling psychologist, I was like Nick. At first, I expected the process to simply entail learning information that I could apply in therapy sessions with patients who were ready and waiting to be heard (let's call this assumption the "wax"). What I had yet to realize was that to effectively, openly, and presently listen to others, I too would need to hone the skill of hearing and listening to myself. I, like Nick, needed to clear the "wax" from my ears. A quote that comes to mind in explaining this dilemma can be found in *Invisible Man*.

> All my life I had been looking for something, and everywhere I turned someone tried to tell me what it was. . . . I was looking for something and asking everyone except myself questions which I, and only I could answer. (Ellison, 1952, p. 15)

My choice to pursue a career in counseling psychology has drawn attention to what had often been lacking in my previous attempts to authentically name my personal and professional values. I had not truly been attuned to myself, had not meaningfully considered the role of my family, my race, my gender, my sexual orientation, my ethnicity, my faith, or my inner voice in shaping who I am.

I consider my own intersecting target and agent identities in shaping my vocational path. As a Black woman, raised in a household where education and professional development were highlighted as core values, I quickly learned, in working with youth of color in diverse settings, that while my skin color may have, in some cases, served as a point of connection, my education status and that of my parents sometimes marked a line of privilege and difference. I needed to learn how to welcome the direct challenges of students wondering how I, a doctoral student at the time, who grew up in a suburban town, could understand their experience. They were right. Again, I was positioned to take the "wax" from my ears to more honestly take in and process their uncertain glances, their questioning tone, and their appropriate inquiry of the authenticity of my desire to "help." Thus, I encourage counselors seeking to implement this intervention to honestly assess their potential biases, sociopolitical identities, assumptions about career choice, notions of career development access, and beliefs of success.

CONCLUSION

Making a career decision influences many aspects of our lives. Without adequate support and knowledge regarding vocational options, it is difficult to ensure job satisfaction and personal fulfillment. Our cultural identities and the sociopolitical barriers that individuals may face in establishing career interests, fostering vocational self-efficacy, and pursuing career goals are critical aspects of social and environmental experience. Crossing Barriers is designed to nurture skills and internal supports to fight against structural barriers by developing critical consciousness to better appreciate the ways in which understanding of self and our social environments can promote career development, access, and outcomes.

APPENDIX 3.1

Module 1: Sample Activities, Readings, and Media Resources

Activity One: What Is Multicultural Identity?

1. Large group: What does the word *multicultural* mean?
2. "Multi" (i.e., many, varied, various, different, etc.)
3. "Cultural": what does the word *cultural* mean to you individually, and how might *cultural* be defined in a dictionary or in society?

Activity Two: My Multicultural Identity

1. Ask each participant to write down the most salient aspects of their own multicultural identities and write them on a note card; ask participants to then write down the ways that their identities are represented in popular media, society, by peers, by family, and others.
2. Provide definitions of social and cultural identity categories.
3. Discussion Questions: What cultural identity dimensions are missing from this list; to what dimensions do you have a strong reaction?

Activity Three: Multicultural Identity Journal

1. Invite students to journal once weekly on one aspect about their identity (age, gender, sexual orientation, race, ethnicity, religion, or SES).
2. Sample Journal Prompts: What aspect of your identity was salient for you today; in what ways has this part of your cultural identity impacted your relationship with others; how has this part of your identity been represented in the community?

Activity Four: Considering Power, Privilege, and Oppression in Our Community

1. In small groups, ask each student to identify the five most important resources needed in their communities; compare each group's list.
2. In small groups, identify ways to solve the problems and challenges presented by the identified community needs.
3. Provide guiding questions: Whom can you contact to help with the task; how much do you think the necessity costs; how can you fundraise to help reduce the cost; who will benefit from having this item or program?

Suggested Reading Preparation for Facilitators

Johnson (2006) (book: *Privilege, power, and difference*)
Maulucci & Menshah (2015) (article: "Naming ourselves and others")

Media Resources (American Academy of Child and Adolescent Psychiatry, 2017)

Hidden Figures (Chernin, Gigliotti, Melfi, Topping, Williams, & Melfi, 2016; Race, Gender)
Higher Learning (Singleton & Hall, 2005; Racial Identity Development)
The Infidel (David & Appignanesi, 2010; Religious Identity)

APPENDIX 3.2

Module 2: Sample Activities, Readings, and Media Resources

Activity One: Values Exploration

1. Define and provide an example of a personal value and professional value.
2. Group students in pairs and invite them to identify three to five personal values and three to five professional values.
3. Ask students to rank values from greatest to least importance with their partner.
4. Administer and explore the online Values Sort to support students in broadening their definition of values (Mucinkas, 2015).

Activity Two: Values Interview

1. Invite students to choose a parent, adult mentor, or teacher to interview on their personal and professional values.
2. Sample interview questions: How do you define your personal values; what informs your personal values; how do your personal values impact your professional values?

Activity Three: Values Assessment

1. Explain the purpose of the COPES to participants.
2. Administer and score the COPES.
3. Review scores with students individually if time allows.

Activity Four: My Multicultural Identity and Values

1. Invite students to journal once weekly on how aspects of their cultural identity inform their values.
2. Sample journal prompts: What aspects of your cultural identity inform your personal values and how; what aspects of your cultural identity inform your professional values; how are professional values represented in your families and the community; of the values you have observed in your community, which are consistent with your own values and which are different?

Suggested Reading Preparation for Facilitators

EdITS (2017). (online assessment: *Career orientation placement and evaluation survey*)
Hirschi (2010). (article: "Positive adolescent career development: The role of intrinsic and extrinsic work values")
Mucinkas (2015). (online activity: "Values sort")

APPENDIX 3.3

Module 3: Career Exploration and Goal Setting

Activity One: Career Exploration

1. Introduce students to the MyNextMove website (https://www.mynextmove.org/; United States Department of Labor, 2017).

2. Ask students to identify the category that best fits their current stage of career exploration: "I want to be a . . ."; "I'll know it when I see it"; or "I'm not sure."
3. Ask students to identify two to three careers of interest based on their exploration of the MyNextMove website.
4. Invite students to download PathSource Careers & Schools (2016) to continue their career exploration.

Activity Two: Speed Networking/Career Panel

1. Preparation: Survey identified careers of interest, as indicated in Activity One; recruit five to six professionals from the career fields of interest to serve as career panelists and interviewees; inform students of networking activity plans; and support students in identifying interview questions for career panelists.
2. Implementation: Organize space into five stations, with one chair for the career presenter and three to four chairs for student interviewers; allow students fifteen to twenty minutes for each station, rotating five to six times to allow each student group to interview each professional.
3. Suggested Interview/Panel Questions: What are your daily professional responsibilities; what led you to choose this career field; how has your cultural identity impacted your experience in the field; were there any barriers that you faced in pursuing your professional goals; if so, how did you overcome them; and what advice might you share to help me pursue a similar career field?

Suggested Reading Preparation for Facilitators

Diemer, Kauffman, Koenig, Trahan, & Hsieh (2010). (article: "Challenging racism, sexism, and social injustice: Support for urban adolescents' critical consciousness development")

Gushue, Clarke, Pantzer, & Scanlan (2006). (article: "Self-efficacy, perceptions of barriers, vocational identity, and the career exploration behavior of Latino/a High School Students")

Gushue & Whitson (2006). (article: "The relationship of career decision-making self-efficacy, vocational identity, and career exploration behavior in African American high school students")

Torres & Fergus (2011). (book chapter: "Social mobility and the complex status of Latino males: Education, employment, and incarceration patterns from 2000–2009")

REFERENCES

American Academy of Child and Adolescent Psychiatry. (2017, March 23). *Movies that may be useful in teaching about culture.* Retrieved from https://www.aacap.org/App_Themes/ AACAP/docs/resources_for_primary_care/diversity_and_cultural_competency_curricu lum/goal_modules_short_list_of_movies_that_include_culture.pdf.

Bandura, A. (1986). *Social foundations of thought and action: A social cognitive theory.* Englewood Cliffs, NJ: Prentice Hall.

Chernin, P. (Producer), Gigliotti, D. (Producer), Melfi, T. (Producer), Topping, J. (Producer), Williams, P. (Producer), & Melfi, T. (Director). (2016). *Hidden figures* [Motion picture]. United States: Fox 2000 Pictures.

David, A. (Producer), & Appignanesi, J. (Director). (2010). *Infidel* [Motion picture]. United Kingdom: Slingshot Productions.

Diemer, M. A., & Blustein, D. L. (2006). Critical consciousness and career development among urban youth. *Journal of Vocational Behavior, 68*, 220–232. doi:10.1016/j .jvb.2005.07.001.

Diemer, M. A., Kauffman, A., Koenig, N., Trahan, E. & Hsieh, C.A. (2010). Challenging racism, sexism, and social injustice: Support for urban adolescents' critical consciousness development. *Cultural Diversity and Ethnic Minority Psychology, 12*, 444–460. doi: 10.1037/1099-9809.12.3.444.

Diemer, W. A., Wang, Q., Moore, T., Gregory, S. R., Hatcher, K. M., & Voight, A. (2010). Sociopolitical development, work salience, and vocational expectations among low socioeconomic status African American, Latin American, and Asian American youth. *Developmental Psychology, 46*, 619–635. doi: 10.1037/a0017049.

EdITS: A Leader in the Field of Assessment and Career Guidance. (2017, March 14). *Career orientation placement and evaluation survey.* Retrieved from http://www.edits.net/prod ucts/career-guidance/copes.html.

Ellison, R. (1952). *Invisible man.* New York, NY: Vintage Books.

Fisher, C. B. (2009). *Decoding the Ethics Code: A practical guide for psychologists* (2nd ed.). Los Angeles, CA: Sage.

Gushue, G. V., Clarke, C. P., Pantzer, K. M., & Scanlan, R. L. (2006). Self-efficacy, perceptions of barriers, vocational identity, and the career exploration behavior of Latino/a high school students. *The Career Development Quarterly, 54*, 307–317. doi: 10.1002/j.2161 -0045.2006.tb00196.x.

Gushue, G. V., & Whitson, M. L. (2006). The relationship of career decision-making self-efficacy, vocational identity, and career exploration behavior in African American high school students. *Journal of Career Development, 33*, 112–124. doi:10.1177/0894845305283004.

Hirschi, A. (2010). Positive adolescent career development: The role of intrinsic and extrinsic work values. *Career Development Quarterly, 85*, 276–287. doi:10.1002/j.2161-0045.2010 .tb00187.x.

Johnson, A. G. (2006). *Privilege, power, and difference.* Boston, MA: McGraw Hill.

Lent, R. W., & Brown, S. D. (2017). Social cognitive career theory in a diverse world: Closing thoughts. *Journal of Career Assessment, 25*, 173–80. doi/10.1177/1069072716660061.

Lent, R. W., Brown, S. D., & Hackett, G. (1994). Toward a unifying social cognitive theory of career and academic interest, choice, and performance [Monograph]. *Journal of Vocational Behavior, 45*, 79–122.

———. (2000). Contextual supports and barriers to career choice: A social cognitive analysis. *Journal of Counseling Psychology, 47*, 36–49. doi: 10.1037//0022-0167.47.1.3.

Lewis, J., Arnold, M. S., House, R., & Toporek, R. L. (2003). *Advocacy competencies.* Endorsed by the American Counseling Association Governing Council. Retrieved from https://www.counseling.org/Resources/Competencies/Advocacy_Competencies.pdf.

Maulucci, M. S., & Menshah, F. M. (2015). Naming ourselves and others. *Journal of Research in Science and Teaching, 52*, 1–5. doi: 10.1002/tea.21196.

Mucinkas, D. (2015, March 27). Value sort. *The good project.* Retrieved from http://thegood project.org/toolkits-curricula/the-goodwork-toolkit/value-sort-activity/.

National Career Development Association. (1997). *Career counseling competencies.* Broken Arrow, OK: Author.

———. (2009). *Minimum competencies for multicultural career counseling and development.* Broken Arrow, OK: Author. Retrieved from https://www.ncda.org/aws/NCDA/pt/fli/12508/false.

Niles, S. G., & Harris-Bowlsbey, J. (2009). *Career development interventions in the 21st century* (3rd ed.). Columbus, OH: Pearson.

PathSource. (2016). *PathSource careers and schools.* [Mobile Application Software]. Retrieved from www.pathsource.com.

Ratts, M. J., Singh, A. A., Nassar-McMillan, S., Butler, S. K., & McCullough, J. R. (2015). Multicultural and social justice competencies. Retrieved from http://www.counseling.org/knowledge-center/competencies.

Singleton, J. (Producer), Hall, P. (Producer), & Singleton, J. (Director). (1995). *Higher learning* [Motion picture]. United States: Columbia Pictures.

Swanson, J. L., & Fouad, N. A. (2009). *Career theory and practice: Learning through case studies* (2nd ed.). Los Angeles, CA: Sage.

Torres, M., & Fergus, E. (2011). Social mobility and the complex status of Latino males: Education, employment, and incarceration patterns from 2000–2009. In P. Noguera, A. Hurtado, & E. Fergus (Eds.), *Invisible no more: Understanding the disenfranchisement of Latino men and boys* (pp. 19–40). New York, NY: Routledge.

United States Department of Labor. (2017, March 14). What do you want to do for a living? Retrieved from https://www.mynextmove.org/.

Watts, R. J., Abdul-Adil, J. K., & Pratt, T. (2002). Enhancing critical consciousness in young African American men: A psycho educational approach. *Psychology of Men and Masculinity, 3*, 41–50. doi: 10.1037//1524-9220.3.1.41.

Watts, R. J., Griffith, D. M., & Abdul-Adil, J. (1999). Sociopolitical development as an antidote for oppression—theory and action. *American Journal of Community Psychology, 27*, 255–271. doi:10.1023/A:1022839818873.

Whiston, S. C., & Keller, B. (2004). The influences of family of origin on career development. *The Counseling Psychologist, 32*, 493–568. doi: 10.1177/0011000004265660.

4

A Program to Promote Career Development and Counseling Services in High Schools with LGBT Students

Jill Huang

Lesbian, gay, bisexual, and transgender (LGBT) high school students experience the normal developmental tasks that their heterosexual peers experience (e.g., attending high school, maintaining friendships, navigating family life). They also have the added task of navigating high school and puberty while processing their sexual orientation and gender identity, which may inhibit their career development (Etringer, Hillerbrand, & Hetherington, 1990). Our school systems consistently underserve the needs of high school LGBT students, including career counseling (Goodrich & Luke, 2009). This chapter outlines a program to address the systemic barriers that LGBT high school students face by invigorating high school and career counselors to be social justice advocates.

SOCIAL JUSTICE NEEDS AND RATIONALE FOR THE CAREER DEVELOPMENT INTERVENTION

In a representative Gallup poll of U.S. adults, 4.1 percent identify as LGBT, suggesting that there are approximately ten million adults who identify as lesbian, gay, bisexual, and transgender (Gates, 2017). Despite the growing LGBT population in the United States (Gates, 2017), little is known about the career counseling and development of high school students who identify as LGBT (Chen & Keats, 2016). Educational institutions consistently underserve the needs of high school LGBT students, which results in inadequate school counseling, of which career counseling is an essential part (Goodrich & Luke, 2009). This population is particularly at higher risk of experiencing harassment, assault, and discrimination at school (Jackson, 2017; Kosciw, Greytak, Giga, Villenas, & Danischewski, 2016). LGBT youth have lower school engagement, lower academic achievement, and frequent absenteeism due to feeling unsafe and uncomfortable at school (Jackson, 2017; Kosciw et al., 2016). The psychological impact of navigating hostile campus environments can lead to depression and low self-esteem (Kosciw et al., 2016). In addition, perceptions of safety and control are core factors hindering their sexual orientation and gender identity development (Jackson, 2017).

While many of their heterosexual counterparts are developing their vocational identities, LGBT students struggle with career indecisiveness (Etringer et al., 1990). One theory to explain the delay in career development is the "bottleneck effect" (Hetherington, 1991), which proposes that typical career development tasks are postponed because much of their psychological energy is focused on navigating their sexual orientation and gender identity. This theory was supported by the findings from a survey of 102 LGB youth that suggested that sexual identity conflict predicted vocational indecision and career immaturity (Schmidt & Nilsson, 2006).

The intervention program with LGBT high school students presented in this chapter is grounded in the career development theories of Donald Super (1980) and Linda Gottfredson (2005). Both of these theories emphasize self-concept in differing ways. Super (1980) emphasizes life span and life space in how career development "is an adjustment process of many vocational choices that are expressions of one's evolving self-concepts made in the developmental course of one's life and changing roles" (Jackson & Verdino, 2012, p. 1163). Super (1980) identified nine common life roles that people hold over the life span (i.e., child, student, leisurite, worker, citizen, spouse, homemaker, parent, pensioner) that can be held concurrently. The importance of each role increases or decreases depending on where they are in their life span and how emotionally involved they feel about that role (Super, 1980). For example, if a gay man deeply values the role of child yet has homophobic parents, he may not pursue a career that is seen as stereotypically gay (e.g., fashion design, makeup artist, hair stylist). However, when the same man gets older, the role of child may decrease in importance for him and he then might decide to pursue the career he wanted. Counselors can help LGBT individuals understand how their unique life circumstances and self-concept influence their life roles across the life span, particularly as they evolve during adolescence.

Gottfredson's (2005) model of circumscription and compromise uses self-concept to explain why vocational expectations are constrained based on stereotypes. For example, a young gay man may grow up highly involved in sports. However, he may notice that most of the gay characters portrayed in the media are fashion designers, makeup artists, and hair stylists. Through a process of circumscription, he may eliminate his dream to pursue any career options in professional football because he knows of no openly gay football player role models. School and career counselors can help LGBT individuals reconsider the vocational options they may have prematurely eliminated from consideration due to these harmful stereotypes. In working with LGBT students, it is important for school or career counselors to understand the interplay of their self-concept, situational factors (e.g., sociopolitical climate), and vocational identity development. Concerns about safety and discrimination should be considered for counselors to effectively guide LGBT individuals in their career decision-making process. In the program proposed in this chapter, counselors will cultivate needed social justice advocacy competencies (Lewis, Arnold, House, & Toporek, 2003) to more helpfully address the systemic barriers that LGBT high school students face in their career self-concept development.

An important clarification to make is that although this chapter discusses LGBT student career development and counseling needs, it is imperative to remember that this population is not homogeneous (Chen & Keats, 2016). Individuals who identify as lesbian, gay, and bisexual share a sexual minority status, but each group has its own struggles and each individual has their own experience. Transgender, in contrast, is an umbrella term that encompasses individuals who do not identify as cisgender (individuals whose gender identity matches the gender they were assigned at birth). Examples of other transgender identities include but are not limited to gender nonconforming, genderqueer, gender nonbinary, transsexual, and drag queen and king (Pepper & Lorah, 2008; Scott, Belke, & Barfield, 2011). This chapter outlines general interventions that school and career counselors can use to advocate for LGBT high school students.

When it comes to career development, school and career counselors need to remember that LGB and transgender individuals have overlapping yet differing concerns. Relevant to identity and career developmental tasks in high school, LGBT students who are struggling to integrate their LGBT identity are more likely to struggle with making effective career plans (Hetherington, 1991; Mobley & Slaney, 1996; Schmidt & Nilsson, 2006). The LGB students who manage to choose a career path often restrict their career choices for stereotypic occupations (e.g., photographer, interior decorator for gay men; mechanic, plumber for lesbians) because of negative environmental influences and perceived barriers of pursuing their true career interests (Chung, 1995). In addition, career assessments that are supposed to help students figure out their career interests (e.g., the Self-Directed Search) have strong heteronormative and reinforcing gender role biases that invalidate the results for LGB and transgender students (Pope et al., 2004).

Transgender individuals have some common and significantly differing needs and career challenges from those of LGB individuals, including the complexities of nonbinary gender identification and presentation. Similar to their LGB peers, transgender students are verbally harassed for their gender expression, with two-thirds of them reporting feeling unsafe at school (Greytak, Kosciw, & Diaz, 2009). With this antagonistic backdrop, the issue of transitioning socially or medically in school or in the future workplace is enormous (Gonzalez & McNulty, 2010; Pepper & Lorah, 2008; Sangganjana-vanich, 2009). Transgender and gender nonconforming individuals contend with gendered microaggressions in multiple areas of their lives, including at work (as cited in Nordmarken, 2014). Specifically, trans-feminine people face both transphobia and misogyny; whereas, trans-masculine people tend to be supported and welcomed into "patriarchal social hierarchies" (Nordmarken, 2014, p. 131). Medically transitioning (i.e., hormone treatment, gender-affirming surgery) in school or in the workplace comes with positive and negative aspects. Students may desire the stability of their peers' support (Pepper & Lorah, 2008), yet may also be misgendered (being addressed by improper pronouns) despite their peers' well-intentions, which can cause emotional distress (Fraser, 2003). Medically transitioning at a new place of employment may be easier in some ways because transgender individuals do not have to out themselves (Pepper & Lorah, 2008), can reinvent their identities and lives (Sangganjanavanich, 2009), and have fewer expectations from coworkers (Walworth, 2003). However, obtaining employment may be more difficult if they have not changed their identifications (e.g., driver's license, social security) to their current gender identification (Pool, 2006), and if their employment history was under a different name (Scott et al., 2011). Consequently, transgender individuals may decide to pursue entry-level positions despite being overqualified because they may want their previous gender identity to remain private (Sangganjanavanich, 2009). The issues mentioned in this paragraph are associated with transgender individuals who adhere or identify with the gender binary and do not necessarily reflect the experience of individuals who are genderqueer, gender nonbinary, or gender nonconforming. There is little to no literature on how nonbinary transgender individuals pursue career decisions or workplace issues.

Fortunately, researchers have found that the presence of supportive school staff was correlated with the strong positive effects on perceived school environment and student well-being (Kosciw, Palmer, Kull, & Greytak, 2013). In particular, with the mental health implications and increased risk of bullying, school counselors and career counselors play a vital role in the students' lives during and beyond school (Singh & Kosciw, 2017). Unfortunately, many high school counselors feel ill-equipped or question their competency in providing support to LGBT students (Luke, Goodrich, & Scarborough, 2011; Singh, Urbano, Haston, & McMahon, 2010). In addition to fulfilling advocacy competencies as proposed by the American Counseling Association (Lewis et al., 2003), the following program aims to help boost the confidence and cultural competency of high school and career counselors in supporting LGBT students.

MEASURABLE OBJECTIVES AND EXPECTED OUTCOMES

The goal of the program is to mitigate the typically hostile high school environment that is a risk factor to the future of many high school LGBT students in their career exploration and decision-making. By improving the cultural competency of high school and career counselors working with LGBT students, this program will go beyond the student level and enact change at the system level. The hope is to create an affirming environment that will assist in the career development of high school students while buffering against potentially hostile school environments.

By the end of this program, high school and career counselors will:

1. Gain self-awareness of their own biases in working with LGBT students (American Counseling Association, 2005; American Psychological Association, 2012, 2015; American School Counseling Association, 2005; Goodrich, Harper, Luke, & Singh, 2013; Pepper & Lorah, 2008; Pope et al., 2004)

2. Understand common LGBT career issues including problems associated with career assessments and gaining familiarity with definitions of terms and LGBT history (Pepper & Lorah, 2008; Sangganjanavanich, 2009)
3. Gain knowledge of the sociopolitical climate and state and federal laws concerning LGBT career issues (e.g., nondiscriminatory regulations) (Pepper & Lorah, 2008)
4. Gain familiarity with LGBT affirming organizations and resources (Gonzalez & McNulty, 2010; Pepper & Lorah, 2008)
5. Advocate and collaborate at the individual, school, community, and legislative level (Gonzalez & McNulty, 2010; Goodrich et al., 2013)

PLAN FOR PROMOTING SERVICES

This intervention is best facilitated by support from the administrative level of the high school. An administration that advocates for LGBT students and promotes providing LGBT responsive services is essential to creating an affirming school environment and eventual social change within the community (Singh et al., 2010). At the outset of the program, a high school counselor, career counselor, or psychologist who is professionally licensed or certified and has the needed expertise should be appointed the facilitator of the training program (see tables 4.1 and 4.2 for relevant competencies in career counseling and social justice advocacy; Lewis et al., 2003; National Career Development Association, 1997, 2009). Responsibilities of this program facilitator should include securing internal or external guests who can provide psychoeducation about LGBT issues and coordinating monthly peer consultations to manage the logistics of the training program. This facilitator will also select two high school and career counselors to receive training from each high school of a participating school district in providing culturally congruent services to LGBT students.

Table 4.1. Relevance to Career Counseling Competencies

Career Counseling Competency	Addressed by Career Intervention	Relevance to Corresponding Competency
1. Career Development Theory	X	Incorporates integrative life-career theory of Super (1980) and Gottfredson (2005) career development theory of circumscription and compromise.

Career Counseling Competency	Addressed by Career Intervention	Relevance to Corresponding Competency
2. Individual and Group Counseling Skills	X	Requires culturally sensitive counseling skills with students and while collaborating with families, other school personnel, community activists, and political leaders.
3. Individual/Group Assessment	X	Career assessment used will be appropriate for LGBT individuals, and evaluations of potential work environments is essential.
4. Information/ Resources/ Technology	X	Resources will be provided to students and other collaborators to assist in career planning and scholarships.
5. Program Promotion, Management, and Implementation	X	Counselors and administration will monitor societal trends and state and federal legislation for changes that influence the development and implementation of the program.
6. Coaching, Consultation, and Performance Improvement	X	Consultation with families, other school personnel, and community members and organizations (e.g., LGBT center, PFLAG) is imperative in counseling LGBT students.
7. Diverse Populations	X	Services are offered to LGBT students of diverse backgrounds.
8. Supervision	X	Peer and external consultations are encouraged to boost the quality of direct service.
9. Ethical/Legal Issues	X	Understanding and adherence to ethical codes and knowledge of district, state, and federal laws.
10. Research/ Evaluation	X	Evaluation of the program will be completed formatively and summatively on students and other stakeholders to evaluate program effectiveness.

Source: NCDA, 1997, 2009.

Table 4.2.   Relevance to Advocacy Competencies

Advocacy Competency	Addressed by Career Intervention	Relevance to Corresponding Competency
1. Client/Student Empowerment	X	Counselors will empower students to become self-advocates.
2. Client/Student Advocacy	X	Counselors are expected to advocate for students with their families, other school personnel, community members, and political leaders to enact change.

(*continued*)

Table 4.2. *Continued*

Advocacy Competency	Addressed by Career Intervention	Relevance to Corresponding Competency
3. Community Collaboration	X	Counselors are expected to develop alliances with community activists, groups, and political leaders in service of LGBT students.
4. Systems Advocacy	X	Counselors are actively identifying and minimizing systemic factors that act as barriers to LGBT student development.
5. Public Information	X	Counselors will disseminate information about their students' perception of safety and career development progress to the public as a form of advocacy.
6. Social/Political Advocacy	X	Counselors are expected to ally with the community, political figures, and policy makers to lobby for LGBT rights.

Source: Lewis et al., 2003.

PLAN FOR DELIVERING SERVICES

Initial program planning will last approximately two to three months (in summer, ideally) to complete the following tasks in preparation for the school year: creating a budget, selecting the school district, searching for a qualified program facilitator, searching for qualified guest experts to teach the material, deciding what training material to teach, and selecting the direct service providers (two high school and career counselors from each district). Subsequently, the following training program will be enacted in four phases throughout the academic year: (1) training of high school and career counselors, (2) direct application of newly acquired knowledge, skills, and self-awareness with LGBT students, (3) advocacy with families, other school personnel, community members, and political leaders, and (4) continued consultations and formative evaluations to ensure efficient program delivery.

One ethical and legal issue that may arise depending on the school district or state is if there are laws that prohibit educators to discuss LGBT issues in school (e.g., Tennessee's unenacted bill that tried to prohibit instructors from discussing human sexuality that was not heteronormative in pre-kindergarten to eighth grade) (Classroom Protection Act, 2013). If this Senate bill had passed, it would have also mandated school officials to disclose students' sexual minority identities to parents and legal guardians (Classroom Protection Act, 2013). With the understanding that legislation varies from state to state regarding the privacy of LGBT students, school administrators and the program facilitator should carefully consider the impact of program implementation on LGBT students.

Privacy and safety of LGBT students are of the highest priority. Counselors will be participating in monthly peer consultation groups to troubleshoot difficult cases they may be working on. They will be instructed to conceal identifying information about their students while consulting. An exception to this rule would be if other counselors are directly involved in providing the student's care and communication about the case is necessary to providing wraparound services. Counselors in this training program should also inform all students with whom they work that they are training to acquire more culturally congruent training about sexual orientation and gender identity. Although anticipation of transferring is very low, all students, LGBT or otherwise, should be given the option to request another counselor, provided that the school has the resources for such a transfer. If a transfer is not possible, conversation between the counselor and the student about their reservations should be discussed openly to foster an environment of transparency and honesty.

INTERVENTION PROGRAM CONTENT

In the first phase, high school and career counselors will receive four weeks of intensive LGBT-affirming training (appendix 4.1) where they will learn about definitions, LGBT history, common development issues, specific career issues concerning LGBT students (e.g., Nicolazzo, 2016), current state and federal laws particularly around LGBT occupational rights, and LGBT-affirming resources (appendix 4.2). High school and career counselors will also be challenged to self-reflect and gain self-awareness about their own biases in working with LGBT students (American Counseling Association, 2005; American Psychological Association, 2012, 2015; American School Counseling Association, 2005; Goodrich et al., 2013; Pepper & Lorah, 2008; Pope et al., 2004).

During and after this training period, counselors may begin to enact phase two where they apply their newly acquired knowledge, skills, and self-awareness to working with LGBT youth. Counselors need to have a sense of the sociopolitical climate and state and federal laws, particularly in the workplace, in order to effectively guide LGBT students in their career planning and decision-making. Knowledge of laws is particularly important for the safety of transgender students (Chen & Keats, 2016; Scott et al., 2011). Sangganjanavanich (2009) suggested that counselors can help transgender students in their career decision-making process by preparing them for predictable consequences or potential difficult situations they may face applying for jobs and while working (e.g., transitioning in the workplace). Safety and discrimination are major concerns that are relevant to students' career exploration and decision-making process (Hook & Bowman, 2008). Hook and Bowman (2008) suggest for counselors to explore previous experiences of discrimination, the coming-out process, and levels of distress over specific life-career issues. They suggested applying career theories that are more integrative, such as Super's (1980) life-span, life-space approach to career development or Gottfredson's (2005) model of circumscription and compromise, and take into account the unique life-career needs of the LGBT students (Hook & Bowman, 2008). Additionally, gaining familiarity with LGBT-affirming organizations and resources can be particularly important for teaching students the highly important skills for self-advocacy (Goodrich et al., 2013; Singh et al., 2010). Singh and colleagues (2010) interviewed school counselors who worked with LGBT students. Participants declared that part of advocating for students is to teach them how to self-advocate, which includes "teaching them how to navigate difficult systems within the school, to value their own voice and perspective, and to access educational resources" (p. 140). One participant stated that because the parents of a student had threatened to not pay for their son's college tuition because he was gay, the school counselor was able to support the student in finding college scholarships for gay students.

Simultaneously, counselors will also advocate for and collaborate with students, families, school personnel, community activists, and political leaders (Goodrich et al., 2013) as part of phase three. This step is especially important in changing the school and local sociopolitical environment for the students. Educating other school personnel is instrumental for fostering a culture of safety for LGBT students (Gonzalez & McNulty, 2010) and promoting their role as allies with LGBT students on campus (Singh et al., 2010). For example, counselors can train instructors on how to address harassment of LGBT students in the classroom (Chen & Keats, 2016). Counselors can collaborate with instructors to discuss homophobia in athletics or incorporate same-gender relationships into the sex education conversation to maximize LGBT visibility and issues in the curriculum (Chen & Keats, 2016). Additionally, supporting families of LGBT students may also be critical in nurturing the development of LGBT students in that high school and career counselors can inform families of the academic, career, personal, and social developmental issues of their children (Jackson, 2017). Particularly for families of transgender students, counselors may have to educate family members on what being transgender means and its implications in the dimensions listed above to ensure continued family support of the student (Sangganjanavanich, 2009). Collaboration with the community (e.g., school officials, allied organizations, community advocates, and political leaders) has the greatest potential for change at the legislative level (Goodrich et al., 2013) because potentially problematic policies may be overturned or protections may be added (e.g., protection for transgender students to use the bathroom consistent with their identified gender) (Gonzalez & McNulty, 2010).

In the fourth phase, high school and career counselors in the same district will have monthly peer meetings to consult about their experiences in providing services to LGBT students, troubleshoot how to engage in school and community advocacy, offer suggestions to each other, and receive support from each other. They will also seek quantitative and qualitative evaluations from LGBT students about perceived high school environment, career decision-making progress, and quality of interactions with counselors.

RESOURCES NEEDED

Although acquiring school administration support enhances the probability of this program's success, investment in the training of high school and career counselors has the strongest positive effects on school environment and well-being (Kosciw et al., 2013). Thus, procuring a sufficient budget to invest in high-quality staff to train these high school and career counselors is necessary. An appointed facilitator of the training program who has the needed expertise will secure guests who can provide psychoeducation about LGBT issues and coordinate monthly peer consultations to manage the logistics of the training program.

To learn about the basics of LGBT identities and being an ally for them, high school and career counselors will need to be trained by professionals who have developed familiarity and competencies with the topic. School districts may utilize their own internal experts or search for professionals outside of the district. Some suggestions for external partners are: local LGBT centers, other LGBT-affirming organizations (e.g., Parents, Families and Friends of Lesbians and Gays [PFLAG]), or local universities that have an LGBT center that offers Safe Zone training. These organizations have professionals who are familiar with LGBT history, common development issues, current state and federal laws, and other LGBT-affirming resources. Connecting with them and visiting their organizations may also create relationships for future referral sources and partnerships for advocacy and consultation. Mental health professionals (e.g., licensed social workers, mental health clinicians, marriage and family therapists, or psychologists) who have expertise working with LGBT populations may also be excellent resources in providing LGBT-affirming training as well.

To learn about career-specific issues and career-specific state and federal laws, psychologists, counseling psychologists in particular, may be able to speak to the efficacy of specific career assessments for LGBT populations. Using only assessments that are congruent and unbiased for LGBT populations is crucial for accurate career counseling (Chen & Keats, 2016; Pepper & Lorah, 2008). Counseling psychologists can train high school and career counselors to think critically about norming standards and heteronormative and gender bias in assessments (Pope et al., 2004). The process for choosing valid assessments is streamlined when high school and career counselors have reflected on their own stereotypes and biases in working with LGBT students and use this knowledge to carefully choose and interpret the career assessments (Chung, 2003; Pepper & Lorah, 2008). To promote self-awareness and combat bias, counselors will attend multiple multicultural workshops, facilitated by culturally sensitive diversity consultants (e.g., psychologists who specialize in facilitating challenging dialogues about bias, stereotypes, and discrimination).

METHODS OF EVALUATION

Data collection is an important aspect of social justice because it is a powerful way to communicate trends that are grounded in data (Singh et al., 2010). Evaluations will be gathered formally, informally, formatively, and summatively. Counselors will complete formal evaluations of their program training and provide suggestions for program change. They may decide that they need more training in certain aspects that the program had not anticipated. The monthly peer meetings for high school and career counselors to consult about their experiences providing services to LGBT students will be informal self-evaluations of their direct service to LGBT students. Counselors can adjust their methods and strategies for intervention through these consultations.

Formal, formative program evaluations will be collected via quantitative and qualitative methods from LGBT students about perceived high school environment (i.e., safety, hostility), career decision-making progress, and quality of interactions with high school or career counselors. Suggested questions include *How would you describe the campus climate for LGBT students? How safe do you feel on campus? How much exploration of your career choices have you done in the past three months? How would you rate the quality of your relationship with your high school or career counselor?* The information gathered from students can be used as a social justice tool for administrators and the public to highlight the needs and barriers of LGBT students.

A random sample of family members, school personnel, and external collaborators (e.g., local LGBT centers, community advocates, political leaders) will also be evaluated for quality of interaction with the high school and career counselors. Administrators and the appointed facilitator of the program training and monthly consultation meetings will complete formative (e.g., every three months) and summative evaluations (at the end of the academic year) weighing the program costs with the efficacy of the overall program (e.g., its impact on LGBT students, family, community, and policy).

PLAN FOR REVISION

Following analysis of the evaluations, administrators and the appointed facilitator of the program training and monthly consultation meetings will consider the usefulness of the program and make appropriate recommendations for revisions about budget, process of selecting counselors, quality of training personnel, quality of training program and materials, and quality of interactions with families, other school personnel, and community members. The feedback should be considered on a formative basis, and revisions to the training program should be regularly incorporated throughout the academic year.

At the end of the academic year, a summative program evaluation will inform the revisions to the program for the upcoming academic year. Just as the initial program planning took two to three months (in the summer, ideally), updates to the program will occur during this planning period.

REFLECTIONS ON COUNSELOR SELF-AWARENESS OF POTENTIAL RESOURCES AND BIASES FROM PRIVILEGED AND MARGINALIZED IDENTITIES

In my clinical and research work, my aim is to support the underserved, forgotten, silenced, and marginalized. I am proud to use my voice and privilege as a fellow queer, cisgender licensed psychologist to advocate for young LGBT folks who do not necessarily feel empowered to change the environment they live in or school they attend. My focus is on developing my colleagues' cultural competency in working with LGBT youth because they have the great power to promote real change and advocacy for others in my community. I also understand that my colleagues in high school and career counseling may not always feel competent or confident in working with LGBT youth. Being an ally is an incredibly powerful position to be in, and I hope that you will borrow some of the passion I put into writing this chapter to fuel your own far-reaching advocacy for LGBT students.

CONCLUSION

This program is designed to boost the competency and confidence of high school and career counselors working with LGBT high school students. Counselors play an integral role for all students and LGBT students in particular because they can be active change agents that buffer against systemic barriers (e.g., hostile school environments, institutional discrimination). Culturally congruent career counseling allows LGBT students to adequately prepare for and compare their career interests with real talk about barriers that they may face in the workplace. This culturally congruent program will only enhance the success of LGBT students as they graduate high school and become the fabulous adults that they are destined to be.

APPENDIX 4.1

Sample LGBT-Affirming Training Schedule and Activities

Week 1
- Terms and definitions (http://itspronouncedmetrosexual.com/2013/01/a-comprehensive-list-of-lgbtq-term-definitions/)
  - Genderbread person (http://itspronouncedmetrosexual.com/2015/03/the-genderbread-person-v3/)
  - Pronouns
- Review of LGBT history (https://www.glsen.org/article/lgbtq-history-1)

Week 2
- Identity developmental models
  - Vivienne Cass (1979) Homosexual Identity Formation
  - Anthony D'Augelli (1994) Homosexual Lifespan Development Model
  - McCarn and Fassinger (1996) Lesbian Identity Development
  - Heather Knous (2005) Bisexual Identity Formation
  - Arlene Istar Lev (2004) Transgender Emergence Model
- Career theories
  - Donald Super (1980) Life-Span and Life-Space
  - Linda Gottfredson (2005) Circumscription and Compromise
- Career assessments (advantages and disadvantages)
  - Self-Directed Search
  - Strong Interest Inventory
  - Strong Interest Explorer

Week 3
- Sociopolitcal climate
- State and federal laws (http://www.hrc.org/state-maps?gclid=Cj0KC Qjwm6HaBRCbARIsAFDNK-hLNZUojDeeiErfRtzJck_FMUfKbhTs-DRjHzSDLDcT6l2e7L1OF5yMaAq3VEALw_wcB)
  - Bathroom laws
  - Marriage equality

Week 4
- How to be an advocate
- LGBT affirming resources (see appendix 4.2)
- Review

APPENDIX 4.2

LGBT Resource List

Political

- Equality Federation (http://www.equalityfederation.org/)
- Human Rights Campaign (HRC) (http://hrc.org/)
- National LGBTQ Task Force (http://www.thetaskforce.org/)
- Victory Fund (http://www.victoryfund.org/home)

Bisexual

- BIENESTAR (http://www.bienestar.org/)
- BiNetUSA (http://www.binetusa.org/)
- Bisexual.org (http://bisexual.org/)
- Bisexual Resource Center (http://www.biresource.net/)

Youth

- Gay, Lesbian & Straight Education Network (GLSEN) (http://glsen.org/)
- GSA Network (http://www.gsanetwork.org/)
- It Gets Better Project (https://itgetsbetter.org/)
- LGBTQ Student Resources & Support (http://www.accreditedschoolsonline.org/resources/lgbtq-student-support/)
- Point Foundation (http://pointfoundation.org/)
- Safe Schools Coalition (http://safeschoolscoalition.org/)
- Stop Bullying (https://www.stopbullying.gov/at-risk/groups/lgbt/index.html)
- The Trevor Project (http://www.thetrevorproject.org/)

Transgender

- National Center for Transgender Equality (NCTE) (http://www.nctequality.org/)
- Sylvia Rivera Law Project (http://srlp.org/)
- Trans Lifeline (https://www.translifeline.org/)
- Transgender Law Center (https://transgenderlawcenter.org/)

- Transgender Legal Defense & Education Fund (http://www.transgen derlegal.org/)

Legal

- American Civil Liberties Union (ACLU) (http://www.aclu.org/lgbt -rights)
- Lambda Legal (http://lambdalegal.org/)
- The LGBT Bar (http://lgbtbar.org/)
- National Center for Lesbian Rights (NCLR) (http://www.nclrights.org/)

General

- Anti-Violence Project (http://avp.org/index.php)
- CenterLink (http://www.lgbtcenters.org/)
- COLAGE (http://www.colage.org/)
- GMHC (http://gmhc.org/)
- GLAAD (https://www.glaad.org/)
- Matthew Shepard Foundation (http://matthewshepard.org/)
- Movement Advancement Project (http://www.lgbtmap.org/)
- Out & Equal (http://www.outandequal.org/)
- Parents, Families and Friends of Lesbians and Gays (PFLAG) (https:// community.pflag.org/)
- Straight for Equality (http://www.straightforequality.org/)
- The Williams Institute (http://williamsinstitute.law.ucla.edu/)

REFERENCES

American Counseling Association. (2005). *ACA code of ethics*. Alexandria, VA: Author.

American Psychological Association. (2012). Guidelines for psychological practice with lesbian, gay, and bisexual clients. *American Psychologist, 67*(1), 10–42. doi: 10.1037/a0024659.

———. (2015). Guidelines for psychological practice with transgender and gender nonconforming people. *American Psychologist, 70*(9), 832–864. doi: 10.1037/a0039906.

American School Counseling Association. (2005). *The ASCA national model: A framework for school counseling programs* (2nd ed.). Alexandria, VA: Author.

Cass, V. C. (1979). Homosexual identity formation: A theoretical model. *Journal of Homosexuality, 4*(3), 219–235. doi:10.1300/J082v04n03_01.

Chen, C. P., & Keats, A. (2016). Career development and counselling needs of LGBTQ high school students. *British Journal of Guidance & Counselling, 44*(5), 576–588. doi: 10.1080/03069885.2016.1187709.

Chung, Y. B. (1995). Career decision making of lesbian, gay, and bisexual individuals. *Career Development Quarterly, 44*(2), 178–190. doi: 10.1002/j.2161-0045.1995.tb00684.x.

———. (2003). Career counseling with lesbian, gay, bisexual, and transgendered persons: The next decade. *Career Development Quarterly, 52*(1), 78–85. doi: 10.1002/j.2161-0045 .2003.tb00630.x.

Classroom Protection Act. (2013). Tenn. Code Ann. § 49-6-1032.

D'Augelli, A. (1994). Identity development and sexual orientation: Toward a model of lesbian, gay, and bisexual development. In E. J. Trickett, R. J. Watts, & D. Birman (Eds.), *Human diversity: Perspectives on people in context* (pp. 312–333). San Francisco, CA: Jossey-Bass.

Etringer, B. D., Hillerbrand, E., & Hetherington, C. (1990). The influence of sexual orientation on career decision-making: A research note. *Journal of Homosexuality, 19*(4), 103–111. doi: 10.1300/J082v19n04_07.

Fraser, J. (2003). Masks and redemptive transformation. In T. O'Keffe & K. Fox (Eds.), *Finding the real me: True tales of sex and gender diversity* (pp. 209–219). San Francisco, CA: Jossey-Bass.

Gates, G. J. (2017, January 11). In U.S., more adults identifying as LGBT. Retrieved from http://news.gallup.com.

Gonzalez, M., & McNulty, J. (2010). Achieving competency with transgender youth: School counselors as collaborative advocates. *Journal of LGBT Issues in Counseling, 4*(3–4), 176–186. doi: 10.1080/15538605.2010.524841.

Goodrich, K. M., Harper, A. J., Luke, M., & Singh, A. A. (2013). Best practices for professional school counselors working with LGBTQ youth. *Journal of LGBT Issues in Counseling, 7*(4), 307–322. doi: 10.1080/15538605.2013.839331.

Goodrich, K. M., & Luke, M. (2009). LGBTQ responsive school counseling. *Journal of LGBT Issues in Counseling, 3*(2), 113–127. doi: 10.1080/15538600903005284.

Gottfredson, L. S. (2005). Applying Gottfredson's theory of circumscription and compromise in career guidance and counseling. In S. D. Brown & R. W. Lent (Eds.), *Career development and counseling: Putting theory and research to work* (pp. 71–100). New York, NY: Wiley.

Greytak, E. A., Kosciw, J. G., & Diaz, E. M. (2009). *Harsh realities: The experiences of transgender youth in our nation's schools*. New York, NY: GLSEN.

Hetherington, C. (1991). Life planning and career counseling with gay and lesbian students. In N. J. Evans & V. A. Wall (Eds.), *Beyond tolerance: Gays, lesbians, and bisexuals on campus* (pp. 131–145). Alexandria, VA: American College Personnel Assocation.

Holland, J. L. (1997). *Making vocational choices* (3rd ed.). Odessa, FL: Psychological Assessment Resources.

Hook, M. K., & Bowman, S. (2008). Working for a living: The vocational decision making of lesbians. *Journal of Lesbian Studies, 12*(1), 85–95. doi: 10.1300/10894160802174359.

Jackson, K. (2017). Supporting LGBTQ students in high school for the college transition: The role of school counselors. *Professional School Counseling, 20*(1a), 21–28. doi: 10 .5330/1096-2409-20.1a.21.

Jackson, M. A., & Verdino, J. (2012). Vocational psychology. In R. W. Rieber (Ed.), *Encyclopedia of the history of psychological theories* (pp. 1157–1170). New York, NY: Springer. doi:10.1007/978-1-4419-0463-8.

Knous, H. M. (2005). The coming out experience for bisexuals: Identity formation and stigma management. *Journal of Bisexuality, 5*(4), 37–59. doi:10.1300/J159v05n04_05.

Kosciw, J. G., Greytak, E. A., Giga, N. M., Villenas, C., & Danischewski, D. J. (2016). *The 2015 National School Climate Survey: The experiences of lesbian, gay, bisexual, transgender, and queer youth in our nation's schools.* New York, NY: GLSEN.

Kosciw, J. G., Palmer, N. A., Kull, R. M., & Greytak, E. A. (2013). The effect of negative school climate on academic outcomes for LGBT youth and the role of in-school supports. *Journal of School Violence, 12*(1), 45–63. doi: 10.1080/15388220.2012.732546.

Lev, A. I. (2004). *Transgender emergence: Therapeutic guidelines for working with gender-variant people and their families.* New York, NY: The Haworth Clinical Practice Press.

Lewis, J., Arnold, M. S., House, R., & Toporek, R. L. (2003). *Advocacy competencies.* Endorsed by the American Counseling Association Governing Council. Retrieved from https://www.counseling.org/Resources/Competencies/Advocacy_Competencies.pdf.

Luke, M., Goodrich, K. M., & Scarborough, J. L. (2011). Integration of the K-12 LGBTQI student population in school counselor education curricula: The current state of affairs. *Journal of LGBT Issues in Counseling, 5*(2), 80–101. doi: 10.1080/15538605.2011.574530.

McCarn, S. R., & Fassinger, R. E. (1996). Revisioning sexual minority identity formation: A new model of lesbian identity and its implications. *The Counseling Psychologist, 24*(3), 508–534. doi:10.1177/0011000096243011.

Mobley, M., & Slaney, R. B. (1996). Holland's theory: Its relevance for lesbian women and gay men. *Journal of Vocational Behavior, 48*(2), 125–135. doi: 10.1006/jvbe.1996.0013.

National Career Development Association. (1997). *Career counseling competencies.* Broken Arrow, OK: Author.

———. (2009). *Minimum competencies for multicultural career counseling and development.* Broken Arrow, OK: Author. Retrieved from https://www.ncda.org/aws/NCDA/pt/fli/12508/false.

Nicolazzo, Z. (2016). *Trans* in college: Transgender students' strategies for navigating campus life and the institutional politics of inclusion.* Sterling, VA: Stylus Publishing.

Nordmarken, S. (2014). Microaggressions. *Transgender Studies Quarterly, 1*(1–2), 129–134. doi: 10.1215/23289252-2399812.

Pepper, S. M., & Lorah, P. (2008). Career issues and workplace considerations for the transsexual community: Bridging a gap of knowledge for career counselors and mental heath care providers. *Career Development Quarterly, 56*(4), 330–343. doi: 10.1002/j.2161-0045.2008.tb00098.x.

Pool, N. (2006). Shirts to skirts: Male to female transsexuals in the workplace. In G. Teague (Ed.), *The new goddess: Transgender women in the twenty-first century* (pp. 65–72). Waterbury, CT: Fine Tooth Press.

Pope, M., Barret, B., Szymanski, D. M., Chung, Y. B., Singaravelu, H., McLean, R., & Sanabria, S. (2004). Culturally appropriate career counseling with gay and lesbian clients. *Career Development Quarterly, 53*(2), 157–177. doi: 10.1002/j.2161-0045.2004.tb00987.x.

Sangganjanavanich, V. F. (2009). Career development practitioners as advocates for transgender individuals: Understanding gender transition. *Journal of Employment Counseling, 46*(3), 128–135. doi: 10.1002/j.2161-1920.2009.tb00075.x.

Schmidt, C. K., & Nilsson, J. E. (2006). The effects of simultaneous developmental processes: Factors relating to the career development of lesbian, gay, and bisexual youth. *Career Development Quarterly, 55*(1), 22–37. doi: 10.1002/j.2161-0045.2006.tb00002.x.

Scott, D. A., Belke, S. L., & Barfield, H. G. (2011). Career development with transgender college students: Implications for career and employment counselors. *Journal of Employment Counseling, 48*(3), 105–113. doi: 10.1002/j.2161-1920.2011.tb01116.x.

Singh, A. A., & Kosciw, J. G. (2017). School counselors transforming schools for lesbian, gay, bisexual, transgender, and queer (LGBTQ) students. *Professional School Counseling, 20*(1a), 1–4. doi: 10.5330/1096-2409-20.1a.1.

Singh, A. A., Urbano, A., Haston, M., & McMahon, E. (2010). School counselors' strategies for social justice change: A grounded theory of what works in the real world. *Professional School Counseling, 13*(3), 135–145. doi: 10.5330/PSC.n.2010-13.135.

Super, D. E. (1980). A life-span, life-space approach to career development. *Journal of Vocational Behavior, 16*(3), 282–298. doi: 10.1016/0001-8791(80)90056-1.

Walworth, J. (2003). *Transsexual workers: An employer's guide.* Bellingham, WA: Center for Gender Sanity.

5

The Step-Up Career Development Program with Unaccompanied Latinx Refugee Youth in Resettlement High Schools

Elizabeth A. Quiñones

Unaccompanied refugee youth are under the age of eighteen, have fled their country of origin, and are without their parents or a previous primary caregiver. A surge of unaccompanied refugee youth, ages thirteen to seventeen, who originated from Honduras, Guatemala, El Salvador, and Mexico recently resettled in the United States. When found, these adolescents have been placed in the custody of the Office of Refugee Resettlement where they receive educational, medical, and social services. With the Step-Up Career Development Program, these vocationally at-risk Latinx (Latino/Latina) youth are enabled to become career- or college-ready high school graduates with concrete goals for the future. Students are provided strong role models with steady careers and research on any career of their choice. School counselors provide one-on-one career counseling in order to prepare students for graduation and the career of his or her choice. The cohesion of their peers participating in this program and the social support from adults may help unaccompanied Latinx refugee youth to develop their resilience while coping with traumatic loss, cultural transitions, and stigma.

SOCIAL JUSTICE NEEDS AND RATIONALE FOR THE CAREER DEVELOPMENT INTERVENTION

A refugee is defined as someone who has been forced to flee his or her country because of persecution, war, or violence. A refugee has a well-founded fear of persecution for reasons of race, religion, nationality, political opinion, or membership in a particular social group. Most likely, they cannot return home or are afraid to do so (USA for UNHCR, 2017a). In recent years, there has been an escalation in gang warfare and violence in Latin America, particularly in El Salvador, Honduras, and Guatemala. The rates of brutal homicides and other human rights abuses, including the recruitment of children into gangs, extortion, and sexual violence, have significantly risen. Thus, thousands of families have fled "and, in many cases, children have made the perilous journey alone. These unaccompanied children are some of the world's most vulnerable refugees—they have witnessed horrific violence and faced extreme risk" (USA for UNHCR, 2017b, p. 1).

The Office of Refugee Resettlement reported that 82 percent of unaccompanied refugee youth who have resettled in the United States of America are between the ages of thirteen and seventeen (Office of Refugee Resettlement, 2016). That is around 48,519 students in America in need of high school education services, including career development. In addition, recent refugee adolescents have arrived, academically behind their peers (Administration for Children and Families, 2015). High school–age unaccompanied refugee youth are an at-risk population for academic achievement and vocational development toward successful transition into adulthood due to their "history of loss and bereavement, exposure to a variety of traumas, and uncertainty about the future" (as cited in Seglem, Oppedal, & Roysamb, 2014, p. 293). This uncertainty comes at a time when youth must begin to think about what they are going to do after high school. American high schools should be prepared to guide unaccompanied refugee youth in the midst of their chaotic and uncertain lives. Additionally, due to increased racial tension and political uncertainty for refugees and immigrants in the United States (Rhodan, 2017), school staff and counselors should be prepared to handle issues such as bullying or racism directed at youth with refugee status or targeted cultural identification.

While in custody of the Office of Refugee Resettlement, unaccompanied youth typically receive six structured education hours a day after their educational level is assessed. At some point, unaccompanied youth are placed with a sponsor or within the foster system to be enrolled in the local public schools (Administration for Children and Families, 2015). Age upon arrival is an important risk factor for these students placed in high schools because they spent their formative school years outside of the United States, must learn English, and assimilate to American culture (Diaz-Strong & Ybarra, 2016).

Seglem, Oppedal, & Roysamb (2014) found that, despite their traumatic background, refugee youth adapt and adjust well to Western cultures. Students in this study exhibited similar levels of life satisfaction as their peers. However, unaccompanied refugee youth exhibited higher levels of depression. Thus, school counselors should be trained in depression assessment and educated about risk factors that can greatly influence high school completion. Refugee adolescents have experienced great loss and may have gone through the Office of Refugee Resettlement to live in foster care or with a relative. Some may have endured maltreatment, including exposure to substance abuse and neglect (Scott, Faulkner, Cardoso, & Burstain, 2014). While they should be treated like any other student with regard to career development, these students might especially need to depend on the social support given by role models in the school environment.

A refugee student may not know how to evaluate his or her interests and abilities in the same way that his or her U.S. peers may in order to become *career ready*. Johnson, Jones, and Cheng (2014) define career readiness as the "acquisition of the knowledge, skills, and behaviors necessary to achieve [future] plans" (p. 144). Johnson et al. (2014) conducted a study about at-risk urban youth's career readiness. They found that students who had grown up around violent scenes and drug activity without vocational support in school were more likely to engage in criminal activity. Their study also found that vocational support in school aided students to become more career ready after high school. They concluded that in order for a high school student to be career ready after graduation, he/she needs appropriate academic preparation, including extracurricular learning, well-developed motivation, engagement, and self-efficacy. Unaccompanied refugee adolescents likewise need this preparation for their own futures. In addition, they likely need extra support to explore their possible abilities and interests in order to navigate the American workforce and be equipped with relevant information and purpose (Diaz-Strong & Ybarra, 2016). Because unaccompanied refugee youth have been shown to exhibit similar levels of life satisfaction as their peers and high levels of adaptability to their resettlement country, school resources and community volunteers can be utilized to target career-readiness with these youth (Seglem et al., 2014).

The Step-Up Career Development Program could give unaccompanied refugee youth in high school the social support they need (a step up) in order to trust adults to help them succeed in a new country. This program helps to develop skills in language, research, analysis, self-evaluation, persistence, and goal setting. When these students arrive in the United States, they do not have a family; they are experiencing culture shock and are emotionally handling dark and heavy problems. This program takes students and fills them with hope that, with hard work and needed support, they can pursue almost any career they would like. Culturally competent role models, tutors, guidance counselors, and teachers/staff will work with them so that they can develop and meet their vocational goals. These positive role models can provide the educational and social support needed to prepare unaccompanied refugee Latinx youth throughout high school to develop their vocational self-concepts, promote their career decision-making skills, and plans after graduation, toward successful transitions to employment or college (Tello & Lonn, 2017; Wibrowski, Matthews, & Kitsantas, 2017). Thus, this career development intervention program in high school may help unaccompanied refugee Latinx youth make positive future contributions to society. With so many unaccompanied refugee youth arriving in America with so little support, this vocational program can be mutually beneficial.

The Step-Up career development intervention outlined in this proposal is grounded in the theory of circumscription and compromise (Gottfredson, 1996, 2005). According to this theory, as children and adolescents grow in their awareness of themselves and their social place in the world, they undergo a process of narrowing down vocational options to those they perceive as more compatible with their evolving self-concept. This career choice process includes four developmental stages: cognitive growth, self-creation, circumscription, and compromise. Counselors can helpfully intervene in this career development process with high school students, particularly with Latinx refugees, by providing educational support and resources to learn about their evolving vocational interests, abilities, and values in relation to accessible vocational options and pathways.

In the first stage of the career development process, the Step-Up Program begins with a strength-based career assessment and exploration learning activity, the Personal Accomplishment/Transferable Skills Career Exercise (see chapter 2 in this book). This assessment exercise allows both the school counselor and the student to realize how much the student's environment and unique background play a role in his or her abilities and/or interests. The resettlement process for an unaccompanied refugee youth could disrupt self-concept development, particularly in a school setting. It is through processing this exercise with the counselor that the student can start to develop a sense of self as a high school student preparing for the future, with many of the same opportunities as his or her U.S. peers.

The next stage in Gottfredson's career development theory is self-creation, or the need to have a sense of belonging in the world (Swanson & Fouad, 2015). By creating a list of possible careers to learn about, then narrowing it down throughout the student's high school career, the student is given the opportunity to create an identity in order to find a niche. Additionally, school counselors research various careers with a student in-session and give students an opportunity to research their desired niche in-session and independently. This is especially important because starting at the age of fourteen, individuals develop an orientation to their internal unique self so that they can explore vocational choices, which is the third stage of career development in Gottfredson's theory (Swanson & Fouad, 2015). Career workshops provide another opportunity to explore various career niches in order to narrow down career choices in informed ways that do not prematurely circumscribe their options.

According to the final stage in Gottfredson's four-stage model of career development, compromise, adolescents begin to think more about their vocational choices in terms of their interests and abilities (Swanson & Fouad, 2015). Unrealistic vocational considerations are abandoned for more realistic paths of action. In order to assist in this process, many high schools prepare their students by educating them about their options to enter the workforce upon graduation, attending vocational school, attending a two- or four-year college, joining the military, and so on (Niles & Harris-Bowlsbey, 2013). A healthy mix of encouragement and realism is recommended in discussions with students regarding the process and requirements of various careers and work, as well as researching relevant application deadlines and developing a timeline and plan of action. Their considerations in developing this vocational plan of action will include students' refugee status, their academic grades, standardized testing scores, and extracurricular activities so that they can apply them in the career-decision process. Counselors will need to be advocates so that refugee youth receive the services they deserve. It is important to note that unauthorized childhood arrivals are not eligible for federal financial aid to support college attendance (Diaz-Strong & Ybarra, 2016).

These stages of the career development intervention, grounded in Gottfredson's theory, are designed to be used effectively in the Step-Up Program. Students write personal reflections about their interests and abilities and are able to reflect aloud to their counselor. Through this process, the counselor is able to provide individualized interpretation and feedback to support the student's reflections. School counselors, teacher workshop leaders, volunteer tutors and volunteer career workshop leaders all provide practical information about the world of work through internet research and role modeling. Consistent with Johnson and colleagues' (2014) findings, role models play a large part in preparing at-risk youth to be career ready. These positive role models provide the social support needed to prepare unaccompanied refugee youth to make a life-changing decision that will help define their contribution to society.

MEASURABLE OBJECTIVES AND EXPECTED OUTCOMES

Freshman Year

Objective: Students will develop a tentative plan for possible elective courses and extracurricular activities for which they might enroll.

Outcome: Students will develop interests and abilities through chosen extracurricular activities and elective courses.

Sophomore Year

Objective: Students will understand varying options in the American workforce and will be able to list possible vocational interests.

Outcome: Students will use their list of vocational interests to research each vocation's requirements and will align their extracurricular activities and academic courses accordingly.

Junior Year

Objective: Students will be able to understand their interests and abilities through personal reflection and exploring results of assessments.

Outcome: Students will use their assessment results and personal reflection to choose a possible vocational path.

Senior Year

Objective: Students will choose their vocational path and prepare accordingly.

Outcome: Students will prepare their college applications, vocational schooling applications, and/or résumé.

PLAN FOR PROMOTING SERVICES

Promotion for this program will begin with having the program coordinator (e.g., a helping professional trained in career counseling in school contexts) speak with the high school principal to construct a team of teachers and staff interested in facilitating the program. In order to promote follow-through with the vocational program, teachers and staff will have freedom to adapt the program content with the program coordinator to fit the structure and needs of their school. The school will send a letter in English and Spanish to the student body announcing the Step-Up program aimed at refugee youth. Students can send back an enrollment form or sign up at school.

PLAN FOR DELIVERING SERVICES

There will be weekly meetings during the summer months with the program coordinator, counselors, and development team before school begins to organize and prepare for the enrolled refugee youth. This will include an orientation by the program coordinator to provide education about (a) career development according to Gottfredson's theory of circumscription and compromise and (b) the background and risk/resilience factors for this population to gain cultural competence in working with Latinx refugee high school students so that they can be supportive to the incoming students' needs.

At the start of the school year, the counselors will make one-on-one appointments with refugee students to create an ongoing plan throughout students' high school years. School counselors are advised to meet with students individually throughout the program, which will normalize access to counseling services. Thus, these counselors could connect youth with appropriate individual therapy or group support as needed. Counselors should have a translator available to them if they do not speak Spanish for sessions. Lack of English proficiency is a risk factor for this population (Diaz-Strong & Ybarra, 2016), so students will be encouraged to use as much English as possible in sessions, as well as in other settings within the school. Latinx refugee students who have traveled alone to the United States are less likely to complete high school than their U.S.-born Latinx counterparts (Diaz-Strong & Ybarra, 2016). According to Diaz-Strong & Ybarra (2016), they are even less likely to attend college due to the hurdles needed to attain federal financial aid. These researchers also stated that many students choose to drop out of high school due to lowered aspirations "when they realize that the 'normal' routes after high school are closed or difficult to achieve" (p. 283). Counselors should be trained by the program coordinator on how to be an advocate for their student.

Based on student plans, counselors implement and facilitate career workshops, where professional Latinx and/or refugee volunteers of varying vocations talk about their careers and jobs. It is important for students to see successful adults with similar background (refugee status and/or ethnicity) as role models (Yancey, Grant, Kurosky, Kravitz-Wirtz, & Mistry, 2011). Students are encouraged to request career education workshops on options they are considering. The program coordinator and school counselors can work together to find culturally appropriate individuals to lead those workshops. Students should have free periods/study hall periods that the school can use to hold college application/résumé workshops, and volunteers can attend to assist with homework. Homework volunteers must speak Spanish fluently.

CAREER DEVELOPMENT PROGRAM CONTENT

Relevant to the freshman year program objective, the program coordinator will set up a group workshop with refugee youth students at the beginning of the year in order to provide an overview of the Step-Up Program. Thereafter, a school counselor will administer the Personal Accomplishments and Transferable Skills Exercise to a volunteer student in front of the group. Then, the large group will split into pairs or small groups to administer the exercise with each other. This exercise will not only allow students to get to know each other, but also allow students to see the skills and abilities they have acquired while accomplishing three chosen accomplishments. Students will be developing their self-concept and working towards self-actualization by using their personal experiences, cultural background, and unique past environment. At the end of the workshop, students will sign up for an individual time slot with their assigned counselor. This workshop may be conducted in Spanish, as needed.

During an individual session with the student, counselors will use the Personal Accomplishments and Transferable Skills Exercise to pick out the transferable skills that have prepared them for high school and extracurricular activities and courses the student could take in the future. Students will begin to develop a cognitive map of possible occupations they might pursue. The list of interests is expected to be long with possibilities.

Relevant to the sophomore year program objective, volunteers of varying vocations (e.g., lawyers, doctors, electricians, plumbers, artists, social workers, psychologists, union workers) will be recruited to provide students with a workshop outlining their vocational path, job description, pros and cons of their vocation, and a Question & Answer segment. These professionals should be a source of empowerment for the students. Thus, the program coordinator and school counselor will find professionals of color, specifically Latinx, and/or those who have had or currently hold a refugee status.

During an end-of-the year meeting with their school counselor, students will develop a list of possible career choices they would like to pursue. With help from their counselor, students can follow up with previous workshop speakers. Counselors will explore with the student the requirements for those careers and related careers using the Occupational Outlook Handbook (OOH) published online by the U.S. Bureau of Labor Statistics (http://www.bls.gov/ooh/). Students will also begin using as much English as possible with counselors and with staff. Student tutors will be provided after school if students are falling behind academically due to their lack of English proficiency. This will be available throughout the duration of the program.

Relevant to the junior year program objective, school counselors will review with students their career interest list created at the end of sophomore year to further research and explore during their meetings. Together, the counselor and each student will engage in considering possible paths and requirements needed for their careers of interest. Considerations will include what post–high school vocational options and pathways are realistically possible for the student to pursue according to the student's academic record, individual interests, abilities, and life circumstance (e.g., state of finances, sources of social and emotional support). School counselors will do their own research to be able to be an advocate for the student's chosen path, with the support and resources of the program coordinator. The students should be aware of any obstacles and be frequently updated on the status of the counselor's advocacy efforts, as well as consider realistic backup options and alternate pathways. Counselors will help each student consider helpful strategies to navigate barriers and access resources for pursuing their post–high school vocational options and pathways.

Relevant to the senior year program objective, students will meet with their school counselors at the beginning of the year to deliver their action plan along with the requirements needed to meet their career goal. The counselor will make an appointment with the student within the next two weeks to provide deadlines for requirements (e.g., college applications). Students will prepare their materials according to the deadlines or timelines they have determined, with active support from their counselors.

RESOURCES NEEDED

A program coordinator, a well-qualified school/career counselor, bilingual in Spanish and English, is needed to plan the program with staff, train staff to develop cultural competence, manage and monitor program success, and evaluate program efficacy to make adjustments (see relevant competencies needed in tables 5.1 and 5.2). Advertising for volunteers may, for example, include outreach to college social work programs seeking to partner with community service opportunities to enroll their students as volunteers. As this program depends on the buy-in of teachers and staff, stipends for the Development Team (four to five members) might help motivate this core group to facilitate vocational, résumé, and career building workshops, as well as conduct outreach for volunteers. Funding for educational materials and refreshments for workshops would be helpful. Workshop speakers' stipends as a small token of gratitude would be helpful for recruiting role models to speak at the school about their careers. Finally, Spanish-speaking translators should be made available as needed.

Table 5.1. Relevance to Career Counseling Competencies

Career Counseling Competency	Addressed by Career Intervention	Relevance to Corresponding Competency
1. Career Development Theory	X	Counselors will apply Gottfredson's theory of Circumscription and Compromise (1996, 2005).
2. Individual and Group Counseling Skills	X	Career counselors will gain competency in one-on-one counseling and in career workshops with refugee students.
3. Individual/Group Assessment	X	Career counselors will assess students' aptitude, achievement, interests, values, and personality traits through SAT/ACT tests, the Personal Accomplishments/ Transferable Skills Career Exercise, personal reflection and feedback, and student exit counseling interviews and evaluations. Career counselors will

Career Counseling Competency	Addressed by Career Intervention	Relevance to Corresponding Competency
		assess students' realistic options by inquiring about his or her lifestyle, assessing their maturity, and his or her choice career/vocation. They will also discuss students' social, gender, and refugee status challenges.
4. Information/ Resources/ Technology	X	Career counselors will provide students with resources about various careers. Students will be able to request certain career workshops and the program coordinator will find a speaker to provide career education. Career counselors will work with students on their large interests list made in their freshman year throughout high school until they have a specific destination with goals in mind. Together, the student and career counselor will use the internet and various career databases (e.g., Occupational Outlook Handbook) in order to explore career interests. Students will also research deadlines and requirements to begin the process of pursuing vocational goals.
5. Program Promotion, Management, and Implementation	X	The program provides high schools with evaluations and exercises to practice with students. With more data, career counselors will be able to manage and implement the program more effectively.
6. Coaching, Consultation, and Performance Improvement	X	The career counselor will be able to consult and supervise the development team of this program. Teachers and staff will need guidance on how to conduct career-building workshops using Gottfredson's theory.
7. Diverse Populations	X	This program identifies the individual needs of unaccompanied refugee youth and supports them in learning about the American workforce and possible career paths. Students will be able to strengthen their English-speaking skills during tutoring sessions with undergraduate volunteers.
8. Supervision	X	Due to the program coordinator's competence in underserved Latinx youth, s/he will supervise members of the development team, including career/ school counselors.

(continued)

Table 5.1. *Continued*

Career Counseling Competency	Addressed by Career Intervention	Relevance to Corresponding Competency
9. Ethical/Legal Issues	X	Career counselors will learn to adhere to relevant ethical codes and standards (NBCC, NCDA, and ACA). Career counselors will learn about the legal issues involved with refugee students who may have undocumented family members.
10. Research/ Evaluation	X	This is an extremely underserved population. There is little research on unaccompanied refugee youth and almost none of Latino refugees. The career counselor will rely heavily on student and teacher evaluations to measure the program's effectiveness. A more experienced career counselor can assist in making needed changes.

Source: NCDA, 1997, 2009.

Table 5.2. Relevance to Advocacy Competencies

Advocacy Competency	Addressed by Career Intervention	Relevance to Corresponding Competency
1. Client/Student Empowerment	X	Counselors will identify strengths and resources of students by administering the Personal Accomplishments and Transferable Skills Exercise. Counselors will undergo cultural competency training by the program coordinator in order to understand the political, economic, and cultural factors that affect unaccompanied refugee youth. Counselors will help students identify the external barriers they may face in pursuit of their chosen career goal. In addition to advocating for the student, counselors will keep students informed about potential barriers so that they can advocate for themselves.
2. Client/Student Advocacy	X	Counselors will inform and work with students to gain access to resources, such as federal financial aid if they choose to attend college. Together, they can develop a way to get around the discussed barriers.
3. Community Collaboration	X	The program coordinator and counselors will work together to build a community for students. Culturally competent mentors

Advocacy Competency	Addressed by Career Intervention	Relevance to Corresponding Competency
		and volunteers will be available to inform students of varying career opportunities and their path to success. Tutoring volunteers will also be available to support academic success and English proficiency.
4. Systems Advocacy	—	—
5. Public Information	—	—
6. Social/Political Advocacy	—	—

Source: Lewis et al., 2003.

METHODS OF EVALUATION

At the end of every school quarter, the program coordinator will hold a Development Team meeting to administer a process evaluation to determine whether students are benefitting from the program, including survey results from students on their perceptions. The team will discuss the results and limitations to student success in order to problem solve and adjust the program accordingly. The first year of the program will be a test run to demonstrate to the school board that unaccompanied refugee youth can benefit from a career intervention program that is focused on their vocational interests post high school.

Career preparedness can be defined as "academic knowledge to qualify for job training . . . [and] has the prerequisite knowledge and skills needed to be placed in a credit-bearing course or training program" (Camara, 2013, p. 22). Requirements considered in the evaluation for preparedness include admission to a vocational school, teacher evaluations of skills needed for chosen vocation skills, academic grades, and relevant extracurricular activities. College preparedness can be defined as "academic knowledge and skills required to qualify for placement into entry-level college credit coursework without remediation" (Camara, 2013, p. 22). The following requirements will be considered in the evaluation for preparedness of the Step-Up Career Development Program for participating high school student participants, unaccompanied Latinx refugee youth: SAT/ACT scores, academic grades, teacher evaluations of improved cognitive skills from high school entry to graduation, and college admission letters. Additionally, there will be exit counseling with the students during their senior year, including a self-report survey evaluating the program's strengths and weaknesses (formative evaluation), and teacher evaluation of the program's strengths and weaknesses (summative evaluation).

PLAN FOR REVISION

With this program, every student enrolled as an unaccompanied refugee youth is expected to choose a career path with significant social and academic support from his or her school counselor, volunteers, and teachers/ staff. If students are not prepared for college or a career, the Step-Up Career Development Program needs to be revised according to teacher process evaluation results and a student self-reported survey aimed at measuring how supported students felt, as well as the teacher evaluation of how well the program seems to be fostering self-actualization in a school setting and beyond. While the staff is dedicated to making sure that students have all resources necessary to build English proficiency and to learn about American occupations, students will still be assimilating to American culture. This process of assimilation is an important part of development for these students. Counselors should be prepared for this to be a hurdle in making career goals. Many students may discover new things about themselves and develop new curiosities as the years go on. Revisions should be implemented in a timely manner across all grades with interim feedback from participating students and staff. All revisions should remain within the budget. The nature of this program allows schools to adapt to the needs of their students and should be subject to complete revision every two years.

REFLECTIONS ON COUNSELOR SELF-AWARENESS OF POTENTIAL RESOURCES AND BIASES FROM PRIVILEGED AND MARGINALIZED IDENTITIES

As a light-skinned Puerto Rican second-generation college student, I have been able to benefit from White privilege. No one has ever assumed me to be incompetent or threatening due to the color of my skin or cultural background. Unlike my mother, no one has ever felt threatened by my presence in a convenience store based solely on appearance. Unlike my father, no one has ever questioned my ability to succeed. Most importantly, no one has questioned whether I should be in this country or not. Unlike Latinos with darker skin, I have never been asked for proof of my citizenship in this country. I do not know what it feels like to be treated like I don't belong in a country, especially one that I bravely traveled to alone. Many of the students who can benefit from the Step-Up program will have lost or left behind their entire family to somehow travel to another country for any opportunity. Students who will attend high school have experienced trauma and may still be experiencing a turbulent home life. My goal was to incorporate in the Step-Up program my privileged high school experience that was dedicated to my success. No one ever doubted that I would go to college or succeed. If I ever came across obstacles, many staff members were available to advocate for me or provide the necessary resources so that I could advocate for myself. I attended an all-girls private high school in an affluent suburb in New Jersey. My high school started preparing me for college as soon as I arrived. Similarly, students that are a part of the Step-Up Program would have an opportunity to have staff ready to advocate and work with them so that they can accomplish realistically set goals.

When I first heard that so many unaccompanied refugee youth were coming into the United States, I was relieved that there were resources if they were found. I was disappointed, however, by the lack of further support for this population. With growing political tensions in the United States about Latinx immigrants, students may find themselves without the emotional and social support necessary to believe that they can accomplish their dreams. It is hard for me to imagine a teenager who no one believes in, so I developed the Step-Up program.

REFERENCES

Administration for Children and Families. (2015). Children entering the United States unaccompanied: Section 3. Retrieved from http://www.acf.hhs.gov/programs/orr/resource/children-entering-the-united-states-unaccompanied-section-3#3.3.5.

Camara, W. (2013). Defining and measuring college and career readiness: A validation framework. *Educational Measurement: Issues and Practice, 32*(4), 16–27. doi: 10.1111/emip.12016.

Diaz-Strong, D. X., & Ybarra, M. A. (2016). Disparities in high school completion among Latinos: The role of the age-at-arrival and immigration status. *Children and Youth Services Review, 71*, 282–289. doi: 10.1016/j.childyouth.2016.11.021.

Gottfredson, L. S. (1996). Gottfredson's theory of circumscription and compromise. In D. Brown & L. Brooks (Eds.), *Career choice and development: Applying contemporary theories to practice* (3rd ed., pp. 179–232). San Francisco, CA: Jossey Bass.

———. (2005). Applying Gottfredson's theory of circumscription and compromise in career guidance and counseling. In S. D. Brown & R. W. Lent (Eds.), *Career development and counseling: Putting theory and research to work* (pp. 71–100). New York, NY: Wiley.

Johnson, S. L., Jones, V., & Cheng, T. (2014). Promoting successful transition to adulthood for urban youths: Are risk behaviors associated with career readiness? *Social Work Research, 38*(3), 144–153. doi:10.1093/swr/svu020.

Lewis, J., Arnold, M. S., House, R., & Toporek, R. L. (2003). *Advocacy competencies.* Endorsed by the American Counseling Association Governing Council. Retrieved from https://www.counseling.org/Resources/Competencies/Advocacy_Competencies.pdf.

National Career Development Association. (1997). *Career counseling competencies.* Broken Arrow, OK: Author.

———. (2009). *Minimum competencies for multicultural career counseling and development.* Broken Arrow, OK: Author. Retrieved from https://www.ncda.org/aws/NCDA/pt/fli/12508/false.

Niles, S. G., & Harris-Bowlsbey, J. E. (2013). *Career development interventions in the 21st century* (4th ed.). Upper Saddle River, NJ: Pearson Education.

Office of Refugee Resettlement. (2016, September). Facts and data. Retrieved from http://www.acf.hhs.gov/programs/orr/about/ ucs/facts-and-data.

Rhodan, M. (2017, April 28). Arrests of undocumented immigrants went up during president Trump's first 100 days. *Time.* Retrieved from http://time.com/4759713/trump-100-days-arrests-undocumented-immigrants/.

Scott, J., Faulkner, M., Cardoso, J. B., & Burstain, J. (2014). Kinship care and undocumented Latino children in the Texas foster care system: Navigating the child welfare-immigration crossroads. *Child Welfare, 93*(4), 53–69.

Seglem, K. B., Oppedal, B., & Roysamb, E. (2014). Daily hassles and coping dispositions as predictors of psychological adjustment: A comparative study of young unaccompanied refugees and youth in the resettlement country. *International Journal of Behavioral Development, 38*(3), 293–303. doi: 10.1177/0165025414520807.

Swanson, J. L., & Fouad, N. A. (2015). *Career theory and practice: Learning through case studies* (3rd ed.). Thousand Oaks, CA: Sage.

Tello, A. M., & Lonn, A. R. (2017). The role of high school and college counselors in supporting the psychosocial and emotional needs of Latinx first-generation college students. *The Professional Counselor, 7,* 349–359. doi: 10.15241/amt.7.4.349.

USA for UNHCR (United Nations High Commissioner for Refugees). (2017a). *What is a refugee?* Retrieved from http://www.unrefugees.org/what-is-a-refugee/.

———. (2017b). *Central America: Families and unaccompanied children are fleeing horrific gang violence.* Retrieved from http://www.unrefugees.org/where-we-work/central-america.

Wibrowski, C. R., Matthews, W. K., & Kitsantas, A. (2017). The role of a skills learning support program on first-generation college students' self-regulation, motivation, and academic achievement: A longitudinal study. *Journal of College Student Retention: Research, Theory & Practice, 19,* 317–332. doi: 10.1177/1521025116629152.

Yancey, A. K., Grant, D., Kurosky, S., Kravitz-Wirtz, N., & Mistry, R. (2011). Role modeling, risk, and resilience in California adolescents. *Journal of Adolescent Health, 48*(1), 36–43. doi: 10.1016/j.jadohealth.2010.05.001.

IV

CAREER DEVELOPMENT INTERVENTIONS FOR SOCIAL JUSTICE NEEDS IN EDUCATIONAL CONTEXTS WITH UNDERSERVED COLLEGE STUDENTS

6

Gen1 Quick-Start

Academic Major and Career Decision-Making Workshop for Latina First-Generation Freshmen

Ariel Sorensen

This chapter outlines an introductory workshop directed toward incoming first-generation Latina freshmen at a four-year commuter college in a low-socioeconomic neighborhood. The specific needs of this population are assessed in terms of the impact of both identity intersectionality and intergenerational cultural capital on college retention and graduation rates. The proposed workshop program is designed to increase both first-year student retention and the four- and six-year graduation rates, reduce late-stage major changes (at three-plus full-time academic years completed), and normalize (and therefore increase) utilization of career service resources in order to bridge the gap between first-generation Latinas and their legacy peers.

SOCIAL JUSTICE NEEDS AND RATIONALE FOR THE CAREER DEVELOPMENT INTERVENTION

The target population for the career development intervention proposed in this chapter is Latina first-generation college freshmen, particularly low-income commuter students at four-year colleges with concerns for their retention and graduation rates. This Gen1 Quick-Start introductory workshop was developed to help address these students' underserved needs for timely information and culturally sensitive academic and career planning support. In this chapter, *first-generation* refers to students whose parents or guardians have not attended any college, regardless of degree status, and does not relate to immigration status. In contrast, *legacy* students are described as students with at least one parent who matriculated into college. *Latina* is based on a self-identification of female gender and ethnic origin from a Latin American country, Puerto Rico, or Spain.

The first-generation college Latina student population is of particular concern because of the additional difficulties related to overlapping marginalized identities. Developing an effective intervention that empowers these students to succeed in academic and career development requires consideration of the intersectionality of gender, ethnicity, and first-generation status.

The unique difficulties faced by first-generation students have been widely documented. First-generation students tend to come from lower-income families and, as a result, are more likely to experience financial stress while in college (Bui, 2002). Similarly, these students are more likely to need to work at least part time to support either themselves or family members, which has been shown to adversely affect academic performance (Saenz, Hurtado, Barrera, Wolf, & Yeung, 2007). Ironically, the cost of academic failure is also higher for many first-generation students, as tuition likely represents a greater proportion of these students' financial assets. According to a Pell Institute study (Engle & Tinto, 2008), the median individual income for low-income first-generation students was $12,100 and the average amount of unmet financial need for each student was roughly $6,000, nearly half of their total income. For these students, going to college poses a significantly greater financial risk with a lower rate of success than their legacy peers.

The differences between first-generation and legacy students are hardly limited to financial resources. *Cultural capital* is a sociological term to describe intangible assets such as knowledge and skills that allow for upward social mobility. Parental college experience often leads to the intergenerational transmission of cultural capital in the form of reinforced positive attitudes toward higher education. In order to maintain the status quo, college educated parents instill in their children an appreciation for higher education as well as provide them with social, educational, and monetary resources that facilitate future success (McDonough, 1997). Essentially, the children of college-educated parents tend to inherit an advantage. According to a study conducted by Padgett, Johnson, and Pascarella (2012), students who had a parent with any amount of college experience tended to be more actively engaged in learning opportunities by the end of their first year. The findings suggest that college-educated parents transmit helpful knowledge and expectations about college to their children and, therefore, first-generation students are placed at a fundamental disadvantage. While some academically helpful traits such as scientific curiosity and passion for math are often considered innate, they are more likely fostered and developed in childhood by caretakers who both value those traits and have the resources to encourage their development.

The literature indicates a need for supportive programming directed toward first-generation college students, but treating these students as a homogenous group ignores important multicultural considerations. Disadvantaged groups are disproportionately represented among first-generation students. A National Center for Education Statistics study found in 2011, 61 percent of Latino/a students aged five to seventeen qualified as first-generation students as opposed to roughly 33 percent of students in the total population (Aud et al., 2012).

A study of the postsecondary aspirations of Mexican American high school seniors found that, compared to their White peers, these students reported more perceived barriers to attending college and described those barriers as more difficult to overcome (McWhirter, Torres, Salgado, & Valdez, 2007). Notably, the students tended to report more anticipated preparation barriers such as not knowing what they wanted to do career-wise. Despite this, both groups reported comparable levels of career aspiration. The researchers suggested that the Mexican American students perceived a disconnect between what they wanted to do and what they personally believed themselves capable of doing.

Latina students may also be forced to overcome a cultural stigma against their choice to attend college. Latino/a culture traditionally prescribes a strict gender-role separation with women taking care of the home and raising children. While an increasing number of Latinas are making the choice to pursue a higher degree, in deference to their culture many may be prematurely foreclosing on traditionally masculine majors, for example, in STEM fields (science, technology, engineering, math). Risco and Duffy (2011) assessed both Latino and Latina students for work-related values and indeed found that Latinas assigned significantly higher importance to caring for others and reported less career decisiveness and identity salience than Latinos. The authors suggested that this was in line with traditional gender-role socialization and may not have reflected actual personal interest.

Similarly, in a study of the congruence between vocational interests and choice of academic major in various marginalized groups, significant correlations were found for Asian and Black students, but not for Latino/a students (Diemer, Wang, & Smith, 2010). This finding indicates that Latino/a students may be less likely to choose a major that directly corresponds with their vocational interests. Cuseo (2005) suggested that 75 percent of all in-coming first-year Latino/a students are actually undecided about an academic major, but many prematurely declare due to extrinsic factors such as family pressure or perceived economic value of a given career path without regard to personal interests or values. More than any other ethnic group, Latino/a students are more likely to choose a major for its perceived economic value (Bui, 2002). This could explain some of these students' later struggles. Cuseo (2005) found that students who eventually changed majors often cited an initial lack of understanding about their own interests and values as well as a lack of information about how various majors developed into careers. This suggests that Latino/a students could greatly benefit from an early ex-ploration of various majors and how they correspond with various interests. Providing information on the education requirements for a major at an early stage of a student's academic career is also important. At a 2001 conference on students in transition, Cuseo (2005) noted that many students reported not knowing the academic requirements for their chosen major. In addition, after completing four-year academic planning sheets, these students realized that the required classes were not in line with their interests. Garriott, Flores, and Martens (2013) also found that low-income students' learning experiences and level of perceived support moderated both career goals and outcome expectations. Therefore, a lack of access to direct learning experiences in STEM fields may lead to lowered outcome expectations for those fields and premature foreclosure of those options as majors.

The significance of these learning experiences is further detailed in Krum-boltz's (1996) social learning theory of career choice and decision making, which states that the interaction between learning experiences and an indi-vidual's innate characteristics, environmental factors, and how the person approaches a task directly influences the possible options that a person may consider when making a career-related decision. Essentially, a person's understanding of and preferences regarding the world of work are products of both direct experience (instrumental learning) and vicarious experience (associative learning), but the number and type of learning experiences to which that person is exposed may be limited by factors such as financial difficulties, lack of access, lack of perceived support, lack of information, or a perceived lack of interest. For example, a student whose parents can-not afford a musical instrument or lessons will not have the same amount or quality of learning experiences regarding music as would a student who has been taking private lessons since age five. In this case, the student with more learning experiences would be more likely to seriously consider music when considering career options than the student without the experiences. From this perspective, the role of a career intervention is to provide growth-oriented career-related learning experiences to broaden the individual's range of possible options, to instill a more realistic idea of the world of work, and to reinforce appropriate problem-solving skills in regard to decision-making. The goal of intervention is not only to help an individual make satisfying career decisions, but also to help the person develop the skills necessary to continue seeking helpful learning experiences and making satisfying decisions.

In line with this, the difference in access to a variety of learning experiences between Latina first-generation students and legacy students can be seen as a factor contributing to the gap in cultural capital. As previously noted, the Latina population must contend with the issues of intersecting marginalized identities and the cultural pressure to take on traditional gender roles. Thus, these identities and cultural factors also shape the number and kind of learning experiences to which a Latina student is exposed. Because first-generation students lack a parental college role model, they also notably lack the substantial associative learning experiences of parents providing information about their own direct experiences. Fouad, Gerstein, and Toporek's (2006) definition of social justice in the counseling environment states that the overarching goal of a targeted intervention is to ensure that every student has an equal chance at success. Thus, the proposed method of empowering this population is to reduce the cultural capital gap between first-generation Latinas and legacy students as quickly as possible by providing vicarious learning experiences and practice in using task-approach skills. On a practical level, this involves providing incoming freshman with much of the college-specific knowledge that legacy peers likely would have received from their parents, yet in a context that promotes needed cultural and social support.

In summary, the barriers that Latina first-generation college students face include a lack of college-specific knowledge, minimally informed vocational guidance, insufficient social support, and an increased likelihood of external stressors, such as family expectations and financial problems.

The specific needs of this population are as follows:

1. To develop an understanding of personal vocational interests
2. To identify possible majors of interest
3. To determine why other majors were not considered and evaluate whether some were prematurely excluded (and if so, why)

4. To know what classes are required for a major
5. To evaluate how personal interests align with academic major prerequisite classes
6. To know how various majors can lead to various careers
7. To understand points 1–6 *before* choosing first-semester courses in order to minimize late-stage major changes
8. To identify and explore how personal and cultural values and expectations have shaped academic and career choices
9. To open channels of communication among peers, provide a model for helpful peer communication, and normalize peer support
10. To develop an understanding of the career services offered by the college

MEASURABLE OBJECTIVES AND EXPECTED OUTCOMES

Based on these identified needs, students who complete this workshop program will be able to:

1. Identify and communicate their own vocational interests
2. Identify at least three prospective majors while recognizing that they do not have to make a one-time choice
3. Use college resources to find a full list of prerequisites for at least three majors of interest
4. Create a hypothetical four-year academic plan for at least two majors of interest
5. List and briefly describe at least five possible careers for at least three majors of interest
6. Describe the education-to-career progression for three of the careers
7. Explain why at least five majors in nontraditional fields were excluded
8. Describe an extracurricular activity that could provide an exploratory experience in both a major of interest and a major not of interest

These students will be expected to:

1. Develop more informed class schedules that will help them both graduate in a timely fashion and efficiently prepare for a desired career
2. Be more informed about majors and careers that will decrease late-stage major changes
3. Be more willing to seek career services assistance

PLAN FOR PROMOTING SERVICES

Because of the high attrition rate for first-generation students (Ishitani, 2006) and specifically because many commuter colleges allow incoming freshman to register for classes online without meeting with an academic advisor, an effective intervention would ideally take place before classes begin to allow for the participants to adjust their schedules without penalty.

Participants would be recruited using demographic data from the existing incoming freshman survey. Students who indicate that they identify as female, Latino/a (or "Other" and write in a specific Latin American country, Spain, or Puerto Rico), and indicate that their parents' or legal guardians' highest attained level of education is high school/GED or below would be contacted via their new campus email address to attend an on-campus pre-orientation first-generation student workshop. This mode of selection would include students with a parent or guardian who matriculated but did not attain a degree. Ideally, to allow these students viable options for attending one of the workshops on campus, four half-day workshops would be offered at least a week before the official start of classes: three on different weekdays and one on a weekend. On-campus childcare would be offered to ease the potential burden for mothers. The recruitment email would contain information in both English and Spanish and would include a link to RSVP for a session. A link stating "I'm interested but I can't make any of the dates" would direct to a career services individual appointment page. Students who do not RSVP would be sent two follow-up invitation emails. Automated reminder emails would be sent out a week prior to each session. A day before the workshop, a career services staff member would make reminder calls and offer individual appointments if a student is no longer able to attend the workshop. In order to attract students, lunch from a local restaurant would be advertised as included with the workshop.

PLAN FOR DELIVERING SERVICES

To reduce the risk of incomplete information due to missed sessions, the workshop would take place over a single four-hour half-day ending in a group lunch. Each session would be planned for no more than ten participants, with additional sessions opening if there is a demand. The program would be delivered first in a standard classroom, then in a computer lab to allow participants access to the course catalogue and internet career exploration and job search resources—specifically to complete the online O*NET Interest Profiler (available in both English and Spanish) and receive results and links to related occupations (National Center for O*NET Development, n.d.). Participants would then move back to the standard classroom to discuss their findings as a group. Alternatively, an open-layout computer lab would allow the entire program to take place in one room. After the didactic component and aside from the administration of the O*NET Interest Profiler, the students would be encouraged to actively consult with their peers throughout the workshop.

INTERVENTION PROGRAM CONTENT

Section 1

This would begin with introductions from the facilitator(s) and students, including name, prospective major if any, and current career aspirations if any. The facilitator would give a presentation on major choice and change statistics, issues faced by students who prematurely or belatedly select a major, where to find major requirements, and career sites that list related majors. This would include a brief presentation of major areas (such as business, generally, and specializations in business administration, accounting, etc.) and various career paths and educational requirements (graduate school, externships, certifications, etc.) associated with each, paying special attention to nontraditional fields for women. The facilitator would discuss how choices should be well informed and ask for reasons why the participants would choose a major.

Section 2

The group would relocate to a computer lab to allow internet access. The facilitator would begin by having the students take the O*NET Interest Profiler online and find matching career options via O*NET links. Students would be instructed to take notes about careers that they find appealing. Then, the facilitator would have students open the college major catalogue and, on a provided sheet of paper divided into three columns, sort every major as "would be interested," "not interested," and "unsure." Facilitators would assist students in finding careers associated with their three top-choice majors, have them write down at least five career options for every major that interests them, have them select three careers of top interest, and instruct them to read about those careers on O*NET and how to prepare for them. Students would be asked to consider if their top interest-based careers lined up with their top major choices and, if not, take a moment to find which majors led to them and consider the similarities and differences. The facilitator would re-convene the whole group and guide a discussion of findings about how their top majors were chosen, which majors were disregarded, and which careers did or did not appeal to the group. Include a break if necessary.

Section 3

The facilitator would provide students with three copies of the college four-year academic planning sheet and project the college's general education requirements on the main screen. Students would be directed to the college major and course catalogues to list the required courses for their top three majors. The facilitator would lead a discussion about any surprises or wor-ries about requirements, then assist students in creating a four-year academic plan for the three selected majors including summer internships and study abroad opportunities. The facilitator would encourage making room for ex-ploratory electives in subjects in which they may want to major.

Section 4

The next task would be to consolidate knowledge and assess for premature exclusion by asking students to pick a major on their "unsure" list and repeat all previous activities (find five career paths, pick one and learn about it, find required courses, and develop a plan). The facilitator would lead a discussion of how the students felt after developing a plan for an "unsure" major, why it was "unsure" in the first place, and whether it was more or less "unsure" after researching options. Introductions would be provided to career services connections to community service, internship fairs, and other exploratory options. The facilitator would have students brainstorm how to test various career and/or major options.

RESOURCES NEEDED

Anticipated resources necessary for each workshop include: (1) at least one facilitator, a career services counselor who is professionally well qualified and trained to address ethical and multicultural considerations throughout the program (ideally a bilingual Latina role model), and who might implement and coordinate evaluation of the workshops (see tables 6.1 and 6.2 for relevant competencies in career counseling and social justice advocacy; Lewis, Arnold, House, & Toporek, 2003; National Career Development Association, 1997, 2009); (2) access to the incoming freshman survey data; (3) access to school email accounts of targeted students; (4) one classroom and one computer lab with ten computers or one computer lab with an open layout (so as not to impede discussion) reserved before classes begin; (5) open internet access; (6) ten pens, ten copies of the columned sheet, and thirty copies of the four-year academic planning sheet per workshop; (7) visual projector capability; (8) access to two or more years of past scheduled academic courses to plan a hypothetical four-year schedule (or, ideally, two or more years of projected courses scheduled if possible); and (9) funding for lunch.

Table 6.1.   Relevance to Career Counseling Competencies

Career Counseling Competency	Addressed by Career Intervention	Relevance to Corresponding Competency
1. Career Development Theory	X	Support from research applying social learning career theory (Krumboltz, 1996).
2. Individual and Group Counseling Skills	X	Ability to quickly establish a productive group climate, moderate and encourage disclosure, and model providing effective feedback.
3. Individual/Group Assessment	X	Make use of a computer-delivered assessment and assist students in interpreting the resulting data.
4. Information/ Resources/ Technology	X	Familiarity with available campus resources in order to provide students with accurate information. Professional career counseling skills to administer and help students explore results with the online O*NET assessment and related career search sites; familiarity with the school's internet-based resources.
5. Program Promotion, Management, and Implementation	X	Developing this intervention to suit the needs of a particular college requires knowledge of the logistical aspects of program development.
6. Coaching, Consultation, and Performance Improvement	—	—

Career Counseling Competency	Addressed by Career Intervention	Relevance to Corresponding Competency
7. Diverse Populations	X	Multicultural sensitivity to the needs of heterogeneous Latina first-generation college students.
8. Supervision	—	—
9. Ethical/Legal Issues	X	Professional ethical attention to helpfully address issues of potential bias and discrimination against participants particularly in the intersectionality of their gender, language, race/ethnicity, SES, first-generation college status, and other cultural factors.
10. Research/ Evaluation	X	Development and delivery of a means of evaluation that suits the specific needs of the school or program.

Source: NCDA, 1997, 2009.

Table 6.2.   Relevance to Advocacy Competencies

Advocacy Competency	Addressed by Career Intervention	Relevance to Corresponding Competency
1. Client/Student Empowerment	X	To recognize the barriers that impact the students' academic aspirations and provide the necessary skills and knowledge to empower the students to self-advocate.
2. Client/Student Advocacy	X	To advocate for the needs of this population to the college administration in order to provide access to resources and information.
3. Community Collaboration	—	—
4. Systems Advocacy	—	—
5. Public Information	—	—
6. Social/Political Advocacy	—	—

Source: Lewis et al., 2003.

ETHICAL AND MULTICULTURAL CONSIDERATIONS

Careful consideration must be given to explaining the purpose of this introductory workshop, as the students may be young and the facilitator may be seen as an authority figure in power. The goals of the workshop must be made clear for all students, including those for whom English may be a second language. Ideally, the facilitator should be bilingual in the students' first language. Similarly, the facilitator's presentations may constitute the students' first serious exploration of major choice, therefore the information and methods for choosing majors as well as the suggestions provided by the online O*NET Interest Profiler must be presented as options for further exploration, not as absolute directives.

Special consideration must also be paid to those who fall under the target demographic but have already decided on a course of study. The purpose of the program is to broaden students' knowledge base in order to help inform decisions, not to actively push them away from a choice if they have already made one. Specifically considering Latina culture and expectations, the facilitator must consider that some students may make very culturally congruent major decisions despite other interests and those may still be entirely appropriate choices. The facilitator must not force Western or other ethnocentric ideas about work and prestige attainment onto others. Relatedly, though the students are grouped together as Latinas, the facilitator must be conscious and accepting of the fact that different students will vary widely in cultural expression, experience, and values.

In line with providing helpful cultural capital, care should be taken to address the fact that, as women, there are (and students have already likely experienced some form of) social barriers to entry in some fields. The students should be aware of the negative aspects as well as the positive, though in a manner that prepares them to challenge adversity rather than discourages them from trying. As appropriate, the facilitator may be in a position to advocate for disadvantaged students to faculty and staff who are not upholding unbiased practices. Moreover, the facilitator should encourage participants to continue to seek helpful support in their studies and career development with each other as well as with accessing college services.

METHODS OF EVALUATION

The following methods are proposed for gauging program effectiveness:

1. Conduct end-of-program exit evaluations gauging knowledge of majors, career paths, academic requirements, and vocational interests prior to

course and after course. Use open-ended questions asking what they learned that was of most value and what should be done differently.

2. Conduct semester/yearly follow-ups to measure attrition rate, major decidedness, feeling of major-decision preparedness, career decidedness, and feeling of career-decision preparedness.

PLAN FOR REVISION

Based on the evaluation results, relevant adjustments may be planned in the delivery or content of this career development intervention for first-generation Latina college students. For example, on one hand, it may be most feasible to offer half-day workshops with childcare and lunch provided for these Latina commuter students with multiple work and family responsibilities. On the other hand, if supported by evaluation feedback, a first-generation Latina support group might be integrated into a longer career development intervention, such as in a semester-long required course for all freshmen college students.

REFLECTIONS ON COUNSELOR SELF-AWARENESS OF POTENTIAL RESOURCES AND BIASES FROM PRIVILEGED AND MARGINALIZED IDENTITIES

The idea of this sample intervention was born from a personal reflection of what would have been helpful during my own college experience as both a first-generation college student and the multiracial daughter of a Caucasian U.S. Army service member and a South Korean immigrant. For much of my early life, my primary identification was "Army brat" with little mind to the other aspects of my identity. Because my family moved every three years and primarily lived on military bases, I was exposed to a wide range of people from various backgrounds and walks of life. However, this was moderated by the pervasiveness of military culture, which from my experience, tended toward conservatism, a blue-collar work ethic, and a glorification of traditional masculinity. I grew up in an environment of working- and lower-middle-class families who blamed the poor for allowing themselves to be poor and believed that the United States was a true meritocracy. A major task of my life since then has involved very consciously unraveling what I now recognize as internalized racism, sexism, classism, homophobia, transphobia, and other prejudices.

I am forced to recognize my privilege in the fact that I did not have to confront the realities of racial inequity until, as an undergraduate, I began working for a social psychology lab that was conducting research on the effects of stereotype threat in women of color. More than the empirical research, the intake and debriefing interviews that I conducted with the participants made me recognize my utter lack of understanding and awareness of oppression. At the same time, I was becoming gradually more aware of the experiential disparities between my fellow first-generation peers and the legacy students. For several years after graduation, I blamed myself for what I perceived to be a lack of resource utilization, inefficient course planning, and unrealistic expectations. I eventually accepted the fact that I had no way of knowing how to be an effective college student. It seems impossible, in retrospect, that I graduated from an Ivy League university not knowing what "networking" actually meant, but I have to concede that no one else that I grew up around knew, either. When I began working with college students in a counseling setting, I started to see the same lack of basic information with which I had struggled. I was outraged that the college did not seem to care that it was itself becoming a tool of oppression through its lack of active effort to support these students. This, more than anything, informed my development as a socially aware and involved counselor.

CONCLUDING REMARKS

The sample intervention outlined in this chapter was developed to provide a targeted, culturally informed, and efficient means to help close the gap between first-generation Latina college students and their legacy peers with a relatively quicker start. Having the knowledge and skills to make informed choices earlier in the process of selecting initial courses, the students will leave with not only the skills and knowledge to make informed decisions about their college experience, but also an increased sense of self-efficacy and confidence for the beginning of the school year. The students will also be encouraged to build a social support network of peers, which will become particularly important as students begin to have experiences to which their families cannot relate. At the most basic level, participation familiarizes students with important campus services and normalizes future help-seeking behavior.

REFERENCES

Aud, S., Hussar, W., Johnson, F., Kena, G., Roth, E., Manning, E., . . . Zhang, J. (2012). *The condition of education 2012* (NCES 2012-045). U.S. Department of Education, National Center for Education Statistics. Washington, DC. Retrieved from http://nces.ed.gov/pubsearch.

Bui, K. V. T. (2002). First-generation college students at a four-year university: Background characteristics, reasons for pursuing higher education, and first-year experiences. *College Student Journal, 36*(1), 3–11.

Cuseo, J. (2005). "Decided," "undecided," and "in transition": Implications for academic advisement, career counseling, and student retention. In R. S. Feldman (Ed.), *Improving the first year of college: Research and practice* (pp. 27–48). Mahwah, NJ: Lawrence Erlbaum.

Diemer, M. A., Wang, Q., & Smith, A. V. (2010). Vocational interests and prospective college majors among youth of color in poverty. *Journal of Career Assessment, 18*(1), 97–110. doi: 10.1177/1069072709350906.

Engle, J., & Tinto, V. (2008). *Moving beyond access: College success for low-income, first-generation students.* Washington, DC: The Pell Institute for the Study of Opportunity in Higher Education. Retrieved from https://eric.ed.gov/?id=ED504448.

Fouad, N., Gerstein, L., & Toporek, R. (2006). Social justice and counseling psychology in context. In R. L. Toporek, L. H. Gerstein, & N. A. Fouad (Eds.), *Handbook for social justice in counseling psychology: Leadership, vision, and action* (pp. 1–16). Thousand Oaks, CA: Sage. doi: 10.4135/9781412976220.n1.

Garriott, P. O., Flores, L. Y., & Martens, M. P. (2013). Predicting the math/science career goals of low-income prospective first-generation college students. *Journal of Counseling Psychology, 60*(2), 200–209. doi: 10.1037/a0032074.

Ishitani, T. T. (2006). Studying attrition and degree completion behaviors among first generation college students in the United States. *Journal of Higher Education, 77*(5), 861–884. doi: 10.1353/jhe.2006.0042.

Krumboltz, J. D. (1996). A learning theory of career counseling. In M. L. Savickas & W. B. Walsh (Eds.), Integrating career theory and practice (pp. 233–280). Palo Alto, CA: CPP Books.

Lewis, J., Arnold, M. S., House, R., & Toporek, R. L. (2003). *Advocacy competencies.* Endorsed by the American Counseling Association Governing Council. Retrieved from https://www.counseling.org/Resources/Competencies/Advocacy_Competencies.pdf.

McDonough, P. M. (1997). *Choosing college: How social class and schools structure opportunity.* Albany, NY: State University of New York Press.

McWhirter, E. H., Torres, D. M., Salgado, S., & Valdez, M. (2007). Perceived barriers and postsecondary plans in Mexican American and white adolescents. *Journal of Career Assessment, 15*(1), 119–138. doi: 10.1177/1069072706294537.

National Career Development Association. (1997). *Career counseling competencies.* Broken Arrow, OK: Author.

———. (2009). *Minimum competencies for multicultural career counseling and development.* Broken Arrow, OK: Author. Retrieved from https://www.ncda.org/aws/NCDA/pt/fli/12508/false.

National Center for O*NET Development. (n.d.). *My next move.* Retrieved July 27, 2017, from https://www.mynextmove.org/.

Padgett, R. D., Johnson, M. P., & Pascarella, E. T. (2012). First-generation undergraduate students and the impacts of the first year of college: Some additional evidence. *Journal of College Student Development, 53*(2), 243–266. doi: 10.1353/csd.2012.0032.

Risco, C. M., & Duffy, R. D. (2011). A career decision-making profile of Latina/o incoming college students. *Journal of Career Development, 38*(3), 237–255. doi: 10.1177/0894 845310365852.

Saenz, V. B., Hurtado, S., Barrera, D., Wolf, D., & Yeung, F. (2007). *First in my family: A profile of first-generation college students at four-year institutions since 1971.* Los Angeles, CA: Higher Education Research Institute, UCLA. Retrieved from https://www.heri .ucla.edu/PDFs/pubs/TFS/Special/Monographs/FirstInMyFamily.pdf.

V

CAREER DEVELOPMENT INTERVENTIONS FOR SOCIAL JUSTICE NEEDS IN EDUCATIONAL CONTEXTS IN DIVERSITY TRAINING WITH COLLEGES AND UNIVERSITIES

7

Coming to Understand and More Constructively Respond to Racial Microaggressions

Margo A. Jackson

The work roles of college faculty, administrators, students, and staff are focused on promoting teaching, learning, understanding, and knowledge. Open exchange of dialogue among diverse perspectives is needed for a learning community to thrive. However, pervasive racial injustice affects campus communities, microcosms of the U.S. national context. In particular, subtle yet chronic forms of racial microaggressions, often committed unintentionally and without awareness, are experienced by students of color on campuses. Exchanges of racial microaggressions are seldom constructively addressed. Thus, students and other people of color on campus are harmed; empathic understanding needed for working relationships is impeded; constructive dialogue is squelched; and learning (the primary goal of the work in education) is limited. As one intervention, the workshop described in this chapter was designed (a) to raise awareness of the pervasive and unintentional racial microaggressions experienced by students of color on campus; (b) to better understand how these experiences are harmful at individual, interpersonal, and systemic levels, including consequences that limit effective teaching, learning, and classroom dialogues; and (c) to practice one approach to constructively address racial microaggressions. Participants are invited to consider underlying negative stereotype messages with examples of racial microaggressions; practice an approach to empathically understand the perspective of the target of these microaggression examples using I-statements; and practice an approach in the offender role to apologize without self-justification.

SOCIAL JUSTICE NEEDS AND RATIONALE FOR
THE CAREER DEVELOPMENT INTERVENTION

The work roles of faculty, administrators, students, and staff at a college or university are focused on promoting teaching, learning, understanding, and knowledge. In order for a learning community to thrive, particularly in higher education, common values are often promoted for the open exchange of dialogue among diverse perspectives. Social justice access is impeded when learners are marginalized by racial injustice experienced in our campus communities, microcosms of our national context. Racial injustice impedes learning, harms marginalized members of our communities, and limits understanding of all community members. Blustein's (2006) psychology of working framework serves as grounding in career development theory for the workshop described in this chapter. In particular, the need for relatedness and connection to one's work (whether in the role of student, faculty member, administrator, or staff on a college campus) is "central to individual psychological health and to the welfare of communities" (Blustein, 2008, p. 234).

I initially created and presented the university community development exercise described in this chapter as a workshop in November 2015 at the Racial Justice Teach-In at Fordham University. In the context of recognizing the deaths of Michael Brown, Eric Garner, and many other unarmed African American victims of police shootings, a grassroots group of members of the university community organized the Racial Justice Teach-In. This day-long program of sessions was designed as one means to bring together faculty, administrators, and students to better understand the realities of racial injustice and take collective action to address personal and structural racism. The focus of the workshop, titled "Coming to Understand and More Constructively Respond to Racial Microaggressions," was (a) to raise awareness of the pervasive and unintentional racial microaggressions experienced by students of color on campus; (b) to better understand how these experiences are harmful at individual, interpersonal, and systemic levels (Jones, 2000), including consequences that limit effective teaching, learning, and classroom dialogues (Sue, 2013); and (c) to practice one approach to constructively address racial microaggressions.

Racial microaggressions are defined as "brief, everyday exchanges that send denigrating messages to . . . people of color" (Sue, 2010, p. 24). Microaggressions include subtle racial insults that are communicated verbally, behaviorally, or environmentally and that may constitute "a pattern of being overlooked, underrespected, and devalued because of one's race" (Sue, 2010, p. 24). Often committed automatically, unconsciously, and unintentionally, racial microaggressions are pervasive and have a cumulative and harmful impact (Sue, 2010). Among the three broad types of microaggressions, *microassaults* (such as calling someone the N-word) are more often deliberate but less common (Sue et al., 2007). In contrast, *microinsults* and *microinvalidations* are likely more prevalent, unintentional (committed outside of the offenders' conscious awareness), and more harmful due to attributional ambiguity (Sue et al., 2007) and taboos against explicit discourse about racism (Sue, 2013).

Among campus interactions, unintentional racial microaggressions are pervasive, harmful, and difficult to constructively address, particularly in classroom dialogues of reflection and exchange centered on an awakening of potentially conflicting views or beliefs or values about racial injustice issues (Jackson & Mathew, 2017). On one hand, most colleges and universities share common values to promote learning through openness and freedom of discourse. On the other hand, difficult dialogues about racial injustice are often impeded by social and academic norms that implicitly privilege dispassionate perspectives and silence other voices (Sue, 2013). Furthermore, these difficult dialogues are often impeded by fears that differ by individuals' racial perspective. Sue (2013) found that White educators and students had "fears of appearing racist, of realizing their racism, of acknowledging White privilege, and of taking responsibility to combat racism" (p. 663). However, educators and students with identities as people of color experienced common threats of being further exposed to microaggressions that minimize, discount, invalidate, or assail their own racial/ethnic identities. Thus, people of color are further harmed and their voices silenced, and potential opportunities on college campuses are squelched for constructive dialogue that promotes learning and understanding.

I developed the following workshop as one means to promote understanding and practice an approach to more constructively respond to racial microaggressions with university community members. My working assumptions included (a) social justice, including racial justice, starts with us; we each need to develop our own self-awareness of hidden biases and blind spots that limit our human understanding and potential growth together; (b) we all have the potential to be offenders or witnesses of unintentional racial microaggressions; in contrast, only people of color can be targets; and (c) offenders, witnesses, and targets may all benefit from developing bias awareness with practice in identifying the possible negative stereotypes or devaluing assumptions underlying racial microaggressions. Thus, I began the workshop by presenting the rationale, citing relevant literature, and sharing these working assumptions.

Then, I proposed that empathic perspective-taking with targets' experiences of racial microaggressions may be facilitated with practice by workshop participants in four additional ways. In the first step of the exercise, participants develop bias awareness with practice in identifying the possible negative stereotypes or devaluing assumptions underlying racial microaggressions. Second, in the role of a target of a racial microaggression, participants practice using I-statements (e.g., Burr, 1990) as one potentially helpful approach to voicing one's perspective in such interpersonal conflicts, including naming an underlying message of the racial microaggression. Third, the participant's partner practices in the offender role using specific steps outlined to non-defensively offer effective apologies (adapted from Scher & Darley, 1997, and Schumann, 2014) in ways that accept one's own responsibility to recognize the harm caused, albeit unintentional, but without justification, by naming an underlying message of the racial microaggression and committing to work to improve going forward. Lastly, participants switch roles in order to practice in both the target and offender roles, thus practicing skills to facilitate more empathic perspective taking with targets' experiences of racial microaggressions.

MEASURABLE OBJECTIVES AND EXPECTED OUTCOMES

This workshop promoted the following objectives:

- To review a definition of racial microaggressions and recognize examples, including racial microaggressions experienced by students on our campus
- To discuss the reasons why it is important to develop our abilities to recognize and acknowledge racial microaggressions as pervasive biases to which none of us is immune
- To learn and practice more helpful approaches to empathically understand the perspective of the target of racial microaggressions and to apologize without self-justification for racial microaggressions we may commit

PLAN FOR PROMOTING SERVICES

As a member of the grassroots network of university members who planned the Racial Justice Teach-In, I offered to develop the workshop presentation and submitted a blurb for promotional and registration materials. Organizers of the event broadly disseminated promotional materials and readings in advance (Jones, 2000) throughout the university community, including formal and informal networks.

PLAN FOR DELIVERING SERVICES

In adaptations of the workshop described in this chapter, I submit that a prerequisite to delivery is to develop the workshop by tailoring it to a needs assessment of the context by a qualified facilitator in consultation with the community. This is an ethical imperative, considering the sensitivity of the topic and potential harm to participants of color if racial microaggressions are not helpfully addressed or perpetuated in the workshop (e.g., regarding ethical standards of competence and human relations, American Psychological Association, 2017). In particular, the facilitator should have relevant training and qualifications (e.g., a licensed professional counselor, psychologist, or social worker) and be engaged in ongoing development of multicultural competencies in career counseling and advocacy (Lewis, Arnold, House, & Toporek, 2003; National Career Development Association, 1997, 2009; Ratts, Singh, Nassar-McMillan, Butler, & McCullough, 2015). These include competencies the facilitator may use for tailoring to the community and career development needs of relevance in the workshop objectives (see tables 7.1 and 7.2).

Table 7.1. Relevance to Career Counseling Competencies

Career Counseling Competency	Addressed by Career Intervention	Relevance to Corresponding Competency
1. Career Development Theory	X	This university community development workshop is grounded in the psychology of working framework (Blustein, 2006).
2. Individual and Group Counseling Skills	X	Facilitators and co-facilitators use individual and group counseling skills with participant pairs in practicing the workshop exercise.

(continued)

Table 7.1. *Continued*

Career Counseling Competency	Addressed by Career Intervention	Relevance to Corresponding Competency
3. Individual/Group Assessment	X	Facilitators develop the workshop by tailoring it to a needs assessment of the context in consultation with the community.
4. Information/ Resources/ Technology	X	The facilitator develops a workshop presentation citing relevant sources to support the rationale and objectives; prepares relevant handout materials with appropriate citations and permissions; and facilitates media arrangements for promoting, conducting, and follow-up to the workshop.
5. Program Promotion, Management, and Implementation	X	Facilitators use skills to develop, plan, implement, coordinate, and evaluate this community development workshop with co-facilitators and stakeholders at the university.
6. Coaching, Consultation, and Performance Improvement	X	In addition to fostering consultative relationships in developing and evaluating the workshop, facilitators prepare co-facilitators to help coach participants to constructively practice the steps in the workshop exercise to improve responses to racial microaggressions.
7. Diverse Populations	X	Workshop facilitators demonstrate competencies to engage university community members in developing greater understanding of and more constructive responses to racial microaggressions experienced by students and others with whom they work on their campuses.
8. Supervision	X	Qualified facilitators ensure that along with their co-facilitators, they seek ongoing consultation or supervision to constructively challenge their own unintentional racial biases, including intersecting biases, to ethically and effectively support their roles in the workshop.
9. Ethical/Legal Issues	X	Workshop facilitators are qualified professionals who demonstrate ethical and multicultural competencies in conducting psychoeducational interventions tailored to the vocational development needs of the participants and community served.

Career Counseling Competency	Addressed by Career Intervention	Relevance to Corresponding Competency
10. Research/ Evaluation	X	The workshop is grounded in relevant theoretical and scientific literature. Facilitators consider adapting evidence-based evaluation data to assess effectiveness and inform revisions.

Source: NCDA, 1997, 2009.

Table 7.2. Relevance to Advocacy Competencies

Advocacy Competency	Addressed by Career Intervention	Relevance to Corresponding Competency
1. Client/Student Empowerment	X	The workshop is designed to empower participants (a) to better understand sociopolitical, multicultural, and psychological influences that pervasively perpetuate racial injustice, harm working relationships, suppress constructive dialogues, and limit teaching and learning; and (b) to practice developing skills to constructively respond to racial microaggressions.
2. Client/Student Advocacy	X	Facilitators advocate on behalf of students experiencing racial microaggressions on campus by raising awareness with university community members of the harm caused and offering an initial plan of action for constructively confronting the harm caused.
3. Community Collaboration	X	Facilitators collaborate with the stakeholders of the university community, serving as allies with students and other people of color subject to racial microaggressions on campus and helping both targets and offenders raise critical consciousness to constructively respond.
4. Systems Advocacy	X	This workshop was initiated as one among many efforts by a university grassroots network for racial justice advocacy. Evaluation data may be used to inform relevant recommendations to leaders for systemic change at the university and broader community levels.
5. Public Information	X	Information shared in the workshop might be ethically communicated and disseminated to the public through a variety of media.
6. Social/Political Advocacy	X	If evaluation data and future research support the effectiveness of the workshop for raising critical consciousness and more constructively responding to racial microaggressions, then results might be used to advocate for broader dissemination of relevant training.

Source: Lewis et al., 2003; Ratts et al., 2015.

Sufficient time is needed for the facilitator to conduct the workshop, sixty to ninety minutes, typically. In advance, it may be helpful to distribute to participants brief foundational readings (e.g., Jones, 2000; Sue, 2013). Adequate, comfortable, and welcoming space is needed for the size of a large group presentation and, subsequently, to break out into pairs of participants to practice the exercise. Arrangements are also needed for audiovisual media or projection equipment, handout materials, and contacts for participants interested in obtaining further information. For larger groups, it is helpful to have co-facilitators (e.g., para-professionals such as counseling graduate students, including people of color) located throughout the space to assist participant pairs when practicing the exercise.

INTERVENTION PROGRAM CONTENT

Following is an overview of the workshop content and sequence. I gave a PowerPoint presentation highlighting key points (see appendix 7.1 for an outline). As our agenda for the workshop, I presented the rationale, cited relevant evidence in scholarly literature, provided instructions for the exercise, circulated throughout the room during the exercise to facilitate participants with practicing the process, and then concluded with wrap-up discussion. To start, I outlined the agenda of our workshop as:

1. Shared values, racial microaggressions, and difficult dialogues
2. Personal and professional reflections on my own evolving racial awareness, including how I initially became aware of the chronic, frequent occurrence of racial microaggressions
3. Practicing an exercise to help better understand and constructively respond to racial microaggressions experienced by students at our university
4. Questions, discussion, next steps? Thanks!

In the workshop presentation, as discussed in the introduction to this chapter, I noted the shared values of our university community; named my working assumptions; and defined, explained, and cited common racial microaggressions. To illustrate that no context is immune to chronic and pervasive racial microaggressions, I presented specific examples of frequent racial microaggression experiences reported by twenty-one students on campus at our own university. To help explain this contradiction with the shared values of our university community, I referred to the pervasive ambient *smog* of racism and its consequences on health outcomes that Jones (2000) illustrated with her gardner's analogy at institutional, personally mediated, and internalized levels. Furthermore, I summarized Sue's (2013) research findings about how and why classroom dialogues about racism are difficult and rare. I posited that without constructive approaches to difficult dialogues about racial microaggressions experienced by our students on campus, the consequences harm our students of color, thus perpetuating racial injustice, and violate our shared values in higher education of openness and freedom of discourse, limiting effective teaching and learning.

To illustrate that no individual, including myself, is immune to blind spots about chronic and pervasive racial microaggressions, I shared some personal and professional reflections on my own evolving racial awareness, including how I initially became aware of the chronic, frequent occurrence of racial microaggressions. I noted how these experiences have influenced and continue to influence my quest in research, teaching, service, and relationships to better discern hidden biases and promote resources for empathic understanding, healthy development, prosocial contributions, and racial and social justice advocacy. Then, I briefly highlighted research evidence to date on implicit biases, attention deficits of people in social positions of power, stereotype threat effects on academic performance, and blind spots in behavioral ethics.

Next, I proposed that social justice starts with each of us. In particular, powerful teaching and learning includes a role in education for raising our *critical consciousness* (Freire, 2000) of racial microaggressions and taking responsible actions to more constructively address these pernicious aspects of racial injustice. The following workshop exercise is one approach to practice constructively addressing racial microaggressions.

As one more working assumption foundational to this workshop exercise, intersectionality analysis is a tool we can use to increase our self-awareness and raise our critical consciousness in difficult dialogues (Jackson & Mathew, 2017). *Intersectionality* is a term first coined by legal scholar Kimberlé Crenshaw regarding the intersecting racism and sexism affecting Black women. Jackson & Mathew (2017) suggested that an analysis of the intersectionality of power dynamics in a relationship can be used to examine not only the influence of individuals' social identities subject to oppression but also the confluence of their social identities with unearned privilege status. Thus, we can help expand understanding of ourselves and others through critical consciousness of our intersectionality in difficult dialogues by considering the complexity of *both/and* aspects that may exist in our lives and relationships in contrast to making *either/or* assumptions limited to Black/White or good/bad. After presenting the foundational rationale for the workshop, following is an outline for facilitating the workshop exercise.

EXERCISE TO BETTER UNDERSTAND AND MORE CONSTRUCTIVELY ADDRESS RACIAL MICROAGGRESSIONS

Purpose

Regarding the unintentional yet harmful racial microaggressions experienced by students in our university community, the purpose of this exercise is to practice raising our critical consciousness of the underlying stereotypes and constructively responding to common examples of racial microaggressions.

Working Assumptions, Instructions, and Prompts for the Exercise

Workshop attendees are invited to participate in the exercise, with an understanding that participation is entirely voluntary. Participants are instructed to find a partner to practice in pairs. Pairs are to select at least one example per participant from the handout on Examples of Racial Microaggressions (see table 7.3). Pairs will practice the following Steps 1–3 of the Exercise Instructions and Prompts, then repeat the process by switching roles (Step 4).

Step 1

While a priority focus of this exercise is on raising critical consciousness for offenders, the first step is relevant for offenders, witnesses, and targets of unintentional racial microaggressions. We all have the potential to be offenders or witnesses of unintentional racial microaggressions. White people in particular are prone to be offenders, yet even people of color may devalue and put down other people of color via racial microaggressions; we all live in the pervasive *smog* of racism. In contrast, only people of color can be targets of racial microaggressions. Thus, offenders, witnesses, and targets may all benefit from developing bias awareness with practice

Table 7.3. Examples of Racial Microaggressions

Theme	Microaggression	Message
Alien in own land Assigning intelligence to a person of color on the basis of race	"What country are you from?" "Where were you born?" "You speak good English." A person asking an Asian American to teach them words in their native language	You are not American. You are a foreigner.
Ascription of intelligence Assigning a degree of intelligence to a person of color on the basis of their race	"You are a credit to your race." "You are so articulate." Asking an Asian person to help with a math or science problem	You are unusual because people of color are not expected to be capable of succeeding. All Asian people are smart and good at math and science.
Color blindness Statements that indicate that a White person does not want to acknowledge race	"When I look at you, I don't see color." "America is a melting pot." "There is only one race, the human race."	Your racial/ethnic experiences are not valid. Race and culture are not important variables that affect people's lives. You should assimilate exclusively to the dominant culture.
Criminality/assumption of criminal status A person of color is presumed to be dangerous, criminal, or deviant on the basis of their race	A White woman clutching her purse or a White man checking his wallet as a Black or Latino man approaches or passes A store owner following a customer of color around the store A White person waits to ride the next elevator when a person of color is on it	You are a criminal. You are going to steal. You are dangerous. You do not belong.
Denial of individual racism A statement made when White individuals deny their racial biases	"I'm not racist. I have several Black friends." "As a woman, I know what you go through as a racial minority."	Because I have friends of color, this proves I have no racial biases. As a person of color, you should ignore or accept this fiction with me. Your racial oppression is no different than my gender oppression. I can't be a racist. I'm exactly like you.

(*continued*)

Table 7.3. *Continued*

Theme	Microaggression	Message
Environmental microaggressions Macro-level microaggressions, which are more apparent on systemic or structural levels	A college or university with buildings that are all named after wealthy White men Television shows and movies that feature predominantly White people, without representation of people of color or only in lesser roles	You don't belong. You won't succeed here. There is only so far you can go. You are an outsider. You don't exist.
Myth of meritocracy Statements that assert that race and racism do not play a role in succeeding in career advancement or education	"I believe the most qualified person should get the job." "Everyone can succeed in this society, if they work hard enough." "Don't try to play the race card."	People of color are lazy and/or incompetent and need to work harder. If you don't succeed, you have only yourself to blame (i.e., ignore racism and blame the victim). People of color are given extra unfair benefits because of their race (in contrast to being provided access to opportunities that affirmatively reduce barriers of racism).
Pathologizing cultural values/communication styles The notion that the values and communication styles of the dominant/White culture are ideal	Asking a Black person: "Why do you have to be so loud/animated? Just calm down." To an Asian or Latino person: "Why are you so quiet? We want to know what you think. Be more verbal. Speak up more." Dismissing an individual who brings up race/culture in work/school settings	You are not allowed to be who you are, especially if it makes a White person uncomfortable. Assimilate to the dominant culture. Leave your cultural/racial/ethnic baggage outside.
Second-class citizen Occurs when a White person is given preferential treatment as a consumer over a person of color	A person of color is mistaken for a service worker Having a taxi cab pass a person of color and pick up a White passenger Being ignored at a store counter as attention is given to the White person behind you	People of color are servants to White people. They couldn't possibly occupy high-status positions. You are likely to cause trouble and/or travel to a dangerous neighborhood. White people are more valued customers than people of color. You don't belong and deserve to be ignored.

Source: Adapted from D. W. Sue, C. M. Capodilupo, G. C. Torino, J. M. Bucceri, A. M. B. Holder, K. L. Nadal, & M. Esquilin, "Racial Microaggressions in Everyday Life: Implications for Clinical Practice," *American Psychologist,* 62 (2007), 282–283. Copyright 2007 by the American Psychological Association.

in identifying the possible negative stereotypes or devaluing assumptions underlying racial microaggressions.

Together, participants in each pair are instructed to reflect on and name the possible underlying negative stereotypes or devaluing assumptions or expectations of the selected racial microaggression. For this dialogue, they may use as prompts the common themes and messages associated with the Examples of Racial Microaggressions in table 7.3.

Step 2

In the role of a target of a racial microaggression, one potentially helpful approach to voicing one's perspective in such interpersonal conflicts may be to practice using I-statements (e.g., Burr, 1990) that include naming an underlying harmful message of the racial microaggression. This is one approach that may promote bias awareness and empathic perspective taking with, and affirmation of, targets' experiences of racial microaggressions.

One participant in the pair is instructed to assume the role of the target of the selected racial microaggression. With the following prompts, this individual practices using I-statements to respond explicitly about his/her/their experience of being the target of that racial microaggression in ways that name the possible underlying negative stereotypes or devaluing assumptions or expectations. Prompts are: (a) When you say (or did) . . . [practice describing the racial microaggression experience]; (b) I feel (or I felt) . . . [practice describing the possible underlying negative stereotypes and how you felt as the target]; then (c) I would prefer (or would have preferred) that you . . . [practice completing this statement].

Step 3

Practice in the offender role is needed to more constructively respond with empathic perspective taking for targets' experiences of racial microaggressions, particularly in ways that focus on making amends for harm versus excusing the offender. One potentially helpful approach proposed may be to practice in the offender role using specific steps outlined in this exercise to non-defensively offer effective apologies (adapted from Scher & Darley, 1997, and Schumann, 2014); specifically, in ways that accept one's own responsibility to recognize the harm caused, albeit unintentional, but without justification, by naming an underlying message of the racial microaggression and committing to work to improve going forward.

The other participant in the pair is instructed to assume the role of the offender for the target of the selected racial microaggression. With the following prompts, this individual practices a non-defensive response that is a sincere apology, and does so briefly, without self-defensive explanations, and without minimizing or rationalizing. Prompts are: (a) I am sorry. (b) I see how my words (or actions) may wrongly communicate . . . [practice naming the possible underlying negative stereotypes or devaluing assumptions or expectations]. (c) I do not believe that about you and it was not my intention to harm you, yet I did and I am sorry. (d) I will try my best to do better going forward. [End there, or perhaps practice ways you might work to affirm the feedback from your partner's preferences expressed previously in the role of target.]

Step 4

Participants may benefit from practice in both the target and offender roles (by switching roles practiced) in Steps 1–3 with examples of racial microaggressions. Thus, the instructions are to repeat Steps 1–3 with another racial microaggression example selected by the pair and reversing roles assumed by participants in Steps 2 and 3.

Conclusion of the Exercise

Reconvening the large group, the facilitator solicits questions, feedback, and discussion including possible next steps for participants' consideration. Concluding remarks include thanks to the attendees for their participation in this workshop and university community development exercise. Raising our own self-awareness in critical consciousness of racial microaggressions is a vital first step toward social justice action in our university communities. Such efforts are moral and ethical imperatives with powerful potential to promote racial justice, constructive dialogues, teaching, and learning in our working relationships on campus and beyond.

RESOURCES NEEDED

In summary, and as discussed above in the plans for promoting and delivering this workshop, resources needed include a well-qualified facilitator to tailor the workshop to community needs. Qualified co-facilitators are also helpful for assisting participant pairs when practicing the exercise. Sufficient time, adequate space, and arrangements are needed for audiovisual media or projection equipment and handout materials (e.g., the brief article by Jones, 2000; the Examples of Racial Microaggressions, table 7.3; and contacts for participants interested in obtaining further information).

METHODS OF EVALUATION

Following are some methods that might be used to assess the degree of effectiveness of this workshop for promoting the objectives outlined. At the end of the workshop, participants might be asked to complete brief written or digital surveys to respond to the following items: (a) define racial microaggressions; (b) give three examples of racial microaggression experiences reported by students on our campus; (c) explain one reason why it is important to develop our abilities to recognize and acknowledge racial microaggressions as pervasive biases to which none of us is immune; (d) describe what you learned from practicing the exercise on approaches to empathically understand the perspective of the target of racial microaggressions; (e) describe what you learned from practicing the exercise on approaches to apologize without self-justification for racial microaggressions we may commit; (f) provide feedback on the most helpful aspects of the workshop; and (g) offer suggestions for improving the workshop. Alternatively, these surveys might be conducted by interviews with participants. Other methods for evaluating the effectiveness of the workshop might be developed through future research studies.

PLAN FOR REVISION

The workshop outlined in this chapter is proposed as one means to promote working relationships in learning communities of higher education through better understanding of and more constructively responding to racial microaggressions. Evaluation feedback should be considered toward developing a plan for revisions to improve future adaptations of this workshop. Evaluation data may be used to target areas of strengths, limitations, and insights to inform specific revisions.

REFLECTIONS ON COUNSELOR SELF-AWARENESS
OF POTENTIAL RESOURCES AND BIASES FROM
PRIVILEGED AND MARGINALIZED IDENTITIES

As a facilitator in interventions for exploring bias awareness and constructive responses, I need to remind myself that I am in a position of power in relation to participants. Thus, I need to patiently and empathically attend to their vulnerabilities in the process of sharing and examining self-disclosures, as well as aim to constructively challenge them to grow in critical consciousness. Furthermore, I need to clearly communicate with participants how I have my own blind spots, have made mistakes, and will likely again "step in it," not only in the process of diversity training but also in perpetrating microaggressions at times despite continual efforts to grow in my own critical consciousness. I see myself as a partner with others committed to lifelong learning toward understanding and constructively responding to racial microaggressions and other forms of stereotyping, discrimination, and injustice. Thus together, I hope to helpfully contribute in ways that develop empathy, communication, access, equity, inclusion, and community.

I can use my evolving awareness of my own intersecting identities of privilege and marginalization as resources to help myself and others to recognize biases and develop more constructive responses. In addition to my status of power as a diversity trainer, my privileged identities include my social positions regarding race (White and of European descent; English, Scottish, Irish), education (PhD in counseling psychology), socioeconomic status (middle class), health and ability status (currently healthy with no major physical or mental health impairments), U.S. citizenship, heterosexual orientation, marital status (married), and religious affiliation (Presbyterian). More subjugated identities include my gender and age, as a middle-aged woman. Finally, my husband of thirty-seven years is a strong, compassionate, intelligent, resilient Black man and extraordinary father. Together we have raised our two biracial daughters, who are now adults and truly beautiful individuals, inside and out (from my "unbiased" perspective). From my social position in our immediate biracial family and extended multicultural family and communities, my perspectives include painful experiences with racism against my loved ones (chronic microaggressions as well as traumatic incidents) and inspiring experiences with progress toward resilient and constructive responses. I developed the university community development workshop outlined in this chapter as one tool that may be used to promote multicultural understanding and racial justice, core values that I hold personally and professionally.

APPENDIX 7.1

Outline of PowerPoint Presentation for Sample Workshop: Coming to Understand and More Constructively Respond to Racial Microaggressions

Presented at Racial Justice Teach-In, Fordham University Anti-Racism Collective, November 5, 2015, by Margo A. Jackson

Agenda

1. Shared values, racial microaggressions, and difficult dialogues
   - Personal and professional reflections on my own evolving racial awareness, including how I initially became aware of the chronic, frequent occurrence of racial microaggressions
2. Brief exercise to help better understand and constructively respond to racial microaggressions experienced by Fordham University students
3. Questions, discussion, next steps? . . . and thanks!

Working Assumptions and Shared Values

College and universities are special places that promote openness and freedom of discourse.

Fordham University mission

- educating and caring for the whole person
- social justice

Powerful teaching and learning includes

- pedagogy of relevance to individuals, social groups, and broader communities
- analysis of complex issues from multiple and alternative perspectives
- in which all voices are heard and considered

Difficult Dialogues

Yet exploring the influences of racial injustices, such as racial microaggressions, are difficult dialogues.

Definition of Racial Microaggressions

Racial microaggressions are "brief and commonplace daily verbal, behavioral and environmental indignities whether intentional or unintentional that communicate hostile, derogatory, or negative racial slights and insults" towards people of color (Sue et al., 2007, p. 271).

Examples of Racial Microaggressions

- "Someone acted surprised at my scholastic or professional success because of my race."
- "I was told that people of color do not experience racism anymore."
- "I observed [few or no] people of my race in prominent positions at my workplace or school."
- "My opinion was overlooked in a group discussion because of my race." (Nadal, 2011, p. 474)

Fordham University students' experiences

- *21 Racial Microaggressions You Hear on a Daily Basis*
  - A photographer at Fordham asked her peers to write down the microaggressions they've encountered
  - http://www.buzzfeed.com/hnigatu/racial-microaggressions-you-hear -on-a-daily-basis#.pcJq99dbm

Effects of Racial Microaggressions

- Chronic stress has negative effects on people of color in health, career development, and well-being (Holder, Jackson, & Ponterotto, 2015; Miehls, 2011; Nadal et al., 2014)
- Limits learning and understanding for all (Sue, 2013)
- Maintains racial injustices systemically, interpersonally, and intrapersonally (Jones, 2000)

We did not ask to grow up in this *smog* of racism, but it is our responsibility to change it!

Difficult Dialogues

Difficult dialogues of reflection and exchange with others in higher education communities and mentoring relationships are defined as centering on "an awakening of potentially conflicting views or beliefs or values about social justice issues (such as racism, sexism, ableism, heterosexism/homophobia)" (Jackson & Mathew, 2017; Watt, 2007, p. 116).

Why are dialogues exploring racial microaggresions so difficult?

- social and academic norms
- to avoid, ignore, silence, or discourage in-depth exploration of potentially offensive, uncomfortable, and emotionally intense topics
- impede difficult dialogues about racial injustice (Sue, 2013)

Why are these difficult dialogues?

- For White educators and students: "fears of appearing racist, of realizing their racism, of acknowledging White privilege, and of taking responsibility to combat racism" (Sue, 2013, p. 663).
- For educators and students with identities as people of color: often exposes them to microaggressions that minimize, discount, invalidate, or assail their own racial/ethnic identities (Mathew, 2010; Sue, 2013).

I acknowledge up front

- As a White educator in a position of power, as well as thoroughly human, I have made and will make mistakes; expect I will put my foot in my mouth
- Ask that you work through, with me, work toward building mentoring and collegial relationships and classroom climates of trust, balancing challenge and support
- Students may choose what they share or self-disclose and/or *pass* [decline their turn for now] at times in difficult dialogues

Social justice, including racial justice, starts with us.

- We each need to develop our own self-awareness of hidden biases and blind spots that limit our human understandings and potential growth together.

Coming to Understand and More Constructively Respond to Racial Microaggressions

Personal and professional reflections on my own evolving racial awareness

- including how I initially became aware of the chronic, frequent occurrence of racial microaggressions

Hidden Biases/Blind Spots

- Attention deficits of people in social positions of power (Fiske, 1998)
- Behavioral ethics research (Bazerman & Tenbrunsel, 2011)

Role of Education in Raising Critical Consciousness

Powerful teaching and learning includes

- *critical consciousness* (Freire, 2000) of social injustices
- intersecting power dynamics
- taking responsible actions (small or large) toward
  - improving human relations understanding
  - expanding access, participation, and growth in all areas of education, work, health, and well-being

Self-Awareness for Critical Consciousness

Intersectionality is

- the confluence of multiple identities in each individual
- social locations, including the advantage and disadvantage associated with each of our identities

We can help expand understanding of ourselves and of others through intersectionality discussions to consider the complexity of *both/and* aspects that may exist in our lives and relationships in contrast to making *either/or* assumptions limited to Black/White or good/bad [Jackson & Mathew, 2017].

Brief exercise to help better understand and constructively respond to racial microaggressions experienced by students and other members of the Fordham University community.

[Here, step-by-step instructions and prompts for this exercise followed in the PowerPoint presentation.]

Conclusion

Raising our own self-awareness for critical consciousness of racial microaggressions is

- a vital first step toward social justice action
- a moral and ethical imperative
- a practice with powerful potential to expand human relations, understanding, knowledge, growth, health, and more broadly thriving communities

Questions, discussion, next steps?
Thanks!

REFERENCES

American Psychological Association. (2017). *Ethical principles of psychologists and code of conduct* [adopted in 2002, with Amendments in 2010 and 2016]. Retrieved from https://www.apa.org/ethics/code/ethics-code-2017.pdf.

Bazerman, M. H., & Tenbrunsel, A. E. (2011). *Blind spots: Why we fail to do what's right and what to do about it.* Princeton, NJ: Princeton University Press.

Blustein, D. L. (2006). *The psychology of working: A new perspective for career development, counseling, and public policy.* Mahwah, NJ: Erlbaum.

———. (2008). The role of work in psychological health and well-being: A conceptual, historical, and public policy perspective. *American Psychologist, 63*, 228–240. doi: 10.1037/0003-066X.63.4.228.

Burr, W. R. (1990). Beyond I-statements in family communication. *Family Relations, 39*, 266–273. doi: 10.2307/584870.

Fiske, S. (1998). Stereotyping, prejudice, and discrimination. In S. Fiske, D. Gilbert, & L. Gardner (Eds.), *The handbook of social psychology* (4th ed., pp. 357–411). Boston, MA: McGraw-Hill.

Freire, P. (2000). *Pedagogy of the oppressed.* New York, NY: Bloomsbury Academic. (Original work published 1970)

Holder, A. M. B., Jackson, M. A., & Ponterotto, J. G. (2015). Racial microaggression experiences and coping strategies of Black women in corporate leadership. *Qualitative Psychology, 2*, 164–180. doi: 10.1037/qup0000024.

Jackson, M. A., & Mathew, J. T. (2017). Multicultural self-awareness challenges for trainers: Examining intersecting identities of power and oppression. In J. M. Casas, L. A. Suzuki,

C. A. Alexander, & M. A. Jackson (Eds.), *Handbook of multicultural counseling* (4th ed., pp. 433–444). Thousand Oaks, CA: Sage.

Jones, C. P. (2000). Levels of racism: A theoretic framework and a gardener's tale. *American Journal of Public Health, 90*(8), 1212–1215. doi: 10.2105/AJPH.90.8.1212.

Lewis, J., Arnold, M. S., House, R., & Toporek, R. L. (2003). *Advocacy competencies.* Endorsed by the American Counseling Association Governing Council. Retrieved from https://www.counseling.org/Resources/Competencies/Advocacy_Competencies.pdf.

Mathew, J. T. (2010). *Exploring the process of multicultural competence development and training of counselor trainees of color* (Unpublished doctoral dissertation). Fordham University, New York, NY.

Miehls, D. (2011). Racism and its effects. In N. R. Heller & A. Gitterman (Eds.), *Mental health and social problems: A social work perspective* (pp. 62–85). New York, NY: Routledge.

Nadal, K. L. (2011). The Racial and Ethnic Microaggressions Scale (REMS): Construction, reliability, and validity. *Journal of Counseling Psychology, 58*, 470–480. doi: 10.1037/a0025193.

Nadal, K. L., Wong, Y., Griffin, K. E., Davidoff, K., & Sriken, J. (2014). The adverse impact of racial microaggressions on college students' self-esteem. *Journal of College Student Development, 55*, 461–474. doi: 10.1353/csd.2014.0051.

National Career Development Association. (1997). *Career counseling competencies.* Broken Arrow, OK: Author.

———. (2009). *Minimum competencies for multicultural career counseling and development.* Broken Arrow, OK: Author. Retrieved from https://www.ncda.org/aws/NCDA/pt/fli/12508/false.

Ratts, M. J., Singh, A. A., Nassar-McMillan, S., Butler, S. K., & McCullough, J. R. (2015). *Multicultural and social justice counseling competencies.* Retrieved from https://www.counseling.org/docs/default-source/competencies/multicultural-and-social-justice-counseling-competencies.pdf?sfvrsn=20.

Scher, S. J., & Darley, J. M. (1997). How effective are the things people say to apologize? Effects of the realization of the apology speech act. *Journal of Psycholinguistic Research, 26*, 127–140. doi: 10.1023/A:1025068306386.

Schumann, K. (2014). An affirmed self and a better apology: The effect of self-affirmation on transgressors' responses to victims. *Journal of Experimental Social Psychology, 54*, 89–96. doi: 10.1016/j.jesp.2014.04.013.

Sue, D. W. (2010). *Microaggressions in everyday life: Race, gender, and sexual orientation.* Hoboken, NJ: Wiley.

———. (2013). Race talk: The psychology of racial dialogues. *American Psychologist, 68*, 663–672. doi: 10.1037/a0033681.

Sue, D. W., Capodilupo, C. M., Torino, G. C., Bucceri, J. M., Holder, A. M. B., Nadal, K. L., & Esquilin, M. (2007). Racial microaggressions in everyday life: Implications for clinical practice. *American Psychologist, 62*, 271–286. doi: 10.1037/0003-066X.62.4.271.

Watt, S. K. (2007). Difficult dialogues: Privilege and social justice: Uses of the Privileged Identity Exploration (PIE) model in student affairs practice. *College Student Affairs Journal, 26*, 114–126.

VI

CAREER DEVELOPMENT INTERVENTIONS FOR
SOCIAL JUSTICE NEEDS IN COMMUNITY
AND EMPLOYMENT CONTEXTS WITH
UNDERSERVED ADOLESCENTS

8

Girls in Action

Career Development with Juvenile Justice–Involved Adolescent Girls

Lauren Ann Sonnabend

Some juvenile offenders, minors who have committed a crime, are sentenced to juvenile detention centers. Adolescent girls involved in juvenile justice face heightened risks to healthy social development that may contribute to unemployment or underemployment in their adulthood. Girls in Action is a voluntary ten-week career development intervention program proposed for adolescent girls in a juvenile detention center. Conducted by clinically supervised paraprofessional facilitators, the program is designed to promote self-awareness, career exploration, self-efficacy, and planning, as well as skills in decision-making, job search, and work adjustment.

SOCIAL JUSTICE NEEDS AND RATIONALE FOR THE CAREER DEVELOPMENT INTERVENTION

Juvenile offenders are a special population with unique needs both during the time they are incarcerated and after they are released (Tarolla, Wagner, Rabinowitz, & Tubman, 2002). Juvenile offenders are at heightened risk for school failure and social maladjustment during adulthood, contributing to unemployment and underemployment (Zabel & Nigro, 2007). Research has suggested that career counseling can be beneficial to juvenile offenders, demonstrating numerous positive effects: decreased hopelessness; increased internalized locus of control; and improvements in career maturity, self-esteem, self-knowledge, self-sufficiency, and interpersonal skills (Allen & Bradley, 2015; Skorikov & Vondracek, 2007).

Although there is a dearth of research on female offenders, it is evident that there is a significant need for services for this population, particularly relating to career development (Chartrand & Rose, 1996). Largely due to an increase in female arrests in the mid-1990s, the proportion of girls in the juvenile justice system has grown (Puzzanchera & Hockenberry, 2013; Walker, Bishop, Nurius, & Logan-Greene, 2016). While researchers draw varying conclusions about the relative emphasis that should be given to gender differences in delinquency risk, in general, they agree that delinquency is impacted by both shared and unique factors (Andrews et al., 2012). Research suggests that girls who become involved in the justice system experience a greater number of risk factors than boys (Fagan, Van Horn, Hawkins, & Arthur, 2007). Juvenile justice–involved girls have higher rates of mental health issues, direct victimization, sexual abuse, and family conflict (Grande et al., 2012). In particular, risk factors related to familial and social relationships have been found to be more significant for female adolescents than for male adolescents (Fields & Abrams, 2010). These findings suggest gender-specific policy and program recommendations emphasizing trauma-informed treatment and empowerment (Walker et al., 2016). In light of the evidence supporting such program designs to address the underserved needs of adolescent girls involved in juvenile justice, the Girls in Action program is proposed to promote their career development and empower their access to gainful employment in adulthood.

The design of Girls in Action is grounded in social cognitive career theory (Lent, Brown, & Hackett, 1994), given its attention to the influence of multiple contexts on individual development and behavior, the bidirectional relationship between individuals and their contexts, and promoting individuals' career self-efficacy. In this program, the impact of one's own behavior is emphasized and associated with personal power (agency) and responsibility for creating change. Research suggests that interventions guided by social cognitive career theory are viable options to address adult inmates' career development needs (Fitzgerald, Chronister, Forrest, & Brown, 2013). Girls in Action is largely adapted for juvenile justice–involved girls from Project PROVE (Preventing Recidivism through Opportunities in Vocational Education; Chartrand & Rose, 1996), a career development program for female offenders who are scheduled to be released into the community within six months. Furthermore, career development interventions are needed for youth who are girls or members of other groups underrepresented in math- and science-related professional occupations (e.g., African Americans and Hispanics) (Blustein et al., 2012). Thus, Girls in Action includes resources for participants to learn about and potentially develop interests, abilities, and occupations related to math and science.

Given the large number of juvenile offenders being reintegrated into communities and the link between unemployment and recidivism, there is a sizable population of adolescents who need services from career counselors (Thompson & Cummings, 2010). Taking into consideration their age, contexts, and experience to date, female juvenile offenders have the following specific career development needs:

1. Learn the process of career planning that they can apply now and will need to continuously apply throughout their lives.
2. Identify their personal interests and abilities.
3. Relate these interests and abilities to possible occupations, including potential math- and science-related occupations.
4. Learn about these occupations.
5. Understand what kind of education and/or training they will need to prepare for these occupations.
6. Prepare the documents needed for searching for jobs and develop skills to identify job openings, secure job interviews, conduct themselves effectively in job interviews, and select a good place of employment.

MEASURABLE OBJECTIVES AND EXPECTED OUTCOMES

At the end of Girls in Action, at least 80 percent of the adolescents who complete the program will be able to take the following steps:

1. Describe the steps of a thoughtful process for making career decisions.
2. State and describe in detail at least five occupations that relate to their personal interests and abilities.
3. Select at least three occupations of highest interest.
4. State the education and training implications of preparing for those three occupations.
5. Describe how to use support networks.
6. Demonstrate enhanced career planning, maturity, and self-efficacy.

PLAN FOR PROMOTING SERVICES

A qualified program coordinator (on staff at the juvenile detention center or serving as a consultant) will initiate the design and promotion process. This individual should be a licensed psychologist or social worker whose qualifications include experience in promoting psychosocial development with resident female juvenile offenders, expertise in providing developmentally and culturally relevant career assessment and interventions, and competence in training and supervising paraprofessionals. Early in the design process, the program coordinator will recruit a committee of female juvenile offenders, parents and/or caregivers, and staff to help design Girls in Action or provide feedback about preliminary plans. In individual meetings with administrators at the juvenile justice center, the program coordinator will explain preliminary plans and negotiate arrangements. These meetings will include reviewing relevant research on the benefits of career counseling for juvenile offenders and ways in which this program may be of value at the center.

PLAN FOR DELIVERING SERVICES

Paraprofessional facilitators (e.g., counseling psychology graduate student interns) will deliver the proposed ten-week intervention. Facilitators will receive at least one hour per week of counseling supervision from the program coordinator to ensure competence in quality of services and adherence to ethical and legal standards (see tables 8.1 and 8.2 for relevant competencies for the program coordinator in career counseling and social justice advocacy; Lewis, Arnold, House, & Toporek, 2003; National Career Development Association, 1997, 2009). Participants may number up to fifteen female offenders per intervention program, delivered at a juvenile justice center or facility designed to house juvenile offenders who have criminal cases pending in family, county, or district courts. Participants are selected based on type of residency. Due to the length of Girls in Action, only residents identified as long-term residents are included as potential participants. Participants may range in age from twelve to seventeen years. A ten-week intervention is necessary because some at-risk adolescents may require career interventions of this length to recognize opportunities available to them (Legum & Hoare, 2004). Each participant is involved in group career counseling one day per week for two hours. In order to evaluate the program, participants are administered a questionnaire and three career assessment measures at the beginning and at the end of the ten-week counseling program. The following section outlines the program content of the Girls in Action career development intervention (see appendix 8.1 for an outline of sessions).

Table 8.1.   Relevance to Career Counseling Competencies

Career Counseling Competency	Addressed by Career Intervention	Relevance to Corresponding Competency
1. Career Development Theory	X	Girls in Action applies major constructs of social cognitive career theory (Lent et al., 1994).
2. Individual and Group Counseling Skills	X	Supervised counselors facilitate group counseling sessions.
3. Individual/Group Assessment	X	Pre-measures could be used to inform tailoring the intervention, and post-measures to evaluate progress.
4. Information/ Resources/ Technology	X	A psychoeducational component includes group work that emphasizes learning about career development and new life skills with goals of prevention and growth. Counselors facilitate the girls' career exploration via O*Net online resources.
5. Program Promotion, Management, and Implementation	X	The chapter discusses the needs, objectives, plan for promoting services, plan for delivering services, and content for the proposed career development program.
6. Coaching, Consultation, and Performance Improvement	X	The results of the evaluation, feedback from female juvenile offenders and staff, and additional creative ideas are used to revise the program and prepare for its next delivery.
7. Diverse Populations	X	This chapter describes a voluntary program for juvenile justice–involved girls varying in ethnicity and socioeconomic status at a juvenile justice center.
8. Supervision	X	Facilitators will receive at least one hour per week of supervision with a licensed counseling professional to ensure competence and equity in quality of services.
9. Ethical/Legal Issues	X	The chapter summarizes ethical considerations.
10. Research/ Evaluation	X	Evaluation of the program's effectiveness is assessed with pre-/post-measures—including career planning, maturity, and self-efficacy.

Source: NCDA, 1997, 2009.

Table 8.2. Relevance to Advocacy Competencies

Advocacy Competency	Addressed by Career Intervention	Relevance to Corresponding Competency
1. Client/Student Empowerment	X	Counselors help the girls learn about the importance of long-term and short-term goals and receive feedback about their strengths from their peers, parents and/or caregivers, and facilitators.
2. Client/Student Advocacy	—	—
3. Community Collaboration	X	Parents and/or caregivers are encouraged to participate in the intervention.
4. Systems Advocacy	—	—
5. Public Information	X	Girls learn more about the education and training implications of preparing for occupations through O*Net online resources.
6. Social/Political Advocacy	—	—

Source: Lewis et al., 2003.

INTERVENTION PROGRAM CONTENT

During *Session 1: Introduction to Group and Process,* consent and confidentiality are reviewed. Beginning in the first session and continuing throughout the program, personal factors such as gender and race, and contextual factors, such as exposure to career role models and discrimination, are included so that the girls can begin to describe and build their career identity. Background factors are discussed and linked to the kinds of learning opportunities to which they have been exposed (Chartrand & Rose, 1996).

During *Session 2: Introduction to Career and Life Planning,* the connection between learning and maladaptive behavior is highlighted to minimize personal attributions that inhibit change and to emphasize the value of taking advantage of enriching and educational opportunities. For instance, one exercise prompts the girls to think about ways in which their past experiences have had both beneficial and detrimental impacts on their lives (Chartrand & Rose, 1996). Steps to career decision-making will also be explored (see appendix 8.2 for the suggested activity).

As a population, offenders often have difficulty taking a long-term perspective (Ross & Fabiano, 1985). During *Session 3: Achievements,* adapted from the Career Horizons Program (O'Brien, Dukstein, Jackson, Tomlinson, & Kamatuka, 1999) for students at risk for vocational underachievement, the girls learn about the significance of long-term and short-term goals and receive feedback about their strengths from their peers, parents and/or care-givers, and facilitators. In an effort to explore the meaning of success, they participate in a guided imagery exercise in which they envision their lives ten years in the future (see appendix 8.3 for the suggested script). They are then asked to develop a lifeline that includes important past and anticipated events and successes. For some participants, the process of identifying and verbalizing success experiences will be both new and challenging. With the support of the facilitators, the girls create, write down, and then discuss three specific short-term goals and three long-term goals. Then, the girls are asked to put their goals in a shoebox and decorate it so that it becomes their "Success Box," a reminder and container of their achievements and ambitions. After participants anonymously write their views of each other's assets on a golden star and put a star in the box of each participant, they are read to the group. Lastly, the girls are given letters written by their parents and/or caregivers expressing what they perceive as their strengths and what they admire about them (O'Brien et al., 1999).

The intervention also includes a psychoeducational component in *Session 4: Personality Preferences and Career Interests*, in which the girls partici-pate in group work that emphasizes learning about career development and new life skills with the purpose of prevention and growth (Aasheim & Nie-mann, 2006). The girls are educated about the importance of learning more about their interests, values, skills, and personalities to make informed career choices over the lifetime. First, the girls are asked to complete the Myers-Briggs Type Indicator (Myers & Myers, 1995). Then, Holland's (1997) theory of vocational choice and hexagon model are incorporated to help the girls organize information about interests, values, and skills. At the comple-tion of this activity, each participant lists and discusses her personality type and three highest-scoring career clusters. For example, a suggested activity is the Career Cluster Match (North Dakota Career Resource Network, 2017).

Session 5: Math and Science Careers is included in their exploration of career clusters because of the well-known underrepresentation of women and members of racial and ethnic minority groups in math- and science-related occupations. The girls are educated about the relation between math and science courses and future educational and vocational opportunities through interactive activities and class discussions.

During *Session 6: Skills*, participants learn more about various career clusters and related occupations. In an activity, the girls match specific careers with the associated career clusters. Then, the girls learn more about the skills, training, and education needed to qualify for selected occupations.

The intervention also aims to help the girls develop skills in goal setting and planning, which are common barriers for offenders (Ross & Fabiano, 1985). During *Session 7: Values and Prioritization*, the connection between school and the world of work is discussed. Consistent with the literature (Bandura, 1986), the girls are encouraged to set goals that are specific, realistic, positively stated, and within their control. Exercises include developing specific short-term and long-term career goals. The girls are asked to consider personally relevant actions that they could embrace to work toward their ambition (Chartrand & Rose, 1996). Additionally, all participants write down at least five occupations that relate to their personal interests and abilities, select at least three occupations of highest interest, and learn more about the education and training implications of preparing for those three occupations through O*Net, the online occupational network database published by the U.S. Department of Labor (https://onetonline.org/). Facilitators give feedback to the girls on their selections and conduct a discussion regarding the qualifications for each career cluster. Facilitators encourage the girls to visualize dreams of academic and vocational success and then work hard to actualize those hopes.

Session 8: Career Self-Awareness is designed to help the girls gain greater understanding of self; learn effective decision-making strategies; understand how alcohol, drugs, and pregnancy affect future career options; and identify ways to improve personal study skills (O'Brien et al., 1999). Contextual factors are featured to highlight the relationships between person, environment, and behavior. The aim is to help the girls foster a balanced view of themselves, their responsibilities, and the events that have shaped their lives. For instance, the girls are encouraged to consider how events that occurred early in their lives may have affected their educational and career opportunities. Incarceration is discussed both as an opportunity for career development and as a stigma in terms of finding a job (Chartrand & Rose, 1996). The facilitators also lead a discussion with the girls on the changing roles of women and men and the implications that these shifts have for education, family, and leisure.

During *Session 9: Written Communication*, the girls are exposed to job application and resume strategies. For example, the girls complete sample job application forms.

During *Session 10: Communication in Employment Interviews*, the girls are shown interviewing techniques. For example, the girls practice their interviewing skills with each other.

Parents and/or caregivers are encouraged to become partners in fostering healthy and proactive career development. Modeling the Career Horizons Program (O'Brien et al., 1999), they are asked to help their daughters with assignments, one of which includes having a conversation with parents and/or caregivers about their career development. Furthermore, parents and/or caregivers are invited to join the final session of the program, which concludes with a luncheon in which all the girls are recognized for their effort and active participation.

RESOURCES NEEDED

In order to implement Girls in Action, the following resources will be needed:

1. A qualified program coordinator—paid as a consultant or, if on staff, dedicated time and support needed
2. One to two hours of time in staff meetings during which the program and materials are explained
3. Counseling internship for graduate student facilitators
4. Use permissions for the Myers-Briggs Type Indicator (Myers & Myers, 1995) and evaluation measures
5. Psychoeducational materials, including photocopies of Holland's (1997) hexagon
6. A meeting room equipped with computers and internet access that will hold seventeen people
7. Allocated time for the paraprofessional facilitators to organize and oversee the group counseling program

METHODS OF EVALUATION

Evaluation measures are administered to participants during the first and final sessions of the program as a means to assess outcomes. A questionnaire will be developed and administered to address Objectives 1–5 pertaining to steps of a thoughtful process for making career decisions, occupations relating to personal interests and abilities, education and training implications, and support networks. For example, this questionnaire might include the following prompts:

1. Describe the seven steps of a thoughtful process for making career decisions.
2. State and describe in detail at least five occupations that relate to your personal interests and abilities and why they appeal to you.
3. Select at least three occupations of highest interest to you and why they appeal to you.
4. State the education and training implications of preparing for those three occupations.
5. Describe how to use your support networks.

To address Objective 6, demonstrating enhanced career planning, career maturity, and career self-efficacy, three instruments will be administered (measures with supporting psychometric evidence for use with adolescents): the Career Development Inventory–Australia–Short Form (CDI–A–SF; Creed & Patton, 2003), the Career Decision Self-Efficacy Scale—Short Form (CDSE-SF; Betz, Klein, & Taylor, 1996), and the Career Maturity Inventory (CMI; Crites & Savickas, 1996).

PLAN FOR REVISION

The results of the evaluation (comparing responses from the first and final sessions), feedback from female juvenile offenders and staff, and additional creative ideas will be used to revise the program and prepare for its next delivery. Revisions may involve changes to content, time allocated to different activities, personnel, and methods of evaluation. Depending on the evaluation results, further program development from a ten-week to a twelve-week intervention may be considered (as the career development intervention by Chartrand & Rose, 1996, was twelve weeks in duration).

CONCLUSION

Adolescent girls involved in juvenile justice face heightened risks to healthy social development that may contribute to unemployment or underemployment in their adulthood. It is not enough for juvenile justice professionals to develop strategies to prevent behaviors that place juvenile offenders in jeopardy. There must be equal attention paid to stating and implementing goals for offenders to achieve—such as education, preparation for employment, community involvement, and development of appropriate life skills (Roos, 2006). Implementing proper interventions, such as career counseling, is paramount to equipping female juvenile offenders with the maturity, self-efficacy, and skills needed to reenter the workforce following incarceration. Furthermore, measuring increases in the career self-efficacy, maturity, and planning of female juvenile offenders may enhance community support for the juvenile justice system and for the social change agents who seek to turn juvenile offenders into prosocial members of society.

REFLECTIONS ON COUNSELOR SELF-AWARENESS OF POTENTIAL RESOURCES AND BIASES FROM PRIVILEGED AND MARGINALIZED IDENTITIES

I grew up in Weston, Massachusetts, a small, upper-middle-class town with a primarily White and socioeconomically homogenous population. I attended Weston Public Schools, which participated in the Metropolitan Council for Educational Opportunity (METCO) Program, a voluntary program intended to expand educational opportunities, increase diversity, and reduce racial isolation by permitting students in certain cities to attend public schools in other communities that had agreed to participate. As a result of studying alongside less privileged peers, I became aware of concepts of privilege and oppression and my own beliefs about justice at a fairly young age. I frequently asked myself why I was fortunate enough to have all the resources and support I could possibly need while so many other children's opportunities were limited. This social awareness prompted a complex reaction of guilt and confusion.

My burgeoning understanding of and interest in issues related to social justice greatly influenced my decision to attend Wesleyan University, a school known for its diversity, open-mindedness, and idealism. As a freshman at Wesleyan, located in Middletown, Connecticut, I experienced significant culture shock. Meeting so many students from different cultures and countries was such an amazing experience for me, and certainly broadened my worldview. My multicultural, activist friends challenged me, held me accountable, and helped me accept responsibility for the role that race plays in my everyday life. I learned from them, as well as the faculty, about activism and advocacy toward social change.

As a student at Wesleyan I also volunteered as a babysitter to a woman recovering from substance abuse and as a classroom tutor in a Middletown public elementary school. Serving as a volunteer played a significant role in helping me understand the relationship between my community and me. As I became more involved, I realized how much giving back to others was important and meaningful to me.

At Wesleyan I found a love of academia and decided to pursue a master's degree in psychology there. When I entered the program, I assumed that I would pursue a PhD in clinical psychology when I graduated. However, while completing my thesis, I realized that I increasingly found the field of clinical psychology to be too narrow for my interests. I came to understand that I was not only interested in individual differences among children, but also how each child is impacted by her family, school environment, and neighborhood. Instead of simply focusing on trying to help individuals resolve personal issues, I came to understand that I also wanted to better understand how individuals are affected by their environments and to study social justice and the environmental systems that impact individuals, with an emphasis on helping underserved and underrepresented populations.

This interest led me to pursue a master's degree in social work at Columbia University. In my counseling positions both during my program and after graduating, I focused on working with and understanding the worldviews of my very ethnically and economically diverse clients, and struggled with my responsibility as a White social worker to try to confront the systems that supported inequity. An increased awareness of the structural challenges in my clients' lives was and continues to be crucial for my efforts toward being accountable as a person with socioracial, economic, and sexual identity privileges, among many others. My interests in continuing my training as a therapist and researcher with underserved populations led me to Fordham University, where I am currently pursuing a PhD in counseling psychology. With Fordham's foundations in multiculturalism and social justice, I feel very much at home. As I reflect on my development, I realize that I grew through community and family values, then later gained greater awareness and understanding through scholarship. My experiences through scholarship in particular have helped me become more culturally aware, give back to my community, and fight against oppression.

APPENDIX 8.1

Outline of "Girls in Action" Career Development Intervention Program Content

Session 1: Introduction to Group and Process

- Introductions
- Review of consent and confidentiality

Session 2: Introduction to Career and Life Planning

- Discussion of connection between learning and maladaptive behavior
- Exercise about impact of past experiences
- Steps to career decision-making (see appendix 8.2)

Session 3: Achievements

- Guided imagery exercise (see appendix 8.3)
- Lifeline (O'Brien et al., 1999)
- Success Box (O'Brien et al., 1999)

Session 4: Personality Preferences and Career Interests

- Myers-Briggs Type Indicator (Myers & Myers, 1995)
- Holland's (1997) theory of vocational choice and hexagon model

Session 5: Math and Science Careers

- Activities and discussions surrounding math and science opportunities

Session 6: Skills

- Bureau of Labor Statistics—career exploration (https://www.bls.gov/k12/content/students/careers/career-exploration.htm)
- LearnHowToBecome.org—career exploration (https://www.learnhow-tobecome.org/)
- KnowItAll.org—career clusters (https://www.knowitall.org/)

- Activity on matching specific careers with associated career clusters (https://www.nd.gov/cte/crn/coug/docs/COUG.pdf)

Session 7: Values and Prioritization

- Exercises on developing specific short-term and long-term career goals
- O*Net (https://onetonline.org/)

Session 8: Career Self-Awareness

- Discussion of girls' understanding of themselves
- Effective decision-making strategies and personal study skills

Session 9: Written Communication

- Development of resumes
- Completion of sample job application forms

Session 10: Communication in Employment Interviews

- Interviewing techniques
- Practice of interviewing skills

APPENDIX 8.2

Session 2 Exercise: 7 Steps to Decision-Making

Choosing a potential career path can be overwhelming for young people. This exercise shows that a seven-step decision-making process works for minor decisions, such as deciding what to wear, as well as for major decisions, such as choosing a career.

1. *Identify the decision to be made:* Try to define clearly the specific nature of the decision you must make.
2. *Gather the information:* Collect some pertinent information before you make your decision: the necessary information, best sources of information, and ways to find them.

3. *Identify the alternatives:* In this step, you will list all possible and desirable paths of action.
4. *Weigh the evidence:* Use your information, emotions, and imagination to consider what it would be like if you carried out each of the alternatives to the end.
5. *Choose among the alternatives:* Once you have considered all the evidence, you are ready to select the alternative that seems to be the best one for you.
6. *Act:* You are now ready to take some positive action by beginning to implement the path of action you chose in Step 5.
7. *Review and evaluate your decision and its consequences:* In the last step, consider the results of your decision and evaluate whether or not it has resolved the need you identified in Step 1.

(adapted from Efird & Wiggins, 2004, pp. 23–24)

APPENDIX 8.3

Session 3 Guided Imagery Exercise

I invite you to sit up straight in your chair. Close your eyes slowly, take a truly calming breath, and begin to relax. Breathe with your belly. Inhale through your nose and exhale through your mouth. Now inhale and exhale more deeply. Repeat this breath cycle until you feel completely relaxed. Maintain a steady rhythm of breaths in and out. Begin to tune out the outside world.

Focus on your breathing. Allow your breath to find its own relaxed rhythm. Let your body soften and settle down. Let go of any tension or discomfort you may be feeling in your body. Imagine breathing in peace and tranquility as you inhale and imagine releasing anxiety and stress as you exhale. Breathe this way for three very slow and deep breaths.

Become more aware in this place in this moment. With each breath you inhale and exhale, let your thoughts come and go, without resistance or attachment.

Reflect on your life. Think about your family and imagine them in your mind. Think about your friends and imagine them in your mind. Think about school and imagine yourself in class. When you think about your current life, how does it make you feel?

Now think about a goal you would like to achieve in the next ten years of your life. It could be a goal related to a relationship, your education, or work. Think about why this goal is significant to you. How will accomplishing this goal add value to your life? Think about your goal and picture it in your mind.

Now envision yourself going forward into the future. Imagine yourself in one year, two years, three years, and four years. You have started on the path to success. What choices have you made? What have you done? How does it feel to be on the path to success?

Continue going forward to five years in the future. You are closer to accomplishing your goal. You are starting to see the benefits of all your efforts. What emotions are you feeling as you move closer toward your goal?

Now imagine yourself in ten years. You have fully achieved your goal. Envision yourself. How old are you? How do you look? What are you doing? What are your relationships like? What degrees have you completed? Where do you work? How does success feel?

Now look back on your accomplishment. Look back on the process of achieving your goal. Look back on all of the effort and time you put in to accomplishing your goal. How did you achieve your goal? What were the daily steps you took to achieve success? Imagine your work and relationships. Take a moment to reflect on all of the steps you took to achieve your goal. Remain in quiet reflection for a moment.

When you feel ready to return, take a deep breath. Relax. Become aware of your surroundings. Feel your body touching your seat. Open your eyes and sit quietly for a few moments.

REFERENCES

Aasheim, L. L., & Niemann, S. H. (2006). Guidance/psychoeducational groups. In D. Capuzzi, D. R. Gross, & M. D. Stauffer (Eds.), *Introduction to group work* (4th ed., pp. 269–294). Denver, CO: Love Publishing.

Allen, K. R., & Bradley, L. (2015). Career counseling with juvenile offenders: Effects on self-efficacy and career maturity. *Journal of Addictions & Offender Counseling, 36*, 28–42. doi: 10.1002/j.2161-1874.2015.00033.x.

Andrews, D. A., Guzzo, L., Raynor, P., Rowe, R. C., Rettinger, L. J., Brews, A., & Wormith, J. S. (2012). Are the major risk/need factors predictive of both female and male reoffending? A test with the eight domains of the level of service/case management inventory.

International Journal of Offender Therapy and Comparative Criminology, 56, 113–133. doi:10.1177/0306624X10395716.

Bandura, A. (1986). *Social foundations of thought and action: A social cognitive approach.* Englewood Cliffs, NJ: Prentice Hall.

Betz, N. E., Klein, K., & Taylor, K. M. (1996). Evaluation of a short form of the Career Decision-Making Self-Efficacy Scale. *Journal of Career Assessment, 4*, 47–57. doi:10 .1177/106907279600400103.

Blustein, D. L., Barnett, M., Mark, S., Depot, M., Lovering, M., Lee, Y. . . . DeBay, D. (2012). Examining urban students' constructions of a STEM/career development intervention over time. *Journal of Career Development, 40*, 40–87. doi: 10.1177/0894845312441680.

Chartrand, J. M., & Rose, M. L. (1996). Career interventions for at-risk populations: Incorporating social cognitive influences. *Career Development Quarterly, 44*, 341–354. doi:10.1002/j.2161-0045.1996.tb00450.x.

Creed, P. A., & Patton, W. (2003). Differences in career attitude and career knowledge for high school students with and without paid work experience. *International Journal for Educational and Vocational Guidance, 3*, 21–33. doi: 10.1023/A:1022674528730.

Crites, J. O., & Savickas, M. L. (1996). Revision of the Career Maturity Inventory. *Journal of Career Assessment, 4*, 131–138. doi:10.1177/106907279600400202.

Efird, B. M., & Wiggins, B. S. (2004). *Career development resource guide and user's guide for "career choices in North Carolina" 2004–2005.* Raleigh, NC: North Carolina State Occupational Information Coordinating Committee. Retrieved from http://digital.ncdcr .gov/cdm/ref/collection/p249901coll22/id/436170.

Fagan, A. A., Van Horn, M. L., Hawkins, J. D., & Arthur, M. W. (2007). Gender similarities and differences in the association between risk and protective factors and self-reported serious delinquency. *Society for Prevention Research, 8*, 115–124. doi:10.1007/s11121 -006-0062-1.

Fields D., & Abrams L. S. (2010). Gender differences in the perceived needs and barriers of youth offenders preparing for community reentry. *Child & Youth Care Forum, 39*, 253–269. doi: 10.1007/s10566-010-9102-x.

Fitzgerald, E. L., Chronister, K. M., Forrest, L., & Brown, L. (2013). OPTIONS for preparing inmates for community reentry: An employment preparation intervention. *The Counseling Psychologist, 41*(7), 990–1010. doi: 10.1177/0011000012462367.

Grande, T. L., Hallman, J., Rutledge, B., Caldwell, K., Upton, B., Underwood, L. A., & Rehfuss, M. (2012). Examining mental health symptoms in male and female incarcerated juveniles. *Behavioral Sciences & the Law, 30*, 365–369. doi: 10.1002/bsl.2011.

Holland, J. L. (1997). *Making vocational choices: A theory of vocational personalities and work environments* (3rd ed.). Odessa, FL: Psychological Assessment Resources.

Legum, H. L., & Hoare, C. H. (2004). Impact of career intervention on at-risk middle school students' career maturity levels, academic achievement, and self-esteem. *Professional School Counseling, 8*, 148–155.

Lent, R. W., Brown, S. D., & Hackett, G. (1994). Toward a unifying social cognitive theory of career and academic interest, choice, and performance [Monograph]. *Journal of Vocational Behavior, 45*, 79–122. doi: 10.1006/jvbe.1994.1027.

Lewis, J., Arnold, M. S., House, R., & Toporek, R. L. (2003). *Advocacy competencies.* Endorsed by the American Counseling Association Governing Council. Retrieved from https://www.counseling.org/Resources/Competencies/Advocacy_Competencies.pdf.

Myers, I. B., & Myers, P. B. (1995). *Gifts differing: Understanding personality type.* Mountain View, CA: Davies-Black Publishing.

National Career Development Association. (1997). *Career counseling competencies.* Broken Arrow, OK: Author.

———. (2009). *Minimum competencies for multicultural career counseling and development.* Broken Arrow, OK: Author. Retrieved from https://www.ncda.org/aws/NCDA/pt/fli/12508/false.

North Dakota Career Resource Network. (2017). *Career outlook user's guide.* Bismark, ND: North Dakota Department of Career and Technical Education. Retrieved from https://www.nd.gov/cte/crn/coug/docs/COUG.pdf.

O'Brien, K. M., Dukstein, R. D., Jackson, S. L., Tomlinson, M. J., & Kamatuka, N. A. (1999). Broadening career horizons for students in at-risk environments. *Career Development Quarterly, 47*(3), 215–229. doi: 10.1002/j.2161-0045.1999.tb00732.x.

Puzzanchera, C., & Hockenberry, S. (2013). *Juvenile court statistics, 2010.* Pittsburgh, PA: National Center for Juvenile Justice.

Roos, L. E. (2006). *The effect of career development on employment and recidivism among juvenile offenders* (PhD dissertation). Retrieved from ProQuest Dissertations & Theses Global (UMI No 3203992).

Ross, R, & Fabiano, E. (1985). *Time to think: A cognitive model of delinquency prevention and offender rehabilitation.* Johnson City, TN: Institute of Social Sciences and Arts.

Skorikov, V., & Vondracek, F. W. (2007). Positive career orientation as an inhibitor of adolescent problem behavior. *Journal of Adolescence, 30*, 131–146. doi:10.1016/j.adolescence.2006.02.004.

Tarolla, S. M., Wagner, E. F., Rabinowitz, J., & Tubman, J. G. (2002). Understanding and treating juvenile offenders: A review of current knowledge and future directions. *Aggression and Violent Behavior, 7*(2), 125–143. doi: 10.1016/S1359-1789(00)00041-0.

Thompson, M. N., & Cummings, D. L. (2010). Enhancing the career development on individuals who have criminal records. *Career Development Quarterly, 58*(3), 209–218. doi: 10.1002/j.2161-0045.2010.tb00187.x.

Walker, S. C., Bishop, A. S., Nurius, P. S., & Logan-Greene, P. (2016). The heterogeneity of treatment needs for justice-involved girls: A typology using latent class analysis. *Criminal Justice and Behavior, 43*(3), 323–342. doi: 10.1177/0093854815615162.

Weinger, S. (2000). Opportunities for career success: Views of poor and middle-class children. *Children and Youth Services Review, 22*, 13–35. doi:10.1016/S0190-7409(99)00071-7.

Zabel, R., & Nigro, F. (2007). Occupational interests and aptitudes of juvenile offenders: Influence of special education experience and gender. *Journal of Correctional Education, 58*, 337–355.

VII

CAREER DEVELOPMENT INTERVENTIONS FOR
SOCIAL JUSTICE NEEDS IN COMMUNITY
AND EMPLOYMENT CONTEXTS WITH
UNDERSERVED ADULTS

9

Addressing Employment Uncertainty of Rural Working Adults

A Telemental Health Community Workshop

Shannon M. O'Neill

With rapid shifts in the United States economy, job instability has become a growing problem impacting many working adults. When one's work is unstable (e.g., perceived job insecurity or unemployment), negative emotional, physiological, and behavioral responses can develop. This work-related threat is even more critical for marginalized groups who depend on work for basic survival and have limited opportunities in their community for future employment. Rural working adults are facing job instability and considered at-risk for unemployment, as an increase in global competition and advances in technology are replacing their positions. This chapter outlines a career program intervention that takes a culturally sensitive social justice approach to delivering adequate evidence-based career counseling to rural working adults within a context that reduces the stigma of mental health care. Using innovative telemental health technology and a day-long community workshop format, the career program intervention aims to address challenges commonly associated with job instability (i.e., psychological distress, self-esteem, and overall life satisfaction). Developing effective coping skills will empower rural working adults to take an action-oriented approach to address the impact of work-related difficulties within their community. (See tables 9.1 and 9.2 for an outline of relevant competencies needed.)

Table 9.1. Relevance to Career Counseling Competencies

Career Counseling Competency	Addressed by Career Intervention	Relevance to Corresponding Competency
1. Career Development Theory	X	Contains brief introduction to a career theory (Psychology of Working; Blustein, 2006) and incorporation of cognitive behavioral techniques for career implication.
2. Individual and Group Counseling Skills	X	Portrays delivery of career services at a community-workshop level.
3. Individual/Group Assessment	X	Entails pre- and post-program measures.
4. Information/ Resources/ Technology	X	Demonstrates the use of partnering with an agency, using resources to effectively serve a specific population. Offers an innovative telemental health approach to reach geographically, culturally, and economically secluded communities.
5. Program Promotion, Management, and Implementation	X	Offers culturally sensitive attention to promotion, management, and implementation from remote locations.
6. Coaching, Consultation, and Performance Improvement	—	—
7. Diverse Populations	X	Portrays the adaptation of career services to disadvantaged group with unequal life opportunities, power, income, education, or resources.
8. Supervision	—	—
9. Ethical/Legal Issues	X	Entails ethical/legal considerations relevant to rural clientele and telemental health.
10. Research/ Evaluation	X	Demonstrates the evaluation of a career program, using local needs, agency feedback, and participant ratings to inform changes.

Source: NCDA, 1997, 2009.

Table 9.2. Relevance to Advocacy Competencies

Advocacy Competency	Addressed by Career Intervention	Relevance to Corresponding Competency
1. Client/Student Empowerment	X	Entails skills/strategies clients can practice independently to create empowerment regarding their world-related circumstances.
2. Client/Student Advocacy	X	Provides the creation of individual action plans clients can use to self-advocate for specific resources.
3. Community Collaboration	X	Uses collaboration of community agencies to serve as resources/referrals for clients.

Advocacy Competency	Addressed by Career Intervention	Relevance to Corresponding Competency
4. Systems Advocacy	—	—
5. Public Information	X	Program is open to the public and entails community-workshop format, creating a discussion around relevant constraints and resources. Provides a discussion and realistic action other mental health providers can take, using services to aid remote communities in their area.
6. Social/Political Advocacy	—	—

Source: Lewis et al., 2003.

SOCIAL JUSTICE NEEDS AND RATIONALE FOR THE CAREER DEVELOPMENT INTERVENTION

The term *urbancentrism*, originally coined by Stamm (2003), is the tendency for professionals as well as the general public to pay more attention to the problems experienced within metropolitan areas and overlook the struggles of rural communities. This urban-centric perspective is evident when referencing the available body of literature, as very little research has dedicated time and energy to investigating geographically diverse, underserved rural populations. Rural America is often overgeneralized with stereotypical homogeneous images of well-adjusted, hardworking White European farmers who possess simple, stable lifestyles. However, rural America is much more complex with distinct community-specific cultures, resources, and barriers that deserve recognition (Rainer, 2010).

Like members of other minority groups (e.g., by race/ethnicity), rural individuals are considered disadvantaged due to inequalities in life opportunities, power, income, and education (Burton, Lichter, Baker, & Eason, 2013). In fact, those within collective rural communities frequently band together for survival similar to other alienated groups (Zur, 2006). Data from the United States Department of Agriculture (2016) suggest that as geographic rurality increases, college education and employment decrease while poverty and uninsured rates increase. Compared to urban counterparts, rural individuals experience similar rates of psychological distress, yet the availability and accessibility of behavioral health services is drastically different (Juntunen

& Quincer, 2017; Smalley et al., 2010). With a ratio of sixteen psychologists for every one hundred thousand individuals residing in rural areas, there is a chronic shortage of adequate mental health care (Whiting, 2006).

Similar to the urban-rural disparity of traditional mental health services, the discrepancy of vocational resources is equally prevalent. Nearly 40 percent of rural high school students are considered work-bound, as they forgo college and transition to employment opportunities within their community directly after graduation (Provasnik et al., 2007). This work-bound transition can occur for a number of reasons, such as restricted educational and career aspirations, limited access to career counseling and college preparatory courses, lack of occupational role models, and lower family socioeconomic status (Griffin, Hutchins, & Meece, 2011; Provasnik et al., 2007). However, these work-bound individuals may face significant challenges, including fewer job opportunities, less job stability, reduced wages, and lower overall life satisfaction (Halperin, 1998).

Rural work-bound youth frequently find employment in the service, labor, extraction, and agriculture sectors. Yet employment opportunities that were once considered mainstay positions within the community are now disappearing due to economic restructuring and interdependence between urban areas (Brown & Schafft, 2011; Lichter & Brown, 2011). With a continuous rise in global competition, low educated, blue-collared manufacturing workers are at a heightened risk for job displacement (Brand, 2006). Tasks that were once completed by blue-collared workers are now done by machines at a faster rate or outsourced to foreign countries for lower wages (Albrecht, Albrecht, & Albrecht, 2000).

A large body of research has acknowledged the negative effects of unemployment (e.g., depression, anxiety, psychosomatic symptoms, low self-esteem; Paul & Moser, 2009). However, uncertainty of future employment stability can be equally harmful (Rocha, Crowell, & McCarter, 2006). Burgard, Brand, and House (2009) found that prolonged job insecurity can create negative emotional, physiological, and behavioral responses due to "ongoing ambiguity about the future, inability to take action unless the feared event actually happens, and lack of institutionalized supports" (p. 784). If an employee does not possess healthy coping skills, chronic job insecurity can increase burnout, reduce job satisfaction, decrease work performance, and pervade home life (Boswell, Olson-Buchanan, & Harris, 2014).

The uncertainty of work threatens much more than psychological health and well-being for marginalized groups who already experience significant contextual barriers. With lower education, higher poverty, and limited options for future work, maintaining employment is vital in order to meet basic needs for survival (e.g., food, water, shelter). Due to the limited and fragile economic base of many rural communities, job uncertainty is a critical threat to both the employed and unemployed rural working class. The current career program intervention can serve as a helpful community resource, offering rural working adults (eighteen years and older) support and skill development to help effectively cope with an overwhelming economic climate.

Theoretical Framework

David Blustein (2006) developed the psychology of working theory (PWT) to recognize those who work for survival and face significant work-related issues beyond career selection (e.g., marginalized group members facing economic constraints). Prior to this relevant social justice perspective, career theories primarily focused on the developmental needs and experiences of the wealthy majority who have the luxury of exploring options and using their career choice as a form of expression or creativity (e.g., Holland, 1997). Unfortunately, *choice* is not a relevant construct for the poor working class who are in need of an immediate income and have limited options for work within their community. According to PWT, the role of work, regardless of employment type, is to be able to fulfill three functions of the human experience, "survival and power, social connection, and self-determination" (Blustein, Kenna, Gill, & DeVoy, 2008, p. 297).

The theoretical perspective of Blustein (2006) encourages the integration of traditional therapy with career counseling, acknowledging the influence of work-related concerns on psychological health and well-being. When meeting with unemployed adults, Blustein (2006) outlines three broad principles to guide career counseling interventions: (1) address the interconnection between job loss and psychological consequences; (2) provide an array of community resources that offer emotional and instrumental support; (3) assist beyond social and emotional support to address all issues associated with job loss (e.g., family discord). The current career program invention has been constructed to adapt these three principles to serve rural adults experiencing work-related uncertainty. Brief cognitive behavioral strategies are incorporated to enhance career counseling applications, offering culturally sensitive, action-oriented services less stigmatized in rural culture (Cook & Heppner, 1997).

MEASURABLE OBJECTIVES AND EXPECTED OUTCOMES

The primary goal of this career program intervention is to reduce the negative impact of an unstable economic climate affecting the rural working class by acknowledging real and perceived barriers, learning effective coping skills, and creating self-advocacy action plans. Integrating cognitive behavioral techniques with the theoretical framework of PWT, the career program will strive to foster empowerment and encourage rural adults to take an action-oriented approach to work-related concerns to live a more satisfying life in spite of uncertainty. With the help of psychoeducation and the teaching of cognitive behavioral strategies, valuable skills will be developed to reduce psychological distress, increase self-esteem, and enhance satisfaction with life that is often limited among rural working adults (Burgard et al., 2009; Halperin, 1998).

Upon completing the rural telehealth community workshop, participants will be able to do the following:

1. Distinguish between real and perceived threats regarding employment concerns.
2. Apply at least two coping skills found to be helpful (e.g., cognitive restructuring, coping statements, behavioral activation, and progressive muscle relaxation).
3. Reference an individualized action plan to manage work-related stress.

PLAN FOR PROMOTING SERVICES

The chosen program leader should be well equipped with specific knowledge and skills to seamlessly execute the community workshop. A competent program leader is mindful of culturally relevant career counseling, particularly within the given rural context. The leader is capable of implementing cognitive behavioral therapy to an array of work-related problems, challenges, and concerns. Lastly, the program leader is qualified to employ telemental health services, where he/she will organize community outreach, deliver psychological services, and conduct relevant supervision.

Promotional efforts begin by creating a partnership with a local agency in the community. Forming a community-based partnership with an accepted and established institution (e.g., medical facility) can reduce skepticism as well as stigma, enhance the dissemination of services, and offer preexisting referral sources (Deen, Bridges, McGahan, & Andrews, 2012; Hauenstein et al., 2007). Upon receiving approval from relevant personnel, the program leader can use the agency's knowledge to network with other community providers for further promotional services and future resource suggestions (Slama, 2004). In order to remain sensitive to the stigma of mental health care in rural culture, the workshop should be advertised as *strategies to improve with work-related challenges* (Cook & Heppner, 1997; Horrell et al., 2014).

PLAN FOR DELIVERING SERVICES

Telehealth has become an effective platform, creating feasibility for adequate health care professionals to reach geographically, culturally, and economically secluded individuals across the country (American Psychological Association [APA], 2013). Similarly, one-day workshops have been developed to address the needs of communities in a less stigmatizing format. Research examining the delivery of services via telemental health (Richardson, Frueh, Grubaugh, Egede, & Elhai, 2009) as well as one-day workshop formats (Horrell et al., 2014) have found significant treatment effectiveness with patient and clinician satisfaction.

The present career program intervention will use internet-based videoconferencing to connect with the partnering community agency to deliver the one-day workshop. This technology-based community workshop is an innovative approach that addresses common barriers related to the availability, accessibility, and acceptability of mental health care within remote locations (Godleski, Darkins, & Peters, 2012). The workshop will be made available on weekends to accommodate employed and unemployed rural adults.

It is important to identify the benefits and challenges of serving rural communities. Since telemental health guidelines are unique to each state, counselors should inform themselves of local licensure requirements, insurance reimbursement, and privacy risks. Helpful information regarding ethical, legal, and clinical challenges can be referenced within APA's (2013) "Guidelines for the Practice of Telepsychology." Equally important are the unique and complex ethical dilemmas experienced in rural community practice (e.g., dual relationships). Helpful information addressing ethical risk management with rural settings can be found within Schank, Helbok, Haldeman, and Gallardo's (2010) "Challenges and Benefits of Ethical Small-Community Practice." Therapists interested in incorporating this career program intervention into their practice are encouraged to familiarize themselves with helpful electronic resources, such as APA's continuing education workshops, the American Telemedicine Association, and APA's Resource Center for Rural Behavioral Health.

RESOURCES NEEDED

To successfully implement the career program intervention, community agency partnership is required. The agency will provide a designated space to host the workshop, two or three on-site volunteers, videoconferencing equipment, and access to a printer and paper. The on-site volunteers will assist with several tasks, such as distribution and scoring of objective measures, preparing handouts, staging the reserved space, and managing the videoconferencing equipment.

INTERVENTION PROGRAM CONTENT

Prior to beginning the community workshop, prospective participants will visit the partnering agency to obtain information and complete objective measures. Baseline levels of psychological distress, self-esteem, and life satisfaction are measured, scored, and documented. To identify adults who are under severe psychological distress, it is important that agency volunteers review scores and offer any necessary referrals prior to starting the workshop.

The daylong workshop is available to all adult community members. Reaching a large number of community members can lay the groundwork for more open communication, offering social support and resources or referrals for those in need. Although the workshop focuses on serving those experiencing job instability, the cognitive behavioral strategies are transferrable to other stressful life circumstances. Workshop steps are outlined below and listed in appendix 9.1. Program leaders are encouraged to reference accompanying citations for a more comprehensive summary of specific techniques. To maintain the attention of participants, case vignettes, role-plays, and group exercises should be incorporated throughout the workshop.

Introduction

The workshop begins with introductions offered by the program leader and volunteers. Workshop packets are also distributed to encourage active participation and application of techniques being discussed (see appendix 9.2 for a sample handout). An outline of the day will be reviewed to offer focused expectations for the experience. To address any foreseeable resistance associated with the discussion of psychological terminology, the presenter should acknowledge the cognitive behavioral model as an active solution-focused theory that contains tools and techniques used to address daily life circumstances.

Step 1: Psychoeducation

The program leader briefly introduces Blustein's (2006) PWT, highlighting the importance of work and its role in the totality of an individual's life. Discussing health-related benefits and the critical necessity of work can offer a better understanding for the distress experienced with job uncertainty. An acknowledgement of marginalization and economic constraints within the community can assist in validating the reality of participants' experiences. The program leader incorporates the cognitive behavioral model using a simple jargon-free explanation to describe the interconnected nature of work instability and poor mental health. Information to address includes: (a) a situation's (e.g., job insecurity) influence on thoughts, emotions, behavior, and physiology; (b) the link between thoughts and emotions; (c) unhelpful thinking patterns (e.g., fortune telling; Beck, 1995).

Step 2: Cognitive Strategies

To demonstrate how unhelpful thoughts create additional unwanted distress, the program leader introduces the ABC model (Adversity, Beliefs, Consequences; Ellis, 1962). A relevant case vignette, discussing the anxiety often associated with an insecure work environment, should be incorporated. Participants then spend time independently completing their ABC model, exploring individual thoughts related to work-related stress. When participants detect the central features of their work-related beliefs, cognitive strategies can be implemented.

It is important to note, marginalized groups hold both distorted and undistorted negative beliefs, which are developed and strengthened by experiences of oppression. When specific cognitive methods (e.g., challenging negative assumptions) are done incorrectly, the intervention can be ineffective and culturally insensitive. Therefore, the program leader introduces three cognitive methods helpful in addressing chronic continual stressors (e.g., poverty, racism, stressful employment; Meichenbaum, 1975): (a) the "Stop" technique, (b) mental distraction, and (c) coping self-statements. Participants will then break into small groups and use their ABC models to practice the three cognitive techniques. These exercises are encouraged to promote flexibility in thinking and tolerance for ambiguity, which is a growing requirement for today's economy.

Step 3: Behavioral Strategies

The program leader introduces three behavioral methods to combat negative effects of work instability: (a) progressive muscle relaxation (Cormier & Cormier, 1991), (b) behavioral activation (Hopko, Lejuez, Ruggiero, & Eifert, 2003), and (c) problem solving (Beck, 1995). Problem solving is a critical piece of the workshop that is used to address additional life circumstances associated with job instability. Dilemmas commonly addressed using problem solving include: communicating with one's partner about job insecurity, coping with anxiety-provoking work-interfering thoughts, and finding child care services for additional skills training. Stages of problem solving include the following SOLVED steps: (S) select a problem, (O) open mind to all solutions, (L) list the potential pros and cons of each potential solution, (V) verify the best solution, (E) enact the plan, (D) decide if the plan worked. Participants pair off to problem-solve, creating goals to carry out selected solutions.

Step 4: Action

With newly acquired skills, participants spend time creating a one-month action plan (i.e., homework) in order to manage work-related stress upon conclusion of the workshop. Resource packets are distributed, including instrumental and emotional resources that participants may find online as well as within their community that can enhance their individual action plans (see appendix 9.3). The action plan should include the preferred cognitive and behavioral strategies learned as well as steps needed to receive additional services (e.g., résumé building, interview skills).

Conclusion

Prior to leaving the workshop, participants evaluate the workshop and obtain a cognitive behavioral resource folder. Packets will include extra copies of featured worksheets as well as detailed outlines that introduce other skills (e.g., sleep hygiene, time management). Participants are also invited to return for a one-month follow-up meeting. During the meeting, participants complete post-workshop measures, discuss successes/difficulties of individual action plans, and troubleshoot any new or existing dilemmas.

METHODS OF EVALUATION

Participants will complete four measures prior to beginning the workshop and will be reevaluated at the one-month follow-up meeting. Psychological distress will be measured using the twenty-one-item Beck Depression Inventory, Second Edition (BDI-2; Beck, Steer, & Brown, 1996) and the twenty-one-item Beck Anxiety Inventory (BAI; Beck & Steer, 1993). Higher total scores on both inventories indicate more severe symptoms of depression or anxiety. Participants' self-esteem will be measured using a ten-item Rosenberg Self-Esteem Scale (RSES; Rosenberg, 1965). Responses are given on a four-point scale ranging from 0 (*strongly disagree*) to 3 (*strongly agree*), with higher scores representing greater self-esteem. Participants' life satisfaction will be measured by a five-item Satisfaction with Life Scale (SWLS; Diener, Emmons, Larsen, & Griffin, 1985). Responses are given on a seven-point scale ranging from 1 (*strongly disagree*) to 7 (*strongly agree*), with higher scores suggesting more satisfaction with current life circumstances.

PLAN FOR REVISION

The program leader will use feedback from participants and the agency to evaluate and revise the career program. Pre- and post-intervention scores will be examined to determine objective success of the program. Participants will complete the eight-item Client Satisfaction Questionnaire (CSQ-8; Larsen, Attkisson, Hargreaves, & Nguyen, 1979), which is commonly used to assess satisfaction with a variety of services. Responses are given on a four-point scale with higher scores suggesting more satisfaction. Along with the CSQ-8, participants will also have the opportunity to write down any memorable workshop moments that were effective or ineffective.

The program leader will meet with the agency point-person and volunteers to discuss their roles as well as the successes and challenges of the workshop. Hearing from the partnering agency can assist the leader in remaining locally informed to the culture, politics, and economic context of the rural community in order to adapt services accordingly. With comprehensive feedback, the community workshop can modify content and incorporate local circumstances.

REFLECTIONS ON COUNSELOR SELF-AWARENESS OF POTENTIAL RESOURCES AND BIASES FROM PRIVILEGED AND MARGINALIZED IDENTITIES

Having been born and raised in central Kansas, I experienced a very traditional Midwest upbringing. With a population just shy of fifty thousand, my world revolved around the ten-mile perimeter of a community still small enough to be considered a large town. Like other rural areas, my town was geographically isolated, requiring community members to travel a significant distance to receive any specialized health care services. Yet I also considered the town to be stable and self-reliant, leaving me unaware and unconcerned with other's experiences beyond these borders. Retrospectively, I understand my privilege greatly influenced this lack of curiosity, as my needs were met and hardships were not evident.

I grew up in a White, middle-class, Catholic family that was well adjusted and highly supportive. My parents made several financial sacrifices to provide my siblings and me with a private Catholic education—an option that was unavailable in their very rural, resource-poor childhood communities. My Catholic education prioritized community outreach and embedded service projects within the curriculum. Reflecting on these initial service opportunities, my awareness of inequality developed and later led to the exploration of career options within the helping profession. Yet I held an urban-centric perspective, believing I had to relocate to a metropolitan area to aid the underserved.

I accepted an exciting opportunity to receive my doctoral degree in one of the most culturally diverse cities in the country. My graduate studies were richly filled with countless opportunities to serve marginalized groups through research, clinical work, and advocacy. Yet with a surplus of opportunities in a resource-rich community, I further recognized the constraints faced in geographically isolated, hard-to-reach communities.

Throughout the development of my career program intervention, my self-awareness of resources and biases has grown exponentially. Childhood experiences within my large town were filled with several resources and limited barriers, leading me to assume others could equally acquire the opportunities I had. However, I am now more aware of the collection of experiences within a given context. With my privilege and the unwavering support of my family, I had the luxury of extending my education and choosing a career that expressed my passion and interests. I look forward to using my education and this career program intervention to serve disadvantaged rural communities.

CONCLUSION

It is the author's hope that this chapter facilitates further discussion and action to address the urban-rural disparity in mental health resources. The career program intervention promotes a realistic platform for metropolitan mental health professionals to extend their services to hard-to-reach, remote communities. The one-day workshop can serve as a tool for resource-poor communities, offering a culturally sensitive evidence-based approach to address the limited and fragile economic climate of many rural areas. As aforementioned, the program leader is encouraged to stay locally informed and adapt services to the targeted community's culture, values, beliefs, needs, and expectations. Yet the general framework strives to empower rural working adults, teaching strategies to overcome work-related difficulties within their community.

APPENDIX 9.1

Outline for a Telemental Health Community Workshop
Addressing Employment Uncertainty of Rural Working Adults

Introductions (*30 min*)
- Facilitator introductions
- Workshop overview
- Anticipated learning objectives

- Introduce a relevant case vignette
  - Use the case throughout the workshop to teach various techniques
- Distribute participant workshop packets, which include the following:
  - Cognitive Behavioral Model, Distorted Thinking Patterns, ABC, Thought Stopping, Mental Distraction, Self-Statements, Progressive Muscle Relaxation, Behavioral Activation, Problem-Solving, SMART Goals, Action Plan

Step 1: Psychoeducation (*90 min*)
- Psychology of working theory (Blustein, 2006)
  - Importance of work
  - Health-related benefits
  - Marginalization and economic constraints
- Cognitive behavioral model (Beck, 1995)
  - Connection between thoughts, emotions, behaviors
  - Unhelpful thinking patterns
- ABC worksheet (Ellis, 1962)
  - Example—case vignette
- Independent completion of one ABC worksheet
  - Identify personal beliefs that create work-related stress

15-minute break

Step 2: Cognitive Strategies (*60 min*)
- Difference between distorted and undistorted negative beliefs
- Rationale for cognitive techniques
- Thought stopping (Meichenbaum, 1975)
  - Interrupt bothersome and unnecessary thoughts
  - Serves as a reminder that thoughts can be repetitive, negative, distorted
  - Can replace with healthier, more productive thoughts
- Mental distraction (Meichenbaum, 1975)
  - Turning attention to another topic
  - Difference between distraction and complete avoidance
- Self-statements (Meichenbaum, 1975)
  - Replace distorted thinking with positive, neutral, productive thoughts
  - Example—case vignette
- Small group exercise
  - Refer to completed ABC worksheet
  - Implement various cognitive techniques

15-minute break

Step 3: Behavioral Strategies (*60 min*)
- Rationale for behavioral techniques
- Progressive muscle relaxation (Cormier & Cormier, 1991)
  - Guided practice
  - Relaxation resources, websites, phone apps
- Behavioral activation (Hopko et al., 2003)
  - Pleasant activities list
  - Scheduled activities
- Problem solving (Beck, 1995)
  - SOLVED steps
  - Example—case vignette

Lunch break

Step 4: Action (*60 min*)
- Discuss importance of planning
- Introduce SMART goals (Doran, 1981)
- Independent development of one-month action plan
  - Helpful cognitive and behavioral strategies
  - Identify additional services needed

Conclusion (*30 min*)
- Briefly review the workshop's four steps
- Anticipated learning objectives
- Participant feedback/evaluation
- Date/time of one-month follow-up meeting
- Distribute cognitive behavioral resource folder

APPENDIX 9.2

Sample Worksheet and Action Plan in Participant Workshop Packet

Please select the two or more strategies you found most helpful and feel confident practicing for thirty days.

Thinking Strategies
  - Thought Stopping
  - Mental Distraction
  - Self-Statements

Thinking Strategy SMART Goal

(S)pecific _____

(M)easurable _____

(A)chievable _____

(R)elevant _____

(T)ime Based _____

Example: *I will practice two self-statements when I wake up at 7:00 am five times each week.*

Behaving Strategies
- Progressive Muscle Relaxation
- Behavioral Activation
- Problem-Solving

Behaving Strategy SMART Goal

(S)pecific _____

(M)easurable _____

(A)chievable _____

(R)elevant _____

(T)ime Based _____

Example: *I will practice progressive muscle relaxation at 8:00 pm three times each week.*

Please reference the participant resource packet* and reflect on any additional services you may need. As needed, create additional SMART goals (Doran, 1981).

To review the participant workshop packet in its entirety, please contact the author, Shannon O'Neill, regarding your request.

APPENDIX 9.3

Participant Resources

Sample List to Consider in Creating a Community-Specific Resource Page

Vocation and Employment:
- USDA—Vocational Education and Job Training (https://www.nal .usda.gov/vocational-education-and-job-training)
- Purdue Online Writing Lab—Resumes and Vitas (https://owl.english .purdue.edu/owl/section/6/23/)
- Career Development—Self-Assessment Tools (https://www.fordham .edu/info/24478/additional_career_resources/330/self-assessment_tools)

Physical and Mental Health:
- Health Finder—Access carefully selected information and websites from over 1,500 health-related organizations (https://healthfinder.gov/)
- Health and Aging—Searchable database lists more than 250 national organizations that provide help to older individuals (https://www.nia .nih.gov/health)
- Directory of Migrant Health Centers and Primary Care Associations— Access information on important migrant health resources by state and region (https://www.migrantclinician.org/community/health-centers .html)

Community:
- USDA—Rural Information Center (https://www.nal.usda.gov/ric)
- U.S. Small Business Administration (https://www.sba.gov/)

Local Collaboration:
- American Legion
- Domestic violence advocate
- Home health care
- Hospice
- Legal services
- Mental health support group
- Public health
- Religious pastor

- School counselor
- Senior center
- Social services
- Twelve-step recovery meetings

REFERENCES

Albrecht, D. E., Albrecht, C. M., & Albrecht, S. L. (2000). Poverty in nonmetropolitan America: Impacts of industrial, employment, and family structural variables. *Rural Sociology, 65*(1), 87–103. doi: 10.1111/j.1549-0831.2000.tb00344.x.

American Psychological Association. (2013). Guidelines for the practice of telepsychology. *American Psychologist, 68*(9), 791–800. doi: 10.1037/a0035001.

Beck, A. T., & Steer, R. A. (1993). *Beck anxiety inventory manual.* San Antonio, TX: Psychological Corporation.

Beck, A. T., Steer, R. A., & Brown, G. K. (1996). *Manual for the Beck depression inventory-II.* San Antonio, TX: Psychological Corporation.

Beck, J. A. (1995). *Cognitive therapy: Basics and beyond.* New York, NY: Guilford.

Blustein, D. L. (2006). *The psychology of working: A new perspective for career development, counseling, and public policy.* Mahwah, NJ: Erlbaum.

Blustein, D. L., Kenna, A. C., Gill, N., & DeVoy, J. E. (2008). The psychology of working: A new framework for counseling practice and public policy. *The Career Development Quarterly, 56*(4), 294–308. doi: 10.1002/j.2161-0045.2008.tb00095.x.

Boswell, W. R., Olson-Buchanan, J. B., & Harris, T. B. (2014). I cannot afford to have a life: Employee adaptation to feeling of job insecurity. *Journal of Personnel Psychology, 67*(4), 887–915. doi: 10.1111/peps.12061.

Brand, J. E. (2006). The effects of job displacement on job quality: Findings from the Wisconsin longitudinal study. *Research in Social Stratification & Mobility, 24*(3), 275–298. doi: 10.1016/j.rssm.2006.03.001.

Brown, D. L., & Schafft, K. I. (2011). *Rural people and communities in the 21st century: Resilience and transformation.* Cambridge, UK: Polity.

Burgard, S. A., Brand, J. E., & House, J. S. (2009). Perceived job insecurity and worker health in the United States. *Journal of Social Science and Medicine, 69*(5), 777–785. doi: 10.1016/j.socscimed.2009.06.029.

Burton, L. M., Lichter, D. T., Baker, R. S., & Eason, J. M. (2013). Inequality, family processes, and health in the "new" rural America. *American Behavioral Scientist, 57*(8), 1128–1150. doi: 10.1177/0002764213487348.

Cook, S., & Heppner, P. (1997). Coping, control, problem-solving appraisal, and depression symptoms during a farm crisis. *Journal of Mental Health Counseling, 19*(1), 64–75.

Cormier, W. H., & Cormier, L. S. (1991). *Interviewing strategies for helpers: Fundamental skills and cognitive behavioral interventions* (3rd ed.). Pacific Grove, CA: Brooks/Cole.

Deen, T. L., Bridges, A. J., McGahan, T. C., & Andrews, A. R., III. (2012). Cognitive appraisals of specialty mental health services and their relation to mental health service utilization in the rural population. *The Journal of Rural Health, 28*(2), 142–151. doi: 10.1111/j.1748 -03 61.2011.00375.x.

Diener, E., Emmons, R. A., Larsen, R. J., & Griffin, S. (1985). The satisfaction with life scale. *Journal of Personality Assessment, 49*(1), 71–75. doi:10.1207/s15327752jpa4901_13.

Doran, G. T. (1981). There's a S.M.A.R.T. way to write management's goals and objectives. *Management Review, 70*, 35–36.

Ellis, A. (1962). *Reason and emotion in psychotherapy.* New York, NY: Stuart.

Godleski, L., Darkins, A., & Peters, J. (2012). Outcomes of 98,609 U.S. Department of Veterans Affairs patients enrolled in telemental health services, 2006–2010. *Psychiatry Services, 63*(4), 383–385. doi: 10.1176/appi.ps.201100206.

Griffin, D., Hutchins, B. C., & Meece, J. L. (2011). Where do rural high school students go to find information about their futures? *Journal of Counseling & Development, 89*(2), 172–181. doi: 10.1002/j.1556-6678.2011.tb00075.x.

Halperin, S. (1998). *The forgotten half revisited: American youth and young families, 1988– 2008.* Washington, DC: American Youth Policy Forum.

Hauenstein, E. J., Petterson, S., Rovnyak, V., Merwin, E., Heise, B., & Wagner, D. (2007). Rurality and mental health treatment. *Administration and Policy in Mental Health and Mental Health Services Research, 34*(3), 255–267. doi:10.1007/s10488-006-0105-8.

Holland, J. L. (1997). *Making vocational choices: A theory of vocational personalities and work environments* (3rd ed.). Odessa, FL: Psychological Assessment Resources.

Hopko, D. R., Lejuez, C. W., Ruggiero, K. J., & Eifert, G. H. (2003). Contemporary behavioral activation treatments for depressions: Procedures, principles, and progress. *Clinical Psychology Review, 23*(5), 699–717. doi:10.1016/S0272-7358(03)00070-9.

Horrell, L., Goldsmith, K. A., Tylee, A. T., Schmidt, U. H., Murphy, C. L., Bonin, E.-M., . . . Brown, J. S. (2014). One-day cognitive-behavioral therapy self-confidence workshops for people with depression: Randomized controlled trial. *British Journal of Psychiatry, 204*(3), 222–233. doi:10.1192/bjp.bp.112.121855.

Juntunen, C. L., & Quincer, M. A. (2017). Underserved rural communities: Challenges and opportunities for improved practice. In J. M. Casas, L. A. Suzuki, C. A. Alexander, & M. A. Jackson (Eds.), *Handbook of multicultural counseling* (4th ed., pp. 447–455). Thousand Oaks, CA: Sage.

Larsen, D. L., Attkisson, C. C., Hargreaves, W. A., & Nguyen, T. D. (1979). Assessment of client/patient satisfaction: Development of a general scale. *Evaluation and Program Planning, 2*(3), 197–207. doi:10.1016/0149-7189(79)90094-6.

Lewis, J., Arnold, M. S., House, R., & Toporek, R. L. (2003). *Advocacy competencies.* Endorsed by the American Counseling Association Governing Council. Retrieved from https://www.counseling.org/Resources/Competencies/Advocacy_Competencies.pdf.

Lichter, D. T., & Brown, D. L. (2011). Rural America in an urban society: Changing spatial and social boundaries. *Annual Review of Sociology, 37*(1), 565–592. doi:10.1146/annurev -soc-081309-150208.

Meichenbaum, D. (1975). Self-instructional methods. In F. H. Kanfer & A. P. Goldstein (Eds.), *Helping people change* (pp. 357–391). New York, NY: Pergamon.

National Career Development Association. (1997). *Career counseling competencies.* Broken Arrow, OK: Author.

————. (2009). *Minimum competencies for multicultural career counseling and development*. Broken Arrow, OK: Author. Retrieved from https://www.ncda.org/aws/NCDA/pt/fli/12508/false.

Paul, K. I., & Moser, K. (2009). Unemployment impairs mental health: Meta-analyses. *Journal of Vocational Behavior, 74*(3), 264–282. doi:10.1016/j.jvb.2009.01.001.

Provasnik, S., KewalRamani, A., Coleman, M. M., Gilbertson, L., Herring, W., & Xie, Q. (2007). *Status of education in rural America* (NCES Publication No. 2007-040). Retrieved from http://nces.ed.gov/puhs2007/2007040.pdf.

Rainer, J. P. (2010). The road much less travelled: Treating rural and isolated clients. *Journal of Clinical Psychology: In Session, 66*(5), 475–478. doi:10.1002/jclp.20680.

Richardson, L. K., Frueh, B. C., Grubaugh, A. L., Egede, L., & Elhai, J. D. (2009). Current directions in videoconferencing tele-mental health research. *Clinical Psychology Science & Practice, 16*(3), 323–338. doi:10.1111/j.1468-2850.2009.01170.x.

Rocha, C., Crowell, J. H., & McCarter, A. K. (2006). The effects of prolonged job insecurity on the psychological well-being of workers. *Journal of Sociology & Social Welfare, 33*(3), 9–28. Retrieved from http://scholarworks.wmich.edu/jssw/vol33/iss3/2/.

Rosenberg, M. (1965). *Society and the adolescent self-image*. Princeton, NJ: Princeton University Press.

Schank, J. A., Helbok, C. M., Haldeman, D. C., & Gallardo, M. E. (2010). Challenges and benefits of ethical small-community practice. *Professional Psychology: Research and Practice, 41*(6), 502–510. doi:10.1037/a0021689.

Slama, K. M. (2004). Toward rural cultural competence. *Minnesota Psychologist, 53*(3), 6–13. Retrieved from https://www.apa.org/practice/programs/rural/cultural-competence.pdf.

Smalley, K. B., Yancey, C. T., Warren, J. C., Naufel, K., Ryan, R., & Pugh, J. L. (2010). Rural mental health and psychological treatment: A review for practitioners. *Journal of Clinical Psychology, 66*(5), 479–489. doi:10.1002/jclp.20688.

Stamm, B. H. (Ed.). (2003). *Rural behavioral health care: An interdisciplinary guide*. Washington, DC: American Psychological Association.

United States Department of Agriculture, Economic Research Service. (2016, November). *Rural America at a glance* (EI Bulletin No. 162). Retrieved from https://www.ers.usda.gov/webdocs/ publications/eib162/eib-162.pdf?v=42684.

Whiting, M. R. (2006, January). Rural America in need. *Monitor on Psychology, 37*(1), 64. Retrieved from http://www.apa.org/monitor/.

Zur, O. (2006). Therapeutic boundaries and dual relationships in rural practice: Ethical, clinical and standard of care considerations. *Journal of Rural Community Psychology, 9*(1), 1–40. Retrieved from http://www.marshall.edu/jrcp/.

10

Life-Design Group Course for Laid-Off Workers

Kathleen Hahn

Many experienced workers who are unemployed due to involuntary layoffs or organizational change feel disempowered and disheartened by the loss of their job. Often the individuals affected include members of marginalized populations who have previous experience of limited opportunities and resources. Low-cost continuing-education programs at local community colleges are often available to these unemployed workers to build job search skills, but the workers' eroded confidence often impedes their ability to apply these skills. While individual career counseling could be helpful for them in making sense of these transitions and considering coping strategies, it may be an expensive option and subject to delays due to the limited number of career counselors available. Therefore, a ten-week group career counseling course is proposed to provide affordable and efficient assistance for laid-off workers in understanding the changes in their lives and the impact of their social, political, and cultural contexts. The goal is to empower individuals to construct their next career stories in ways that integrate their life themes and to advocate for themselves by taking the necessary actions to advance their employability and career adaptability.

SOCIAL JUSTICE NEEDS AND RATIONALE FOR THE CAREER DEVELOPMENT INTERVENTION

Due to globalization, technology, and outsourcing, employers are periodically conducting significant layoffs, which have created an unstable work environment. Consequently, one in five workers in the United States has experienced unplanned termination of employment (Bureau of Labor Statistics, 2009). While involuntary layoffs affect the general population, members of socially oppressed groups by race, class, disability, immigrant status, sexual orientation, age, gender, poverty, or lack of access to resources are even more impacted by unemployment (Bureau of Labor Statistics, 2017). Vocational assistance to these marginalized populations facing unemployment is imperative from a social justice perspective. Failure to provide access to such assistance could result in greater inequalities, propagating further disparities in employment and other domains of psychosocial well-being (Blustein, Kozan, & Connors-Kellgren, 2013).

Career counseling practices that are tailored to marginalized individuals can be used to foster empowerment and critical consciousness (Blustein, 2006). Empowerment refers to interventions that help individuals become aware of the power dynamics in their life, develop the skills to regain some control without infringing on the rights of others, and support the empowerment of others in the community (McWhirter, 1994). *Critical consciousness* relates to the process where socially oppressed individuals come to identify their day-to-day experiences in the context of larger sociopolitical issues and take action against the oppressive elements (Freire, [1970] 2000). Furthermore, developing employability skills for members of marginalized groups may require multiple layers of intervention including counseling, case management, and social advocacy (Blustein, Kenna, Gill, & DeVoy, 2008).

The Life-Design Group Course (LDGC) is a targeted and efficacious intervention that promotes empowerment and critical consciousness as individuals integrate their life themes to make meaning of their unexpected career transitions. The ten-week program for unemployed workers assists individuals in making new career choices using their own life narrative. While this chapter describes the course in a local community college setting, the LDGC may be readily adapted to community clinics or outplacement settings for employers seeking to provide transition support for their former employees. Community colleges typically offer continuing education courses on job search, networking, and interview skills.

The LDGC is proposed to be implemented in a local community college specifically for experienced workers who are seeking employment largely due to involuntary layoffs or organizational change. Many of the students attending these courses feel disempowered and disheartened by the loss of their job midway through their career, which in turn adversely affects their ability to be motivated to learn the skills taught in the course and apply the skills out of the classroom. Research suggests that those who lose their job to layoffs can experience a range of psychological distress including stress, changes to perceived control, loss of self-esteem, shame, loss of status, grief, and financial strain (Anafl, Baum, Newman, Ziersch, & Jolley, 2013). Career transition courses often do not address these psychological impacts of job loss or the need for students to learn to make sense of the change, particularly in light of their social, political, economic, and cultural contexts. Additional social and emotional supports are required for students to develop their self-advocacy skills in taking ownership of their situation, reviewing their career options, making career decisions, and taking actions to implement their decisions.

Effective career counseling would assist the students to work through their thoughts and feelings around the job loss and support them in making new career choices. Unfortunately, career counseling services are often under-resourced with a long waitlist of students seeking guidance. The LDGC is an alternative option for access to aid participants in coming to terms with the current and ongoing changes in their lives since being laid off and in learning how to advocate for themselves to promote their employability and career adaptability. Furthermore, delivering this intervention in the format of psycho-educational group counseling allows participants to gain support from each other, learn through observations of each other, and experience the therapeutic factors of groups (Yalom, 1995).

MEASURABLE OBJECTIVES AND EXPECTED OUTCOMES

At the end of this course, participants will be able to:

1. Articulate the current career concerns that they want to address in their next career choice
2. Articulate the life themes (including the effect of social, political, and cultural factors) that provide sense and meaning in their lives that would be used in selecting their next career
3. Identify future careers and jobs that match their life themes
4. Complete a plan of activities that participants could implement to pursue the identified careers and jobs that take into account the identified barriers (including environmental barriers) and their own developmental needs

PLAN FOR PROMOTING SERVICES

The promotion of LDGC might be coordinated with career counselor instructors, both externally and within the college, via the following ways:

1. Listing an advertisement of the course on the college webpage for continuing education
2. Email to current students and alumni
3. Flyers advertising the course at local government employment agencies, local libraries, and local churches
4. Focus group session with the instructors of the current career development skills courses on the feedback that they have received from participants, their perception of participants' needs, and their feedback on the proposed course content
5. Pilot the course with existing participants in the job search course to be provided free of charge in return for their detailed feedback

PLAN FOR DELIVERING SERVICES

Delivery of the course would be through a combination of online assessments, homework, and group meetings on a weekly basis at the college. The ten group sessions of the course might be scheduled at the community college for two hours on the same night in ten consecutive weeks with the maximum number of participants being eight. The course should be facilitated by instructors who are professionally qualified career counselors (see tables 10.1 and 10.2 for relevant competencies in career counseling and social justice advocacy; Lewis, Arnold, House, & Toporek, 2003; National Career Development Association, 1997, 2009).

Table 10.1.   Relevance to Career Counseling Competencies

Career Counseling Competency	Addressed by Career Intervention	Relevance to Corresponding Competency
1. Career Development Theory	X	Career construction theory and life-design counseling approach (Savickas, 2012); psychology of working (Blustein, 2006).
2. Individual and Group Counseling Skills	X	Individual and group counseling competencies needed to facilitate CCI and group process.

Career Counseling Competency	Addressed by Career Intervention	Relevance to Corresponding Competency
3. Individual/Group Assessment	X	Ethical and multicultural competencies to administer and interpret career assessments and life-design CCI.
4. Information/ Resources/ Technology	X	Develop knowledge/networks to secure labor market information and make professional referrals. Utilizing appropriate technology to promote the program and administer career assessments.
5. Program Promotion, Management, and Implementation	X	Skills to develop, plan, implement, and manage career development program in a college setting.
6. Coaching, Consultation, and Performance Improvement	X	Consultation skills in collaborating with other college instructors to optimize program content.
7. Diverse Populations	X	Develop cultural competencies to deliver ethical and helpful career counseling group course intervention with laid-off workers, members of groups with diverse identities.
8. Supervision	—	—
9. Ethical/Legal Issues	X	Monitor for mental health issues and financial assistance needs of the participants; ethical and multicultural competencies required of the LDGC counselor/instructor.
10. Research/ Evaluation	X	Develop program evaluation skills in assessing feedback and outcomes for further revisions.

Source: NCDA, 1997, 2009.

Table 10.2. Relevance to Advocacy Competencies

Advocacy Competency	Addressed by Career Intervention	Relevance to Corresponding Competency
1. Client/Student Empowerment	X	Skills to help clients understand their own lives in context to advocate for themselves through their career transitions.
2. Client/Student Advocacy	X	Skills to help clients access needed resources such as financial aid, job opportunities, and mental health assessments.

Table 10.2. *Continued*

Advocacy Competency	Addressed by Career Intervention	Relevance to Corresponding Competency
3. Community Collaboration	X	Skills to communicate with other college instructors and relevant student affinity groups to collaborate on changing clients' environmental barriers.
4. Systems Advocacy	—	—
5. Public Information	—	—
6. Social/Political Advocacy	—	—

Source: Lewis et al., 2003.

INTERVENTION PROGRAM CONTENT

The content and format for the LDGC is grounded in career construction theory, and it applies life-design counseling assessment and techniques outlined by Savickas (2012). In particular, the LDGC adapts a life-design intervention described by Barclay, Stoltz, & Wolff (2016), a career counseling group course for undergraduate freshmen; it modifies this intervention to help people experiencing job loss, and it extends and integrates the development of critical consciousness and empowerment (Blustein et al., 2008).

The career construction theory and life-design counseling methods developed by Savickas (2012) uses clients' narratives to help them understand their identity and appreciate their life story. The goals of the LDGC intervention are to enable individuals to capitalize their awareness of self and their stories to cope with the uncertainties evoked by changes in their work life and to construct the next phase of their work life in a way that is congruent with their life themes. The life-design career counseling approach of Savickas (2012) is used to elicit personal narratives and help connect participants from different multicultural contexts (e.g., by culture, age, race/ethnicity, gender, sexual orientation, and socioeconomic status) in the process of finding their personal meaning of work in their individual contexts. Along the way, the instructors facilitate participants in discovering how their behaviors and concerns may have been influenced by systematic factors or internalized oppression that they may have experienced (Blustein, 2006).

Thus, this process of career counseling exploration goes beyond the traditional psychometric career assessment approach designed for more affluent Western contexts, which may not be as congruent for the individuals from more diverse cultural contexts, such as those of the participants attending the workshop (Setlhare-Meltor & Wood, 2016).

An outline of the ten-week LDGC program and homework associated with each week is highlighted in appendix 10.1. The first session of the LDGC for laid-off workers would include an introduction to the course and plan for the ten sessions. In preparation for the following sessions, participants would be asked to think about the people they admire the most, their favorite magazines or TV shows, their favorite stories or movies, their favorite saying or motto, and three of their earliest memories that they could share with the group (Savickas, 2012). Also, as homework, participants would be given instructions to complete the following online assessments for career exploration: the Strong Interest Inventory (SII; Strong, Donnay, Morris, Schaubhut, & Thompson, 2004), Skills Confidence Inventory (SCI; Betz, Borgen, & Harmon, 1996), and Adult Career Concerns Inventory (ACCI; Super, Thompson, & Lindeman, 1988). Their results would later be provided to them individually and considered in relation to their evolving life and career stories. In the following eight sessions, one group member would be highlighted each week to share the individual's career concern and construct career episodes. In the first hour, the career counselor/instructor would focus on using the Career Construction Interview (Savickas, 2013) framework and exploring relevant critical consciousness and empowerment issues (Blustein, 2006) with the individual group member. The second hour would focus on facilitating further processing with feedback from the group and might include exploring assessment results of relevance to the highlighted group member's life/career story.

The counselor begins the Career Construction Interview (CCI) with the highlighted group member by asking the question, "How can I be useful to you as you construct your career?" (Savickas, 2013, p. 657). Thereafter, the counselor uses the CCI framework of five questions to elicit concrete examples of the participant's life stories. These questions are used to focus the participant's self-awareness, reflect on what matters most to them, and consider how to reconstruct meaning that helps move them forward for the next chapters in their life/career story. Following are the CCI prompts (Savickas, 2013, p. 657):

1. Whom did you admire when you were growing up?
2. What attracts you to your favorite magazines or TV shows?
3. What is your favorite book or movie? Tell me the story.
4. Tell me your favorite saying or motto.
5. What is your earliest recollection?

The small stories or micronarratives shared by each group member in response to the interview questions will demonstrate how they have construed their self, identity, and career as actor and agent of their life story. The stories and themes may then be used by the individual group members to author the next episode of their career in the context of their life story (Savickas, 2012).

It will be important for the counselor to be culturally sensitive to gender, race, ethnicity, sexual orientation, social status, and other identities subject to social injustices, as well as the diverse strengths and values that may inform the counselor's interpretations of each group member's life story (Savickas, 2012). Each group member's small stories, or micronarratives, may contain dominating expectations and self-limiting ideas that may contribute to the disheartenment and sense of disempowerment that the group member is experiencing from the job loss. Some of these ideas and expectations are likely to have been developed through experiences of oppression, marginalization, and confrontation of systemic barriers that can also affect the layoff process. For example, Kalev (2014) found downsizing organizations with layoffs significantly decreased the representation of White women, Black women, and Black men in management positions. Naming and examining these experiences can be used as an opportunity for the group to distinguish discrimination from perceived deficiency of skills and abilities, develop critical consciousness, and consider empowerment strategies for each group member (Blustein, 2006; McWhirter, 1994). The career counselor/instructor should look to deconstruct the stories to reveal what the story assumes, overlooks, omits, forgets, or inadequately addresses to access different meanings and knowledge for the group member as well as strengths and sources of helpful resources.

In the second hour of the session, the peer group members and the counselor will provide feedback to the highlighted group member that links the small stories to portray general life themes, values, passions, and cognitive maps that intermingle with emotions and goals. The career counselor may use ThemeMapping (Stoltz & Barclay, 2015) to reconstruct a statement of identity, adaptabilities or transferable skills, preferred work environments, and self-actualization for the highlighted group member to consider (Barclay et al., 2016).

As homework, the highlighted group member will need to reflect upon, edit, and revise the draft of their life portrait to co-construct where they are in the context of their life story. Using the new perspectives and knowledge of themselves gained through the micronarratives, the group member will be encouraged to write what they want the next episode of their career story to be (Savickas, 2012).

As an additional source for potential exploration in drafting their next life/career narratives, the results of the assessments (SII, SCI, and ACCI) will be considered. Thus, each group member may make further adjustments to their revised identity narratives for their lives and careers (Barclay et al., 2016). Using the revised identity narrative, the group member will be encouraged to identify the activities that would address the career concerns that brought them to the LDGC to create a plan of action. This may involve reviewing the other skills-based courses that the college offers in order to consider matches with possible professions; seek targeted job information; or actively explore their choices through volunteering, internships, and contract work. In some cases, the counselor may need to step in to advocate for the group member in negotiating and accessing resources and services that can help the person overcome career barriers.

In the final workshop session, the group will reflect on the narratives and the progress of each member and provide feedback on the workshop. They might also generate a plan for follow-up contact and support that includes the counselor and group members.

RESOURCES NEEDED

Resources needed to deliver the course as designed are as follows:

1. Professionally qualified career counselor/instructor with competencies relevant to this intervention (e.g., ethical and multicultural consideration in administering and interpreting the SII, SCI, and ACCI, as well as career counseling with individuals and groups using the Life-Design methods of Savickas, 2012)
2. Career counselor/instructor time—two hours per week for ten weeks to conduct the course and estimated twelve hours per week for course

preparation and follow-up (e.g., via office hours or contact availability to respond to students' questions)

3. Meeting room for two hours per week for ten weeks
4. Funding promotion and marketing expenses for website additions, email distribution, flyers, and resources to gather feedback and course evaluation
5. Funding for the qualified counselor's purchase of access to administer the online assessment system and obtain results
6. Funding to purchase the SII, SCI, and ACCI assessments for each student (if not charged as part of the course fee)
7. Funding for the initial pilot course to gauge feedback and adapt the content and format as necessary.

The cost of the LDGC per participant is expected to be lower than individual counseling for group members. However, an ethical issue to be considered for each setting is what course fee should be charged for the participants when they are unemployed and may be in need of financial assistance. It may be necessary to consider a sliding scale on a case-by-case basis, or explore possible government grants or other resources that would be available to subsidize the provision of these courses. Also, access to secure computer use for participants should be provided to facilitate their completing online assessments, exploring relevant online career development resources, and promoting their implementing subsequent career plans.

METHODS OF EVALUATION

Recommended methods of evaluation are as follows:

1. At the end of the final session, ask group members to complete detailed feedback on the effectiveness of the workshop in addressing their career indecision, and any changes to the level of motivation, drive, and direction that they have experienced in completing the LDGC.
2. After three months following the final course session, contact the participants by phone or email and evaluate their progress in actions taken from the plan of activities at the end of the LDGC and their current employment status.

3. After twelve months, contact the participants by phone or email and compare the current career direction of the participant with the next career story constructed in the course, as well as assess their current employment status.

PLAN FOR REVISION

Based on the participants' feedback, revisions to the LDGC content and format require consideration. One of the areas to monitor is whether the length of the course is optimal at ten weeks, or if it presents the risk of dropouts because the time commitment is a deterrent for potential participants. In order to allocate a week for each participant to share career construction and receive feedback from the group, the length of the course was set at ten weeks. If the feedback suggests that the course is too long, an alternative may be to consider reducing the LDGC length with a maximum number of participants to six or four. Evaluation of the corresponding increase in the cost of smaller workshops against the greater efficacy of the workshops would need to be undertaken.

Another area to explore is whether the participant experience of providing feedback to other group members on their narratives is a therapeutic benefit or an impediment. The ability to draw themes and patterns from the small stories may be difficult for a diverse range of participants with varying degrees of abstract reasoning and intuition skills. However, the opportunity to help others in the group by giving feedback and recognizing that they are not alone in facing occupational transition may also improve self-efficacy for the participants in the group setting. One option to determine the suitability of participants to the group workshop experience may be a detailed description of what is expected from participants on the website for self-selection into the workshop or pre-screening by way of intake questionnaire.

CONCLUSION

Overall, the LDGC presents a way of delivering an efficient and inclusive career counseling intervention to experienced workers who have been laid off. The course allows participants to process the mixed emotions elicited from their job loss in the context of their life story, to rebuild their confidence and sense of identity. The resulting self-awareness and knowledge can empower individuals to make deliberate and intentional career choices, advocate for themselves, and cope with future career changes.

The value of life-design counseling is that it fulfills two functions of reflection and design at the same time (Maree & Twigge, 2016). These functions align with the needs of marginalized group members in building critical consciousness and empowerment. For marginalized workers who have been focused on survival, the LDGC may present a rare opportunity to process the systemic and internalized oppressions that they have experienced in their lives and explore how they wish to respond through their future career and life choices.

The emphasis on the individual's context lends flexibility for the LDGC to be helpfully applied to that individual's relevant multicultural and lifespan contexts. As an additional source for exploration in drafting one's next life/career narratives, the individual's career assessment results can be used to consider how subjective interpretations may be corroborated for validity and consistency or constructively challenged. Further, the group format in the college or other settings provides a means to address client needs in an efficient manner regarding cost and time.

Without an effective career development intervention, individuals involuntarily laid off are at the risk of becoming unemployable. For counselors committed to taking social action toward social justice, the LDGC may be a viable intervention in assisting this population.

REFLECTIONS ON COUNSELOR SELF-AWARENESS OF POTENTIAL RESOURCES AND BIASES FROM PRIVILEGED AND MARGINALIZED IDENTITIES

I am an immigrant of South Korean descent who migrated to Australia when I was eight years old with my family. We settled in a predominantly White, middle-class neighborhood where I truly identified with the Australian culture of equality, individualism, and multiculturalism. Yet my Asian features and gender attracted unwanted attention and stereotyping that offended me deeply, and it caused me to withdraw and brew with resentment. Conversely, interactions that were flexible, tolerant. and open-minded brought out the best in me. In my youthful idealism, I vowed never to assume that I know another person from the surface and to strive for understanding and respect in my interactions.

When I returned as a young adult to work in South Korea, I encountered prejudice for different reasons. My young age, foreign education, and gender automatically categorized me into lower employment opportunities and lower social hierarchy, without any consideration of my capabilities and contributions that I could make to the workplace and society. I was outraged but felt helpless and hopeless against the ingrained cultural bias, and what I felt was a rejection of the individual that I was, by my country of origin.

Focusing so much on what I felt were my oppressions, I only came to realize the full extent of the privilege that I had when I commenced my mental health counseling internship working with at-risk youth. These youth represented the devastating cycles of economic and social disempowerment that come from inequalities between the privileged and the oppressed, and I was clearly a part of the privileged. Blinded by my race and gender, which I thought held me back, I failed to recognize the far greater privileges of my education, sexual orientation, socioeconomic status, health, and growing up with both parents.

Coming to terms with my privilege has been a difficult process, but I now acknowledge myself as a person with privileged and marginalized identities. I am developing my critical consciousness through scholarship and a community of colleagues and friends who challenge my biases and support me through my feelings of guilt. Most importantly, my diverse clients' worldviews are teaching me how I can play a role in sharing my privilege, to empower and advocate for those who unjustly have less.

APPENDIX 10.1

Outline of the Life-Design Group Course for Laid-Off Workers

Week	Content	Homework
1	Introduction to the workshop Workshop plan Instructions to complete the career assessments	Consider: • people you admire the most • favorite magazines/TV shows, favorite stories/movies • favorite saying or motto • three earliest memories Complete: • Strong Interest Inventory • Strong Confidence Inventory • Adult Career Concerns Inventory

(continued)

Week	Content	Homework
2	Participant 1 Career Construction Interview and Group Feedback	Reflect on, edit, and revise current life story and next career story, and create a plan of action.
3	Participant 2 Career Construction Interview and Group Feedback	Reflect on, edit, and revise current life story and next career story, and create a plan of action.
4	Participant 3 Career Construction Interview and Group Feedback	Reflect on, edit, and revise current life story and next career story, and create a plan of action.
5	Participant 4 Career Construction Interview and Group Feedback	Reflect on, edit, and revise current life story and next career story, and create a plan of action.
6	Participant 5 Career Construction Interview and Group Feedback	Reflect on, edit, and revise current life story and next career story, and create a plan of action.
7	Participant 6 Career Construction Interview and Group Feedback	Reflect on, edit, and revise current life story and next career story, and create a plan of action.
8	Participant 7 Career Construction Interview and Group Feedback	Reflect on, edit, and revise current life story and next career story, and create a plan of action.
9	Participant 8 Career Construction Interview and Group Feedback	Reflect on, edit, and revise current life story and next career story, and create a plan of action.
10	Sharing of each participant's next career story and plans to implement. Feedback on the workshop	

REFERENCES

Anafl, J., Baum, F., Newman, L., Ziersch, A., & Jolley, G. (2013). The interplay between structure and agency in shaping the mental health consequences of job loss. *BMC Public Health, 13*(110), 1–12. doi: 10.1186/1471-2458-13-110.

Barclay, S. R., Stoltz, K. B., & Wolff, L. A. (2016). The Life-Design Group: A case study assessment. *The Career Development Quarterly, 64*(1), 83–96. doi:10.1002/cdq.12043.

Betz, N. E., Borgen, F. H., & Harmon, L. W. (1996). *Skills Confidence Inventory applications and technical guide.* Palo Alto, CA: Consulting Psychologists Press.

Blustein, D. L. (2006). *The psychology of working: A new perspective for career development, counseling, and public policy.* Mahwah, NJ: Erlbaum.

Blustein, D. L., Kenna, A. C., Gill, N., & DeVoy, J. E. (2008). The psychology of working: A new framework for counseling practice and public policy. *The Career Development Quarterly, 56*(4), 294–308. doi:10.1002/j.2161-0045.2008.tb00095.x.

Blustein, D. L., Kozan, S., & Connors-Kellgren, A. (2013). Unemployment and under-employment: A narrative analysis about loss. *Journal of Vocational Behavior, 82,* 256–265. doi: 10.1016/j.jvb.2013.02.005.

Bureau of Labor Statistics. (2009). *TED: The economics daily.* Retrieved from https://www.bls.gov/home.htm.

———. (2017). *Economic news release.* Retrieved from https://www.bls.gov/home.htm.

Freire, P. (1970; 2000). *Pedagogy of the oppressed.* New York, NY: The Continuum International Publishing Group.

Kalev, A. (2014). How you downsize is who you downsize: Biased formalization, account-ability, and managerial diversity. *American Sociological Review, 79*(1), 109–135. doi: 10.1177/0003122413518553.

Lewis, J., Arnold, M. S., House, R., & Toporek, R. L. (2003). *Advocacy competencies.* Endorsed by the American Counseling Association Governing Council. Retrieved from https://www.counseling.org/Resources/Competencies/Advocacy_Competencies.pdf.

Maree, J. G., & Twigge, A. (2016). Career and self-construction of emerging adults: The value of life designing. *Frontiers in Psychology, 6,* 1–12. doi: 10.3389/fpsyg.2015.02041.

McWhirter, E. H. (1994). *Counseling for empowerment.* Alexandria, VA: American Counseling.

National Career Development Association. (1997). *Career counseling competencies.* Broken Arrow, OK: Author.

———. (2009). *Minimum competencies for multicultural career counseling and develop-ment.* Broken Arrow, OK: Author. Retrieved from https://www.ncda.org/aws/NCDA/pt/fli/12508/false.

Savickas, M. L. (2012). Life design: A paradigm for career intervention in the 21st century. *Journal of Counseling & Development, 90,* 13–19. doi: 10.1111/j.1556-6676.2012.00002.x.

———. (2013). The 2012 Leona Tyler Award address constructing careers–actors, agents, and authors. *Counseling Psychology, 41,* 648–662. doi:10.1177/0011000012468339.

Setlhare-Meltor, R. & Wood, L. (2016). Using life design with vulnerable youth. *Career Development Quarterly, 64*(1), 64–74. doi: 10.1002/cdq.12041.

Stoltz, K. B., & Barclay, S. R. (2015). *The life design ThemeMapping guide.* Retrieved from http://www.vocopher.com.

Strong, E. K. Jr., Donnay, D. A. C., Morris, M. L., Schaubhut, N. A., & Thompson, R. C. (2004). *Strong Interest Inventory* (Revised ed.). Mountain View, CA: Consulting Psycholo-gists Press, Inc.

Super, D. E., Thompson, A. S., & Lindeman, R. H. (1988). *Adult Career Concerns Inven-tory: Manual for research and exploratory usage in counseling.* Palo Alto, CA: Consulting Psychologists Press.

Yalom, I. D. (1995). *The theory and practice of group psychotherapy* (4th ed.). New York, NY: Basic.

11

Empowering Battered Women with BRAVER

Adia Tucker

This chapter details the various components of BRAVER (Breaking the Reins of Abuse and Violence through Employment Reeducation), a career development intervention aimed at women whose vocational growth has been hindered by previous or ongoing experiences with intimate partner violence. Lack of economic independence can be a major deterrent in leaving abusive relationships. Therefore, BRAVER aims to empower women vocationally—and by extension, economically and personally—so that they might take steps to lead lives independent of their abusers and free from violence. This chapter describes the social justice issues and career development needs of battered women, the objectives and expected outcomes of the intervention, a plan for promoting the program, guidance for providing services, the program content, the resources required, proposed methods of evaluation, and a few ideas for revising the program based on evaluation data. Lastly, the author has incorporated some thoughts on her growing multicultural self-awareness and evolving identity as a social justice counselor, reflecting upon how BRAVER might tap into her resources and biases from privileged and marginalized identity standpoints.

SOCIAL JUSTICE NEEDS AND RATIONALE FOR THE CAREER DEVELOPMENT INTERVENTION

This career development intervention is called BRAVER—Breaking the Reins of Abuse and Violence through Employment Reeducation—and targets women whose career development has been stunted by intimate partner violence (IPV). Clients may vary in age, race, ethnicity, sexual orientation, educational level, and socioeconomic background. The program will be most beneficial to battered women who need to learn the tools of job searching, résumé writing, and interviewing as well as those who require assistance in identifying jobs or careers that align with their skills and interests. The program will take place at a community center or women's shelter that provides a range of services, such as housing, basic material needs, crisis intervention, individual and group counseling, and advocacy.

The social justice needs of this population are varied. Women experiencing IPV, especially those from economically poor communities, may navigate several systems—criminal justice, welfare, child protective services, and immigration, to name a few—which can ultimately reinforce a feeling of disempowerment and compromise efforts to leave abusive relationships. As van Wormer (2009) illustrates, even in cases when a perpetrator is successfully prosecuted, the battered woman may not get legal justice. The victim typically has little control over whether she might withdraw charges; sometimes she is forced against her will to testify against her abuser; she may be subject to a dual arrest and criminal charges if she physically defends herself; and child welfare might get involved, determining that a child is safer out of the custody of the mother if the child is continually exposed to the violent behavior of the abuser. With all these forces potentially working against her, and by systems that allege to protect, it is no wonder that so much IPV goes unreported. Too many victims feel marginalized once law enforcement becomes involved, and thus the cycle of abuse and the social conditions that contribute to continued poverty and powerlessness are reaffirmed (van Wormer, 2009).

Economic disempowerment lies at the heart, as there is a strong correlation between lower socioeconomic status and higher rates of domestic violence (Coker, 2016). Therefore, an intervention to foster economic independence via employment and career exploration is necessary, as vocational development can allow battered women not only to enjoy higher self-esteem, greater financial independence, and positive social relationships, but also to help them better cope with IPV or leave their abusive partners altogether (Rothman, Hathaway, Stidsen, & de Vries, 2007). Battered women often need assistance in finding and maintaining employment. Their ability to do so is compromised by the physical and psychological abuse they endure from their partners, who may view employment as a sign of independence and exert control tactics to limit women's career opportunities and prevent them from accruing resources (Brown et al., 2005). By obtaining and maintaining employment, battered women can begin a journey to becoming financially independent of their abusers.

In addition to procuring steady employment is the need for self-awareness and career exploration. According to Morris, Shoffner, and Newsome (2009), IPV among women is most highly reported between the ages of twenty and twenty-four; the second highest incidence rates according to reporting occurs among women ages twenty-five to thirty-four. These are typically the years when young adults come to know themselves and the World of Work better, and make the connection between the two. Because many battered women have had these years compromised by IPV and have not yet engaged in thorough exploration of their career interests and values, they are in a state of career "arrested development" (Morris et al., 2009, p. 45). Furthermore, the building of self-efficacy—the belief in one's ability to succeed in particular situations—and the development of a positive self-concept will be a goal of BRAVER. Because abusers often isolate women and curtail their attempts to explore educational and career activities, battered women may not have had access to opportunities to increase self-efficacy in both general life tasks and work tasks. Therefore, this population needs help in the building of self-efficacy and the transforming of negative perceptions of their abilities (Morris et al., 2009).

As suggested by the program's aim to address self-efficacy, the goals and content of BRAVER are primarily grounded in social cognitive career theory (SCCT). As summarized by Lent, Brown, and Hackett (1994), the building of self-efficacy, which greatly influences outcome expectations, is a core element of this theory. Through session discussion and exercises, participants will have an opportunity to reflect upon and share the factors that have contributed to high or low self-efficacy as it pertains to certain careers. What are the circumstances that have led a participant to think "I can't do that career" or "yes, I can do this job"? What are the expected outcomes for pursuing particular jobs, and why? What have been the primary sources of performance accomplishments, role modeling, social feedback, and emotions that have resulted in self-efficacy or lack thereof? Furthermore, SCCT, more so than other career development theories, accounts for meaningful environmental factors that impact one's ability to pursue careers, such as personal barriers and supports. It would be neglectful not to explore the vocational barriers that may exist for these survivors of IPV and brainstorm ways to cope with them, such as irregular employment due to the interference of their abusers, lack of childcare options, financial restrictions that may prevent them from getting to and from interviews, or threats from their abusers who are invested in keeping the participants emotionally or financially dependent on them. Equally important is an exploration of supports—helpful individuals, personal strengths, or circumstances—which can aid in the development of a more positive self-concept and increase optimism for their futures.

Some of the program activities which are rooted in SCCT principles are a job satisfaction history inventory designed to elicit performance accomplishments (see appendix 11.1); a self-efficacy inventory (Chronister & McWhirter, 2004); a transferable skills exercise also aimed at revealing sources of self-efficacy; and an exercise that asks participants to reflect upon a major barrier to realizing their job or career goal and a source of support. In addition, some of the activities in BRAVER incorporate aspects of Holland's (1997) theory of personality-environment fit as well as career assessment and counseling methods advanced by Bolles (2012), Chronister & McWhirter (2006), and Morris et al. (2009). Overall, program interventions aim to address participants' low self-efficacy, explore the relationship between self-efficacy and the development of career interests, reinforce beliefs about underutilized capabilities, and provide opportunities to pursue more sources of self-efficacy and employment.

MEASURABLE OBJECTIVES AND EXPECTED OUTCOMES

There are five main learning objectives for this intervention. By the end of BRAVER, the participants will be able to:

1. Name at least three transferable skills from their life experience to potential employment
2. Identify one or two jobs or career fields which they wish to further explore or pursue
3. Write a one-page résumé
4. Describe two job-searching techniques
5. Create a career action plan, indicating at least two short-term and two long-term goals

In addition to achieving these objectives, it is expected that clients will experience the following outcomes:

1. Have a greater sense of the beneficial role that work can play in their lives.

2. Possess a more positive self-concept and enjoy greater self-efficacy in their ability to successfully maintain employment.
3. Benefit from the support of other program participants who have been affected by IPV.
4. Be more effective in applying and interviewing for jobs.

PLAN FOR PROMOTING SERVICES

BRAVER will be conducted at a community center or women's shelter that provides a plethora of services to battered women. Intake counselors should notify clients of the opportunity to partake in career services, and staff counselors should refer clients for whom they have noted significant vocational needs. The counselor will advertise BRAVER by hanging flyers around the center, requesting referrals, and taking a few minutes to speak to clients about the mission of the program at the start of group counseling sessions. In addition, the counselor will promote the program and advocate for participants by seeking out organizational allies within the community. Prior and concurrent to the running of BRAVER, the counselor should engage in outreach to solicit collaborations from organizations that believe in the mission of BRAVER, are sensitive to the needs of the population it serves, and are committed to supporting the participants by potentially developing roles suited to their unique strengths or considering them as candidates for existing open positions. Alternatively, an organization might offer support via company visits or mentorship by current employees. At the conclusion of the program, the counselor can connect group members with these organizational allies while following up and maintaining community partnerships for future iterations of the program.

PLAN FOR DELIVERING SERVICES

Services will be provided via a series of five two-hour group workshops held on the same day at the same time over consecutive weeks. Clients will also receive three hour-long individual sessions: one held prior to the first workshop, another held approximately midway through the program, and a final one held within a couple weeks of the conclusion of the program. A counselor experienced in career counseling and knowledgeable about the complex dynamics and impact of IPV will conduct the individual and group sessions (see tables 11.1 and 11.2 for relevant competencies in career counseling and social justice advocacy; Lewis, Arnold, House, & Toporek, 2003; National Career Development Association, 1997, 2009). Up to eight clients may participate in the program. To reach a wider swath of women, and assuming there are multiple counselors qualified to run BRAVER, more than one program could run concurrently—for example, a Tuesday evening and a Thursday afternoon program. The program could also be implemented periodically throughout the year with each iteration incorporating any modifications that are appropriate. An important ethical consideration is that the battered woman's pursuit of employment and financial independence can escalate the level of violence she receives from an abusive partner (Brown et al., 2005; Chronister & McWhirter, 2006); therefore, participation in the program could put clients at further risk. Since joining BRAVER could increase the risk of IPV for its participants, counselors and the center as a whole should make the physical and emotional safety of clients a priority by offering additional support in the form of extra counseling sessions, emergency shelter, clear safety plans, and other resources. Lastly, since lack of childcare can act as a barrier to battered women's participation in career services (Chronister, Linville, & Kaag, 2008), childcare will be provided on site.

Table 11.1.   Relevance to Career Counseling Competencies

Career Counseling Competency	Addressed by Career Intervention	Relevance to Corresponding Competency
1. Career Development Theory	X	Holland's (1997) theory and social cognitive career theory (Lent et al., 1994).
2. Individual and Group Counseling Skills	X	Counselor meets clients individually and in groups.
3. Individual/Group Assessment	X	Counselor will administer and interpret vocational instruments.
4. Information/ Resources/ Technology	X	Counselor will demonstrate and enhance knowledge of job-hunting resources and the World of Work.
5. Program Promotion, Management, and Implementation	X	Counselor will be involved in all stages of promoting, implementing, and managing program.
6. Coaching, Consultation, and Performance Improvement	—	—
7. Diverse Populations	X	Clients may vary in age, race, class, ethnicity, and sexual orientation.

Career Counseling Competency	Addressed by Career Intervention	Relevance to Corresponding Competency
8. Supervision	—	—
9. Ethical/Legal Issues	X	Counselor will deepen knowledge of ethical and legal issues pertinent to this population.
10. Research/ Evaluation	X	Counselor will analyze evaluation results and make modifications to future iterations of the program.

Source: NCDA, 1997, 2009.

Table 11.2. Relevance to Advocacy Competencies

Advocacy Competency	Addressed by Career Intervention	Relevance to Corresponding Competency
1. Client/Student Empowerment	X	Increasing clients' awareness of systemic barriers and personal strengths are core features.
2. Client/Student Advocacy	X	Counselor will advocate on behalf of clients when seeking collaborations with organizations.
3. Community Collaboration	X	Counselor will seek alliances with community organizations that are sensitive to the needs of program participants.
4. Systems Advocacy	X	Counselor will work at the organizational and community level to promote career development work as an automatic service provided to battered women.
5. Public Information	—	—
6. Social/Political Advocacy	—	—

Source: Lewis et al., 2003.

INTERVENTION PROGRAM CONTENT

Individual Session 1

The establishment of trust is essential when working with this population. Without a sense of trust and the assurance that they will not be judged for their involvement in abusive relationships, battered women may be less inclined to partake in a career development program or remain until its completion (Chronister et al., 2008). Therefore, BRAVER will include a mandatory intake interview during which the counselor will begin the process of building a supportive and empathic relationship with the client. Together they will explore the client's relationship status and history, discuss her career or educational goals, and clarify what the client hopes to get out of BRAVER. A job history and assessment of prior vocational satisfaction and dissatisfaction should also be completed (see appendix 11.1 for an example of a form that can be used for this purpose). The counselor will also detail the structure of the program and allow the client to ask questions or express concerns. The client will also be given a tour of the facilities and have the opportunity to meet staff members and the on-site childcare provider so that she can become more comfortable in the space. After the intake, the client will be asked to complete a career interest inventory and a values inventory, the results of which will be shared and discussed at the next individual session.

Group Workshop 1

During the first group workshop, the counselor will encourage the clients to share their experiences with IPV and reflect on how abusive relationships have impacted their vocational development or ability to maintain employment. Clients will be able to air any concerns they have about making career decisions, procuring work, or accomplishing goals. The counselor will provide psycho-education about how career development can empower them, enhance their well-being, and help them achieve independence. The counselor will also lead a discussion of the clients' strengths. By helping the women to identify potential strengths such as managing domestic tasks, keeping themselves safe, and navigating an abusive partner's moods, the counselor can reframe these abilities as desirable vocational skills and traits, such as multitasking, perceptiveness, and good judgment (Morris et al., 2009). At the conclusion of the workshop, the clients will be given an inventory that assesses their self-efficacy in performing general vocational tasks (Chronister & McWhirter, 2004). As an assignment for the following workshop, clients should come up with three personal accomplishments that demonstrate skills that are transferable to the workplace.

Group Workshop 2

During the first half of the workshop, using Bolles's (2012) transferable skills exercise as a model, the counselor will demonstrate how to reframe personal accomplishment stories into tangible job skills. The women will break into pairs to share their personal accomplishment stories, discuss the skills they developed from those experiences, and provide feedback and support to one another. During the second half, the counselor will give a presentation on job-hunting resources including but not limited to internet advertisements, staffing agencies, and personal referrals. As an assignment for the following workshop, clients should tap into these resources and identify at least three positions or companies of interest. They should also consider how their transferable skills might match the requirements of the jobs. Any clients who have a résumé should bring a copy to the next workshop.

Individual Session 2

This session should be scheduled sometime between the second and fourth workshops. During this session, the counselor and client will discuss the results of the interest and values inventories and explore occupations that may be a good fit for the client. Using the previously administered self-efficacy assessment as a guide, the counselor will also investigate the client's self-efficacy regarding work tasks. Additionally, the counselor will examine the client's barriers and supports to career development, challenge any misguided beliefs, and help foster more positive outcome expectations (Morris et al., 2009). Together, the counselor and client will begin to set both short-term and long-term career goals (see appendix 11.2 for a sample worksheet that can be used for career action planning).

Group Workshop 3

The counselor will give a presentation on résumé writing by employing examples of effective and ineffective résumés and demonstrating how to tailor a résumé to the requirements of a specific position. Clients will have the rest of the session to begin drafting or revising their résumés (using their identified job postings for guidance) with the counselor's assistance. In advance of the next session, clients should complete a draft of their résumé.

Group Workshop 4

After responding to any remaining questions on résumé writing, the counselor will give a presentation on the most effective interviewing strategies. The counselor will also explain the value of informational interviewing and networking. With the help of a volunteer staff member, the counselor will conduct a mock informational interview. The group will then process the role-play and raise any questions or concerns. As an assignment for the final session, clients should complete a draft of their career action plan (begun in the second individual session) that describes both short-term and long-term career goals.

Group Workshop 5

This is for those clients who are willing may share their action plan with the group and receive suggestions or feedback. Clients will be encouraged to express any fears or anxieties regarding ending the program, pursuing their career goals, or navigating their relationships. Clients will also identify the personal supports and barriers to the accomplishment of their goals (Morris et al., 2009). Before departing, clients will retake the vocational skills self-efficacy assessment (Chronister & McWhirter, 2004).

Individual Session 3

Clients will meet with the counselor within two weeks of the final group workshop and complete a brief questionnaire about the program, indicating which elements they found most helpful and offering suggestions for improvement. Counselor and client will discuss and compare the results of the pre- and post-assessments of self-efficacy. Together they will process the client's overall experience in BRAVER, fine-tune the career action plan, and address any concerns about ending the program or taking steps toward identified goals. The counselor will also share with the client notice of any opportunities for employment or networking within the organizations that have partnered with BRAVER. The counselor will encourage the client to follow up on any potential leads among partnering companies, continue to utilize the center for counseling as needed, and stay in touch with the counselor to provide updates on any career or educational progress or roadblocks.

RESOURCES NEEDED

BRAVER will require the following resources:

1. A professionally qualified counselor with competencies relevant to this intervention
2. Counselor time for ten hours of group work and up to twenty-four hours of individual counseling

3. Counselor time for the preparation of presentations and handouts on job hunting, résumé writing, and interviewing
4. Counselor time for researching and reaching out to various organizations to solicit collaborations that could vocationally benefit program participants
5. A meeting room that will hold up to ten people for two hours on one evening per week for five consecutive weeks
6. Funding to purchase for each of the eight clients the selected inventory measures of career interests, values, and self-efficacy, by the counselor who is professionally qualified to administer and interpret these assessments
7. At least eight copies of handouts on job hunting, résumé writing, and interviewing
8. A childcare provider on site for the ten hours of group workshops

METHODS OF EVALUATION

The evaluation process is critical to ensuring that BRAVER meets the vocational needs of battered women. Listed below are some methods to assess the program's effectiveness:

1. Within two weeks of the final group workshop, clients will fill out a questionnaire that assesses the quality of their experience in the program.
2. The counselor will ask clients for feedback during the individual sessions.
3. The counselor will compare scores between the first and second administrations of the self-efficacy inventory to determine whether the program has increased the women's confidence in career decision-making and goal attainment.
4. Clients will be contacted approximately three months, six months, and one year after the program to determine whether the action plans are being followed and career or educational goals are being pursued.
5. The counselor will communicate with her contacts at the partnering organizations to learn whether any successful placements have been made between group participants and the companies and assess how to improve such collaborations in the future.

6. In overall evaluation of the program's effectiveness, the counselor will consult with clients, partnering organizations, and staff at the community center/women's shelter where BRAVER is conducted to include consideration of briefer and more targeted intervention strategies that might offer greater flexibility in helpfully addressing the inherent instability of the lives of many women subjected to IPV.

PLAN FOR REVISION

Future iterations of the program will be revised in accordance with evaluation results. The counselors who serve as program directors should take particular note of whether clients feel that the environment was an emotionally supportive, non-judgmental one and whether they experienced an increase in their self-efficacy. Based on the feedback of the clients, program directors might decide to reduce or expand group size, increase the number of sessions, or utilize a second counselor to provide an alternate voice during group discussions. It is also important to allow clients to process their IPV experiences as well as their vocational needs (Chronister et al., 2008). If clients indicate that they would benefit from more group sharing of the abuse they have experienced, program directors should consider allotting more time during each workshop for discussions that center specifically on IPV concerns. In addition, the degree of success of partnerships with community organizations should be analyzed. While it should be noted whether any of the program participants were able to establish working, networking, or mentoring relationships with the organizations, new ways of working together might be explored, such as inviting representatives to speak at a BRAVER workshop about their company's mission or values, or engaging the companies to take part in a more structured meet-and-greet with the women prior to the conclusion of the program.

REFLECTIONS ON COUNSELOR SELF-AWARENESS OF POTENTIAL RESOURCES AND BIASES FROM PRIVILEGED AND MARGINALIZED IDENTITIES

In proposing a career intervention for battered women and considering the competencies set forth by Ratts, Singh, Nassar-McMillan, Butler, and

McCullough (2015) as well as the personal stories outlined by Toporek, Sapigao, and Rojas-Arauz (2017), I have reflected upon my own multicultural self-awareness and my continued development as a social justice counselor. As an African American and a woman who grew up lower-middle class in Boston—a vibrant city with a particularly complicated racial history—it is not difficult to pinpoint the ways in which my identity has been historically marginalized. While only some of the aforementioned characteristics may be apparent when I enter a room, they all inform the work I do as a counselor and impact in some way my relationships with clients. As a marginalized counselor, I have firsthand knowledge of and experience with systemic barriers. I am keenly aware that members of an oppressed racial or ethnic group frequently experience additional barriers to their ability to not only obtain employment but also access career development programs (Chronister & McWhirter, 2004). Therefore, any BRAVER participants who fall into such groups are coping with career development challenges from both IPV and structural racism. Especially for these women of color, achieving steady employment and economic independence will not be as simple as matching interests to careers and following their dreams. Unfortunately, there are systems in place that will complicate their efforts to better their situations, and thus it is critically important to seek alliances with organizations or individuals who will throw tangible support behind their attempts to succeed vocationally.

The bigger awakening in my developing consciousness has been the gradual awareness of the ways in which I have been enormously privileged. I can recall an exercise during a graduate school class that rather bluntly required participants to face and acknowledge their own privilege. On one hand, there were the predictable questions that centered on race, sex, and socioeconomics—questions that reinforce any young, lower-middle-class Black woman's self-perception as a generally underprivileged member of society. On the other hand, there were questions that caught me off guard, as I realized they were, in fact, indications of my privilege: the fact that I regularly attended museums, ballets, and the cinema as a child; the preponderance of books around my childhood home; my parents' steadfast interest in my school performance; and my education at an Ivy League university. This recognition of my privileged identity, which is as meaningful and as impactful on my counseling relationships as is my marginalized self, is especially important when working with survivors of IPV, as my educational background and vocational path have afforded me career advantages and social capital to which many participants of BRAVER will not have had access. As a privileged counselor, keeping any assumptions or biases I have in check—for example, a myopic belief that a career (as opposed to a job) is something everyone should value, or an assumption that once one has the support of the program, leaving an abusive relationship should be easy—will be vital. In examining the interplay of my privileged and marginalized selves while aiming to grow in my abilities as a social justice advocate, I would hope to truly connect with BRAVER participants and foster an environment in which the women feel free to express themselves without fear of judgment.

CONCLUSION

As Chronister, Wettersten, and Brown (2004) note, IPV can significantly restrict educational and vocational development. Women in abusive relationships may suffer setbacks such as harassment at work by their partners, frequent absenteeism, difficulty concentrating, poor self-concept, and an inability to maintain steady employment. As a result, their career advancement is severely compromised and their ability to amass resources is limited. A steady and supportive workplace can offer battered women many emotional benefits, including higher self-esteem, a mental respite from abuse, the opportunity to form positive professional and personal relationships, and a motivation to achieve. More critically, economic independence via employment can serve as an asset in battered women's desire and ability to leave abusive relationships. Career services are integral to battered women's overall health and futures. BRAVER recognizes the power that lies in every woman who has survived IPV to fulfill her career potential, grow in self-esteem, and lead a safer, healthier life that is free from violence.

APPENDIX 11.1

Job Satisfaction History

Please consider up to five jobs you have had. List them and indicate one or two things you liked and did not like about each position. You may also consider school projects, volunteer work, family roles, or caretaking responsibilities in addition to paid work experience.

Table A11.1.

JOB/ASSIGNMENT	I ENJOYED . . .	I DID NOT ENJOY . . .
1.		
2.		
3.		
4.		
5.		

How would you describe your ideal job?

_____

_____

_____

Name _____ Date _____

APPENDIX 11.2

Job/Career Action Planning Worksheet

All goals should be **SMART**: **S**pecific, **M**easurable, **A**chievable, **R**elevant, and **T**ime-Framed (Doran, 1981).

1. List three short-term goals for the **next one month** below. Some examples may include completing a résumé, learning a computer program, or signing up for a class. Rank your goals in order, 1 being highest. Working in pairs, evaluate it based on SMART factors by checking each SMART letter.

   a. _____   Rank# _____

       S__ M__ A__ R__ T__

   b. _____   Rank# _____

       S__ M__ A__ R__ T__

   c. _____   Rank# _____

       S__ M__ A__ R__ T__

2. List three steps you need to take to accomplish your #1 goal within the next one month.

   A.

   B.

   C.

3. What resources or materials will you need to accomplish this goal?

   _____

   _____

4. Who is one person you can call for help, support, or encouragement in accomplishing your goal?

   _____

5. What is one thing you can do toward your #1 goal today?

   _____

6. List three medium-term goals for the **next six months** below, ranked in order of importance:

   a. _____   Rank# _____

       S__ M__ A__ R__ T__

   b. _____   Rank# _____

       S__ M__ A__ R__ T__

c. _____ Rank# _____

S__M__A__R__T__

7. List one long-term goal for the **next one year.**

Name _____ Date _____

REFERENCES

Bolles, R. N. (2012). *What color is your parachute? Job-hunter's workbook* (4th ed.). Berkeley, CA: Ten Speed Press.

Brown, C., Linnemeyer, R. M., Dougherty, W. L., Coulson, J. C., Trangsrud, H. B., & Farnsworth, I. S. (2005). Battered women's process of leaving: Implications for career counseling. *Journal of Career Assessment, 13*, 452–475. doi:10.1177/1069072705277928.

Chronister, K. M., Linville, D., & Kaag, K. P. (2008). Domestic violence survivors' access of career counseling services: A qualitative investigation. *Journal of Career Development, 4*, 339–361. doi:10.1177/0894845308316291.

Chronister, K. M., & McWhirter, E. H. (2004). Ethnic differences in career supports and barriers for battered women: A pilot study. *Journal of Career Assessment, 12*, 169–187. doi:10.1177/1069072703257754.

———. (2006). An experimental examination of two career interventions for battered women. *Journal of Counseling Psychology, 53*, 151–164. doi:10.1037/0022-0167.53.2.151.

Chronister, K. M., Wettersten, K. B., & Brown, C. (2004). Vocational research for the liberation of battered women. *Counseling Psychologist, 32*, 900–922. doi: 10.1177/001100000426930.

Coker, D. (2016). Domestic violence and social justice: A structural intersectional framework for teaching about domestic violence. *Violence against Women, 22*(12), 1426–1437. doi: 10.1177/1077801215625851.

Doran, G. T. (1981). There's a S.M.A.R.T. way to write management's goals and objectives. *Management Review, 70*, 35–36.

Holland, J. L. (1997). *Making vocational choices: A theory of vocational personalities and work environments* (3rd ed.). Odessa, FL: Psychological Assessment Resources.

Lent, R. W., Brown, S. D., & Hackett, G. (1994). Toward a unifying social cognitive theory of career and academic interest, choice, and performance [Monograph]. *Journal of Vocational Behavior, 45*, 79–122. doi: 10.1006/jvbe.1994.1027.

Lewis, J., Arnold, M. S., House, R., & Toporek, R. L. (2003). *Advocacy competencies*. Endorsed by the American Counseling Association Governing Council. Retrieved fromhttps://www.counseling.org/Resources/Competencies/Advocacy_Competencies.pdf.

Morris, C. A. W., Shoffner, M. F., & Newsome, D. W. (2009). Career counseling for women preparing to leave abusive relationships: A social cognitive career theory approach. *Career Development Quarterly, 58*(1), 44–53. doi: 10.1002/j.2161-0045.2009.tb00172.x.

National Career Development Association. (1997). *Career counseling competencies*. Broken Arrow, OK: Author.

————. (2009). *Minimum competencies for multicultural career counseling and development.* Broken Arrow, OK: Author. Retrieved from https://www.ncda.org/aws/NCDA/pt/fli/12508/false.

Ratts, M. J., Singh, A. A., Nassar-McMillan, S., Butler, S. K., & McCullough, J. R. (2015). *Multicultural and social justice competencies.* Retrieved from http://www.counseling.org/knowledge-center/competencies.

Rothman, E. F., Hathaway, J., Stidsen, A., & de Vries, H. F. (2007). How employment helps female victims of intimate partner violence: A qualitative study. *Journal of Occupational Health Psychology, 12,* 136–143. doi:10.1037/10768998-12.2.136.

Toporek, R. L., Sapigao, W., & Rojas-Arauz, B. O. (2017). Fostering the development of a social justice perspective and action: Finding a social justice voice. In J. M. Casas, L. A. Suzuki, C. M. Alexander, & M. A. Jackson (Eds.), *Handbook of multicultural counseling* (4th ed., pp. 17–30). Thousand Oaks, CA: Sage.

van Wormer, K. (2009). Restorative justice as social justice for victims of gendered violence: A standpoint feminist perspective. *Social Work, 54*(2), 107–116. doi: 10.1093/sw/54.2.107.

12

Career Progression Workshop for the Internationally Educated

Fanny Kuang

This chapter outlines a preliminary plan for a career development workshop for the large influx of immigrants who hold degrees from a university outside of the United States and are underemployed. Professionals who enter the country without the support or resources needed to navigate the U.S. labor market often experience that their skills and training are underutilized or wasted. Moreover, these many highly educated and skilled immigrants are hindered from obtaining relevant employment to support their own and their families' well-being. The Career Progression Workshop for the Internationally Educated is designed to provide participants with a foundational road map for obtaining employment that more fully uses their skills and qualifications.

SOCIAL JUSTICE NEEDS AND RATIONALE FOR THE CAREER DEVELOPMENT INTERVENTION

The intended population for this workshop is immigrants with foreign degrees who are underemployed in New York City (an example of a large metropolitan area that attracts immigrants and has a range of potentially useful resources). "In 2014, 10.5 million immigrants had a college degree or higher, representing about 29 percent of the total 36.7 million U.S. foreign-born population ages 25 and over" (Zong & Batalova, 2016, p. 1), and from 2011 to 2015 nearly half of all immigrants who arrived in the United States were college-educated ("Immigrants to America," 2017). Yet U.S. immigrants beyond the traditional college age are less likely to be employed in a job related to their highest college degree (Arbeit & Warren, 2013).

The possible impact of this professional dissonance is highlighted by the theory of work adjustment (Dawis, 2005), which suggests that individuals working in environments with ability requirements that do not correspond with their existing abilities will have a low degree of satisfaction. The theory of work adjustment describes the reciprocal relationship between satisfaction and satisfactoriness while focusing on the individual's experience. An individual's level of *satisfaction* depends on how well their job's rewards match with their needs. On the other hand, *satisfactoriness* is their ability to fulfill the duties dictated by their job. The interaction between these two dimensions is affected by differences in adjustment and personality styles. To the degree to which they can adapt with *flexibility* and *perseverance*, individuals may remain in a job characterized by mismatched needs and rewards. Individuals may try to make adjustments through an *active mode*, by making changes in the work environment, or through a *reactive mode*, by making changes within themselves (Dawis, 2005).

This is evident in internationally educated immigrants who are working in jobs or careers that do not match their level of skill or educational attainment. They stay in occupations that require low skilled labor in order to afford autonomy and safety for their current life status. These individuals exhibit a flexibility that enables them to tolerate a mismatch between the environment and their needs. There is also the variable of perseverance among the target population for this workshop, as they are adjusting their acceptable expectations of satisfaction from their jobs. By settling for a job that is unrelated to the field of their highest degree, they are adjusting in reactive mode to what is available to them in their current environment. However, by participating in this workshop, they will have entered action mode. This workshop aims to be the adjustment that an individual can make in order to gain better satisfaction in their career, ultimately promoting maintenance behaviors.

Another potential group for this workshop could be immigrant women from cultures where they are expected to remain at home to assume primary care for their newly established families. This gender role expectation may be a contributing factor in discouraging them from seeking employment (Bulut, 2016). Depending on their country of origin, immigrants with college degrees from outside the United States may have varying proficiencies in English needed for relevant employment in the United States. One study found that many skilled immigrants were unable to transfer their existing professional skills to the American labor market, leading to a higher rate of employment in unskilled jobs (Mattoo, Neagu, & Özden, 2008). Opportunities for skilled workers to contribute to the American economy may be limited; moreover, many highly educated and skilled immigrants are thwarted from obtaining relevant employment to support their own and their families' well-being. Another possible reason for the underemployment of this population concerns the finding that immigrants with higher levels of education perceive higher levels of discrimination in the host society (De Vroome, Martinovic, & Verkuyten, 2014). This may cause them to prematurely foreclose consideration of possible paths for advancement, preventing them from pursuing a full range of career possibilities (Swanson & Fouad, 2015).

Informed by the findings above, the Career Progression Workshop for the Internationally Educated will teach participants how to find and navigate the resources that are publicly available. Some participants may need to evaluate their language skills as well to effectively gauge their employment potential. A needs-assessment questionnaire should be administered to the group prior to the workshop to better prepare handouts and curate websites with relevant material. Translators will be provided to aid any participants who do not speak English as their first language. Information about the certifications required for specific fields and degree equivalencies will be provided for the participants. Refreshments and childcare should be provided on-site to foster access to the workshop for women or parents.

MEASURABLE OBJECTIVES AND EXPECTED OUTCOMES

After this workshop, all participants should be able to do the following:

- Begin the search for a more fulfilling job with the option to earn better wages
- Identify at least two existing skills and sources of experience that they may have overlooked
- Find at least two job opportunities in a field related to their degree
- Identify and challenge potential employment barriers in the American labor market
- Implement a step-by-step plan for obtaining employment in said field
- Receive referral to an adult English course if needed

- Create or improve on a resume that accurately reflects their skills and qualifications
- Identify resources to continue to support their career progress in their chosen field

PLAN FOR PROMOTING SERVICES

Promotion of this workshop can be done in a variety of ways, the most cost effective of which is through schools or referrals from mental health professionals. Flyers can be given to children to bring home to their parents, distributed through career counseling centers, and posted on community boards and digitally on social media platforms. If there is enough revenue stream in the future, or if there are sponsors for this workshop, subway advertisements could be used. Outreach events in immigrant communities can be utilized to promote the workshop and generate confidence for the services provided. New York City will serve as a pilot location for this workshop due to its high concentration of immigrants.

PLAN FOR DELIVERING SERVICES

A basic requirement for implementing this workshop is its dependence on publicly available community resources in any location, whether urban or rural, including computers with internet connection. With a group of ten to fifteen participants in New York City, the first workshop will be conducted by a professionally qualified career counselor/instructor. Tables 12.1 and 12.2 outline competencies in career counseling and in advocacy, respectively (Lewis, Arnold, House, & Toporek, 2003; National Career Development Association, 1997, 2009) and highlight how adapting and implementing this workshop might help the career counselor/instructor develop needed relevant skills. The venue can either be in the form of a webinar or a face-to-face session. In the face-to-face option, the workshop can be conducted in locations such as the New York Public Library's Electronic Training Center, where each computer laboratory has fifteen workstations and one instructor terminal. Two rooms can be combined to create one if necessary in future workshops. Other possible locations that may be more cost effective are grade school computer laboratories after hours or any other setting that provides access to computers and an internet connection. Also, separate but nearby and appropriate space should be secured for volunteers providing childcare during the workshop.

Table 12.1. Relevance to Career Counseling Competencies

Career Counseling Competency	Addressed by Career Intervention	Relevance to Corresponding Competency
1. Career Development Theory	X	A better understanding of the utilization of the work adjustment theory (Dawis, 2005) with diverse populations, which is currently lacking evidence in research.
2. Individual and Group Counseling Skills	X	Group career counseling skills would improve through facilitating discussion and mutual help among the participants.
3. Individual/Group Assessment	X	The intervention has less emphasis on standardized assessments and more on promoting psychoeducational process with individual and group participants.
4. Information/ Resources/ Technology	X	Gain experience in seeking out potential resources for clients. Identifying workshop platforms that can support long-distance learners, as well as familiarity with available facilities for workshop implementation.
5. Program Promotion, Management, and Implementation	X	Familiarity with advertisements, budgeting, management of a group of people, and implementation of a workshop.
6. Coaching, Consultation, and Performance Improvement	X	Improved coaching skills through showing clients where to find information and enabling them to take the first steps on their own.
7. Diverse Populations	X	Immigrants from all over the world may take part in this workshop, and competencies will improve from exposure if the counselor is open to learning as well as seeks culturally relevant consultation and resources.
8. Supervision	X	The first few counselors who run the workshop can serve as supervisors or teachers to later generations of counselors who wish to use the workshop in their own settings.
9. Ethical/Legal Issues	X	Ongoing development of multicultural competencies are ethically required to well serve underemployed immigrants. Familiarity with current legal and other resources to support immigrants, tax incentives for inviting companies to participate in the program, and the ethical issues surrounding the use of technology to facilitate a group are needed.
10. Research/ Evaluation	X	The workshop is grounded in relevant research and evaluation data will be solicited and used to improve future workshops.

Source: NCDA, 1997, 2009.

Table 12.2. Relevance to Advocacy Competencies

Advocacy Competency	Addressed by Career Intervention	Relevance to Corresponding Competency
1. Client/Student Empowerment	X	Engages counselors to help workshop attendees become knowledgeable about their available resources and options.
2. Client/Student Advocacy	X	Identification of barriers to success and development of plans to achieve the goals of each workshop attendee.
3. Community Collaboration	X	Counselors will build alliances within a community, strengthen existing relationships, and bring awareness to patterns that may arise after multiple cohorts have graduated from this workshop.
4. Systems Advocacy	X	Counselors will recognize and learn to work within the confines of existing bureaucracies while advocating for change.
5. Public Information	X	Demographic information and patterns found through this workshop will serve as a primary source of research data to advocate for change in immigration and employment policies.
6. Social/Political Advocacy	—	—

Source: Lewis et al., 2003.

INTERVENTION PROGRAM CONTENT

This program is intended to be an intensive four-hour workshop aimed at helping immigrants who have obtained a degree from a country other than the United States and have had difficulty finding a job that utilizes their degree. It will only be one session long, due to considerations for the time constraints of the population. Information about each participant's education level, degree, country where the degree was obtained, level of English-language proficiency, preferred language, and desired occupation will be requested at the time of registration (see appendix 12.1, Sample Questionnaire for Preliminary Preparation). This will allow the instructor to research relevant information about the fields that pertain to the people in the workshop that day. Also, the questionnaire should include requests for childcare needs during the workshop.

Appendix 12.2 is a Sample Checklist for the Workshop Agenda. The beginning of the session should have five to ten minutes for the instructors to introduce themselves and their credentials for leading this workshop. The workshop will be conducted in English, with relevant language translators provided (arranged in advance, based on the preferred language indicated by participants at registration). The first segment of the session will consist of showing the participants the various resources available to them via government-based websites. There will be explanations for how to use the search engines with appropriate terminology. In-depth information will be provided for how to find accredited agencies that can evaluate their degrees (for example, a national service, http://www.naces.org/, or in New York State, https://www.cs.ny.gov/jobseeker/degrees.cfm). Participants will also be provided information about how to obtain the missing credentials to make their degrees valid for use in the United States.

The middle portion of the session will be dedicated to forming a plan that the participants can use as a guideline for how to move forward after completing the workshop. A bare-bones example of the plan is: Step 1, Information gathering; Step 2, Contact; Step 3, Implementation; and Step 4, Follow-up. In Step 1, participants will conduct a mass collection of information and utilize identified resources to guide goal setting. This step should be completed before forming an action plan to foster autonomy and self-efficacy in doing their searches. In Step 2, participants will contact accredited agencies that can validate their existing degrees or identify relevant degree or certification requirements needed to be considered a qualified candidate for a specific job. During Step 3, the implementation stage, participants will initiate the process of translating and tailoring their degree to the American equivalent; ultimately, participants will begin to apply for and attend job interviews. An alternative path for the implementation step is to apply for and attend training or attend classes that will lay a foundation for the Contact and Implementation phases. Follow-up is the next step; here participants will evaluate their progress and satisfaction with the outcomes of their plan.

The last portion of the workshop will be dedicated to résumé building and referrals. Participants can improve upon an existing résumé, or create one from the ground up. In an ideal situation, the more experienced members of the group will help their peers with proofreading, editing, and suggestions. If there is time, mock interviews would be done by pairing off the participants. This segment will also be the part of the workshop where volunteers from the community give presentations, or if the program partners with specific companies in the future, they will take part in the workshop as well. These presentations are aimed at providing examples of what workshop participants should expect from their efforts to obtain employment after completion of the workshop. The ideal presenters would be immigrants who have found employment related to their degree. Other presenters should also include employers who can provide insight in regard to what skill sets each industry is lacking in or seeking. Alumni are encouraged to attend future workshops.

At the completion of the Career Progression Workshop, participants will have garnered contact information to help them access employment opportunities relevant to their skills and qualifications. For further progress in their career development, participants should also leave the workshop with resources for support with acculturation, discrimination, health care, and other human services. The instructor/career counselor should assist participants with referrals and resources regarding these multicultural, ethical, and legal considerations toward expanding their access to relevant employment and well-being. For example, see appendix 12.3, Sample Take-Home Resources: Career Progression Workshop for the Internationally Educated. Resource lists and workshop content should be adapted to the specific context and needs of the participants.

RESOURCES NEEDED

The possible settings include any community setting where computer and internet access can be provided to the group participants and instructor/career counselor. At the time of this writing, the New York Public Library Electronic Training Center cost was $850 per two hours of usage, and a one-time fee of $150 to prepare the instructor on how to use the facilities. Funding (estimated at $200) would be allotted for both refreshments and supplies such as printouts. An estimate for each page printed may be ten cents each, affording each participant about ten sheets of information that they can print out (leaving $50 for refreshments from the $200 funding estimate). The webinar option may be more cost effective, ranging from free web hosting to an estimated $500 per month. The free hosting comes with minimal to no technical support, whereas the costlier options provide a comparatively more stable connection and technical support that can be tailored to the needs of the workshop. The estimated overall cost for using the library as a venue would be $2,050 per workshop and up to $500 for webinars. Depending on the experience of the professionally qualified instructor/career counselor conducting the workshop, an additional $100–$200 per hour cost should be added to these estimates. Also, the cost of any language translators needed should be included. Volunteers to provide childcare and donated, appropriate space nearby would need to be secured.

Costs for advertisement would make up the bulk of the budget if promotion via public transportation ads is implemented. The estimated cost for advertising on the subway were acquired through a *New York* magazine article from 2005 (Glassberg, 2005) and calculated with inflation in mind. A static subway entrance advertisement would run $3,700. Placements in two hundred stations throughout the city would cost around $50,000. It would cost $55,000 to have the advertisements placed inside subway cars, taking up 25 percent of the available space. These price approximations are subject to change depending on the market, medium, and time of the year. Taking these into account, it may be more cost effective to go through an agency.

Depending on the results of the preliminary questionnaire completed by participants at registration for the workshop, volunteer representatives from local businesses or corporations in the community could give a short presentation about requirements for entering a specific industry. These same companies could be incentivized to contribute to this workshop through the Federal Work Opportunity Tax Credit and Excelsior Jobs Program, both of which reward job creation and retention (New York City Economic Development Corp., 2011).

METHODS OF EVALUATION

There will be a questionnaire administered at registration to determine what field the participants are interested in, and a follow-up interview will be conducted to evaluate the effectiveness of the intervention. A satisfaction survey and comment card will be handed out at the beginning of the workshop for participants to fill out and hand in when they leave (or the digital equivalents, if it is a webinar).

PLAN FOR REVISION

Feedback given after the workshop will be considered and a follow-up phone or face-to-face interview three to six months after the workshop will be used to determine long-term effects of the program. Depending on feedback, the location of the workshop may change. The time allocated to the workshop may change as well; splitting the workshop into more than one session might benefit those who cannot devote time for a four-hour session.

REFLECTIONS ON COUNSELOR SELF-AWARENESS OF POTENTIAL RESOURCES AND BIASES FROM PRIVILEGED AND MARGINALIZED IDENTITIES

The inspiration for the development of this career workshop came from the past experiences and observations of this author growing up in a community of immigrants. In becoming comfortable with the identity of an Asian American woman, I have come to understand a number of factors that influenced my early life as well as my decisions to pursue a graduate education in mental health counseling. I grew up within the Chinese immigrant enclave of New York City, sheltered from many harsh realities that my parents had to face on a daily basis. My first exposure to the world of social justice occurred in primary school. This school was located in the heart of Chinatown and placed emphasis on diversity, community service, and advocacy for the people who were less privileged. This collectivistic attitude was echoed throughout the curriculum as well as the extracurricular activities available to the students. I took part in fundraising events for charities and faculty-led projects aimed at improving our existing community resources.

The values emphasized in school were not seen the same way at home. My parents were preoccupied with earning enough money to provide my brother and me with the opportunities that they did not have. Although these values were seen as ideal in their eyes, it was also the first on the chopping block when it came to "realistic" aspirations. At home, it was emphasized that we were not part of mainstream American society and would never be seen as such. This was engrained by my parents' conversations with their peers in which they shared that we would never be given the same chance as a White American. I grew up denying ideas of privilege without realizing that, because of where I went to school, I was fortunate to not be exposed to social discrimination on a level that overtly affected my day-to-day life. The development of the maturity needed to acknowledge the existence of these invisible webs required significant introspection toward my own identity.

My exposure to more literature concerning historical patterns of migration and awareness of current social movements began when I entered college. Through these classes, I was able to look back with clearer eyes on the community that I grew up in. Themes of self-sacrifice and barriers to accessing available resources permeated this image. Many from my parents' generation chose to come to a new country and take up employment in fields that were completely foreign to them. They did this for the sake of their children and coped by throwing themselves into the singular goal of earning money for their children's future. The stereotype of an educated immigrant who came to this country only to wash dishes in the back room of a restaurant was a common story. It pained me to realize how much talent and education was stagnating in areas of unskilled labor. A common reason behind the saturation of educated immigrants in unskilled jobs was a lack of knowledge regarding resources available for this very population. As a child of an immigrant family, I feel the responsibility to act as a bridge for this group of people. I applied for graduate studies at Fordham University because the school placed emphasis on social justice, an ideal that I carried with me since primary school. With training in mental health counseling, I can realize this ideal by giving support to the population of selfless individuals who gave to my generation without a second thought for themselves.

APPENDIX 12.1

Sample Questionnaire for Preliminary Preparation

1. **What is your degree?**
   [This will help the instructor gather appropriate websites or relevant materials before the workshop; local job agencies for specific areas; existing professional connections that may already be available.]
2. **What university did you obtain your degree from?**
   [This will give the instructor a direction to guide the participant based on the available resources in the area that can translate degrees.]
3. **What is your proficiency in English; native language (if applicable)?**
   [Referrals to language classes may be necessary, and accommodations in the participants' native language should be made if available.]

4. **What job/career would you like to have right now?**
[The ideal job for each participant. This is to be used as a goal for the participant to keep in mind while doing job market research during the information-gathering phase of the workshop.]

5. **Will you need childcare for the duration of this workshop (if applicable)?**
[Libraries often have workshops aimed at children that last for a few hours. The career workshop could be planned at the same time so that both parent and child can benefit. Otherwise, the instructor should prepare a child-friendly activity, supervised by a childcare volunteer, for the duration of the workshop.]

APPENDIX 12.2

Sample Checklist for the Workshop Agenda

Participants will be asked to bring their mobile devices and résumés to the workshop.

Hour 1: Introduction

☐ Introduction of instructors
☐ PowerPoint presentation about search engines to be used [Careerzone, Glassdoor, Google, Indeed, O*Net, US.jobs, etc.]
☐ Explanation about how to use these resources effectively
☐ Information about accredited companies that are capable of evaluating foreign degrees
☐ Explanation about the plan that each participant should have at the end of the workshop

Hours 2 and 3: Application of New Information

☐ Provide assistance for participants based on their preliminary questionnaire responses
☐ Participants will identify an accredited company to translate their degree
☐ Participants will contact the aforementioned company

☐ *Participants will identify job openings that fit their translated degree

☐ Participants will identify any barriers that may prevent them from gaining new employment and consider strategies to helpfully address barriers

☐ Participants will identify methods to supplement their degrees via certificates training or language courses

Hour 4: Resume Building and Referrals

☐ Provide individual assistance for editing resumes

☐ Mock interviews

☐ Referrals to any resources that may be needed [Instructors should be familiar with community resources or have a list with them]

☐ Presentations from local companies and alumni

☐ Q&A

*This is a mock search in order to help participants familiarize themselves with the resource.

APPENDIX 12.3

Sample Take-Home Resources

Career Progression Workshop for the Internationally Educated Resources in New York
[Would need to be updated or adapted for expansion of this workshop outside the New York metro area]
https://council.nyc.gov/immigrant-resources/
Includes phone numbers and websites for:

• Education
• Child care for low-income families
• Access to health care
• Mental health
• Immigration legal help
• Support for participation in the democratic process

New Americans Hotline 1-800-566-7636 (Monday–Friday, 9:00 a.m.–8:00 p.m.)
Hotline for information regarding all immigration-related programs with referrals.

REFERENCES

Arbeit, C. A., & Warren, J. R. (2013). Labor market penalties for foreign degrees among college educated immigrants. *Social Science Research, 42*(3), 852–871. doi:10.1016/j.ssresearch.2013.01.001.

Bulut, E. (2016). The labor force participation of Arab women in the United States. *Women's Studies International Forum, 55*, 10–17. doi:10.1016/j.wsif.2015.11.006.

Dawis, R. (2005). The Minnesota theory of work adjustment. In S. D. Brown & R. W. Lent (Eds.), *Career development and counseling: Putting theory and research to work* (pp. 3–23). New York: Wiley.

De Vroome, T., Martinovic, B., & Verkuyten, M. (2014). The integration paradox: Level of education and immigrants' attitudes toward natives and the host society. *Cultural Diversity and Ethnic Minority Psychology, 20*(2), 166–175. doi:10.1037/a0034946.

Glassberg, B. K. (2005, November 28). New ad city. Breaking down the cost of getting our attention. *New York*. Retrieved from http://nymag.com/nymetro/news/people/columns/intelligencer/15156/.

"Immigrants to America are better educated than ever before." (2017, June 8). *Economist*. Retrieved from http://www.economist.com.

Lewis, J., Arnold, M. S., House, R., & Toporek, R. L. (2003). *Advocacy competencies*. Endorsed by the American Counseling Association Governing Council. Retrieved from https://www.counseling.org/Resources/Competencies/Advocacy_Competencies.pdf.

Mattoo, A., Neagu, I. C., & Özden, Ç. (2008). Brain waste? Educated immigrants in the U.S. labor market. *Journal of Developmental Economics, 87*, 255–269. doi:10.1016/j.jdeveco.2007.05.001.

National Career Development Association. (1997). *Career counseling competencies*. Broken Arrow, OK: Author.

———. (2009). *Minimum competencies for multicultural career counseling and development*. Broken Arrow, OK: Author. Retrieved from https://www.ncda.org/aws/NCDA/pt/fli/12508/false.

New York City Economic Development Corp. (2011). NYCEDC business incentives guide. Retrieved from New York City Economic Development Corp. http://www.nycedc.com/system/files/files/service/NYCEDC_BusinessIncentivesGuide_0.pdf.

Swanson, J. L., & Fouad, N. A. (2015). *Career theory and practice: Learning through case studies* (3rd ed.). Thousand Oaks, CA: Sage.

Zong, J., & Batalova, J. (2016). *College-educated immigrants in the United States*. Retrieved from Migration Policy Institute. https://www.migrationpolicy.org/article/college-educated-immigrants-united-states.

13

Gradually Reintegrating Ex-Offenders into the Workforce

Allyson K. Regis and Gary L. Dillon Jr.

There has been a significant increase in recent decades of people incarcerated for criminal offenses in the United States, particularly of low-income people and Black and Hispanic men. When released from prison, many ex-offenders face extreme difficulties gaining employment due not only to their stigmatizing criminal record but also to limited formal education or work experience. Furthermore, many ex-offenders face reentry issues with housing, physical and mental health, and family reunification. Post-incarceration employment plays a crucial role in reducing recidivism rates. The proposed career development intervention, Gradually Reintegrating Ex-Offenders into the Workforce (GREW), would supplement a partnership program with community and law enforcement resources that helps ex-offenders successfully transition from prison to home. This intervention should be implemented both pre- and post-release in order to assist adult ex-offenders in examining societal and self-imposed barriers to work and life adjustment as well as strategies and resources to constructively promote their career development and community reintegration.

SOCIAL JUSTICE NEEDS AND RATIONALE FOR THE CAREER DEVELOPMENT INTERVENTION

As late as 2013, estimates from the United States Bureau of Justice Statistics indicated that over 2.2 million adults were incarcerated in U.S. federal prisons, state prisons, and county jails, while over 4.7 million adults were either

on probation or parole (Glaze & Kaeble, 2014). With these combined figures, approximately seven million adults—or over 2 percent of the U.S. adult
population—were under some form of correctional supervision. Though the
number of individuals who are currently incarcerated in the United States has
decreased steadily over the past few years, approximately 650,000 offenders
are released from U.S. prisons each year, with over half of released prisoners
getting reconvicted within three years of their release (Carson & Anderson,
2016; Durose, Cooper, & Snyder, 2014; Pew Center on the States, 2011). A
major factor that can influence offenders' return to prison is whether they
can secure stable employment (Varghese & Cummings, 2012). Upon release,
many ex-offenders have difficulty finding employment, which makes them
unable to obtain a stable source of income and ultimately negatively affects
their ability to successfully reintegrate into society.

Offender status often prohibits an ex-offender's ability to access certain
resources once this status is known to government officials and potential
employers. Depending on the offense, ex-offenders may be denied credit,
loans, nutrition assistance, public benefits, and housing, which further
hinders the job search and reintegration process. Additionally, according
to Thompson and Cummings (2010), "State laws regarding professions
that require occupational licenses (e.g., security personnel, teacher, barber,
funeral director) may ban ex-offenders" (p. 210). At times, those exiting
prison are not financially stable on their own and may have to rely on
support from others. Visher, Debus, & Yahner (2008) found that at eight
months post-release, about 50 percent of ex-offenders were relying on
financial support from family and friends while a smaller number of ex-
offenders also earned money from channels such as informal work, legal
employment, government programs, and illegal activity. Thus, Uggen and
Shannon (2014) found that many individuals began to reengage in criminal
behavior due to the lack of legitimate income.

While offender status alone can be a barrier, individuals also find it
extremely difficult to become employed upon their release due to lack of
formal education, limited job experience, low human capital, mental health
concerns, and substance abuse issues (Thompson & Cummings, 2010;
Visher, Debus, & Yahner, 2008; Yang, 2017). Goodwill Industries International (2011) highlights reentry challenges faced by particularly vulnerable
ex-offender populations such as youth, women, elderly individuals, and
those with physical health, mental health, or substance abuse problems.
The issue of finding employment for those with criminal histories is further

complicated by race as racial/ethnic minority groups are disproportionately represented in the criminal justice system. In 2015, approximately 60 percent of sentenced prisoners identified as Black or Hispanic (Carson & Anderson, 2016), though these racial/ethnic groups comprised only about a quarter of the U.S. population (United States Census Bureau, 2011). Thus, systemic and legal barriers that keep ex-offenders from successfully returning to their communities tend to adversely affect Black and Hispanic people more than others.

On a legislative level, there have been efforts to address reentry concerns for ex-offenders. The Second Chance Act was designed to provide federal funding for programs that help individuals leaving prison reenter their communities. Programs that received funding through this act were designed to address barriers such as housing, education, employment, and well-being. This piece of legislation was first signed in 2008 and later renewed as the Second Chance Reauthorization Act in 2011. Over the last decade, the United States Department of Labor created a Reentry Employment Opportunities program in order to address these concerns utilizing faith-based and community organizations. This program granted funding to over one hundred organizations providing services focused on addressing the needs of youth, young adults, and adults who were formerly incarcerated. The following career development intervention, Gradually Reintegrating Ex-Offenders into the Workforce (GREW), focuses on a strength-based approach to helping ex-offenders navigate the reintegration process by providing both individual and group support during pre- and post-release.

Theoretical Framework

The purpose of this intervention is to enhance existing resources by further addressing the needs described above. With the many obstacles that ex-offenders must face, such as race-based and offender-status-based discrimination, it may be hard to develop an intervention that is entirely grounded in one career development theory. Thompson and Cummings (2010) suggested that "given the lack of research on the vocational development of ex-offenders and the absence of this group in traditional vocational theories, career counselors should draw from multidisciplinary research in their approaches to working with this population" (p. 211). Along these lines, Johnson (2013) proposed the self-determination cognitive career theory (SDCCT)—which integrates self-determination theory (SDT; Ryan & Deci, 2008) and social cognitive career theory (SCCT; Lent, Brown, & Hackett, 1994)—for facilitating ex-offenders' career development. SDT is a theory of motivation that focuses on how social and cultural factors facilitate or undermine people's sense of volition and initiative. According to this theory, some of the most important factors that influence people's self-modification of disruptive behaviors are their sense of autonomy, competence, and relatedness. SCCT focuses on the role of environmental influences on people's vocational trajectory. In particular, this theory individually can be relevant to the ex-offender population as these individuals have significant environmental obstacles that can impede vocational attainment.

Taken together, SDCCT's five-step model is sensitive to the needs and considerations of special populations—such as ex-offenders—and focuses on environmental challenges that arise and influence job decisions (Johnson, 2013). The five steps of the SDCCT include: managing environmental barriers, building environmental supports, strengthening self-efficacy, developing realistic outcome expectations, and clarifying job goals. Utilizing this theory as the basis of this intervention allows participants to focus on positive interactions, self-modification of disruptive behaviors, and addressing their psychological needs, which will likely be important in the reintegration process. SDCCT as a basis for this intervention will help ex-offenders explore their life and job options, as well as their job readiness by creating a positive, nonjudgmental, and autonomously supportive context (Johnson, 2013).

MEASURABLE OBJECTIVES AND EXPECTED OUTCOMES

At the end of this intervention, ex-offenders who participate will be able to:

1. engage in career goal identification and planning (e.g., listing three goals and associated deadlines to assist in job attainment)
2. develop skills to establish, build, and maintain healthy relationships (e.g., identify and utilize two sources of support, as needed)
3. discover, anticipate, and cope with systemic and self-imposed barriers to employment (e.g., reflecting on and processing potential barriers and discrimination)
4. increase community and personal functioning (e.g., avoid recidivism and maintain employment for at least a year)

Related to the five-steps of SDCCT, the expected outcomes of this intervention are to (a) increase participants' chances of employment by utilizing career development resources [managing environmental barriers, developing realistic outcome expectations, and clarifying job goals]; (b) increase participants' quality of relationships/social support [building environmental supports]; and (c) obtain lower recidivism rates due to increased attention to psychological and social factors [strengthening self-efficacy].

PLAN FOR PROMOTING SERVICES

To promote the GREW intervention, U.S. federal prisons, state prisons, and county jails should be contacted by the GREW Services Coordinator in an effort to develop professional relationships and a network by which participating future ex-offenders can be funneled. By connecting to the U.S. Department of Justice, and more specifically the Federal Bureau of Prisons, this will enable the GREW intervention to utilize the established systems to increase the number of participants gained, make connections to help with the delivery of our services to its participants, and increase the likelihood of positive outcomes. Additionally, government and community social service agencies will be contacted to promote GREW services as they may ultimately serve ex-offenders. These organizations may also be asked to become partners and collaborate with the GREW intervention. Forms of promotion will include stakeholder meetings with the aforementioned agencies. Scholl, Perry, Calhoun, and Robinson (2016) created a career support workshop series geared toward ex-offenders. Based on their experiences, they recommended that programs serving the ex-offender population develop partnerships with those who oversee the provision of local services as: (1) this may provide access to a familiar meeting place and (2) these individuals may be aware of important factors (e.g., avoiding a particular group time as it may conflict with important community events).

PLAN FOR DELIVERING SERVICES

Services will be delivered by clinical staff to intervention participants in two phases. The first phase will occur while participants are still incarcerated. During this phase, participants will attend group seminars addressing:

(a) communication styles and skills—to help effectively communicate in employment interviews and within interpersonal relationships; (b) job training—to provide skills that can be used in the workforce which will help ex-offenders become more competitive and desirable applicants; (c) resume writing—to help conceptualize and finalize materials; and (d) coping and resilience training—to make participants aware of the potential barriers they may face as ex-offenders and to develop appropriate strategies to get past them. Participants will also be involved in groups that focus on various topics, such as how to (a) avoid reoffending, (b) provide and receive support from peers, (c) cope with triggering situations, (d) manage relationships, and (e) live a productive life after incarceration.

The second phase will occur once participants are released from incarceration. This phase will be similar to the first with regard to the group seminars offered. In addition, social events will be offered to help foster community among participants, thereby encouraging socialization with others who are working toward making positive changes in their lives and avoid recidivism. Participants will also be matched with a peer mentor who will serve as a support that can be utilized at any time. Schinkel and Whyte (2012) described the term "peer" as someone with a common experience who works to provide practical and emotional support in ways that transcend a professional relationship. In a systematic review of literature on peer support services and peer worker benefits with ex-offender programs and their participants, Schinkel and Whyte (2012) found that peer support was more cost effective than using professional staff and that ex-offenders were likely to see professional staff as figures of authority. Additionally, they found that use of peers in interventions such as support groups and/or mentoring was found to deter, prevent, or decrease the likelihood that ex-offenders would engage in antisocial behavior or commit a crime. In addition, participants will also have access to substance abuse and mental health treatment, transitional housing resources, and job referral services. Lastly, participants will have the option to partake in a refresher course that will allow them to retake any seminar that was offered during their incarceration. Scholl and colleagues (2016) recommend that group seminars be co-facilitated, as this allows facilitators to respond to the needs of individual participants. They highlighted that in some cases a participant may not be able to function within a group and that an alternative could be to provide individual instruction as needed.

Services will be offered to adult inmates (ages eighteen and older) who: (a) have six months or more to serve and (b) contractually agree to make the intervention a part of their parole requirements. Additionally, participants' sobriety, job searching behaviors, and medication compliance (if prescribed psychotropic medications) will be monitored and expected to meet program standards. Participants will be required to remain in the program and adhere to all rules and requirements for at least twelve months. After the initial twelve months, participants will be allowed to continue on a voluntary basis. Upon completion of the program, participants who showed exceptional growth, dedication, and success—as measured by their accomplishment of the program's objectives—will be offered the opportunity to apply for a peer mentor position.

INTERVENTION PROGRAM CONTENT

Some methods of instruction throughout the GREW intervention include videos, written materials, role-playing, assessments, peer support, peer feedback, and group discussion. Materials and discussion will primarily focus on criminogenic needs. Dynamic criminogenic needs are changeable characteristics, traits, and risk factors that directly relate to recidivism, such as antisocial behavior, lack of job skills, and positive interpersonal relationships.

Following is an outline of methods for meeting the "Measurable Objectives and Expected Outcomes" noted earlier (for additional information, see appendix 13.1, Sample Program Outline).

In order to help participants engage in career goal identification and planning, using career development resources to increase their chance of employment, the GREW service providers will

a. provide assessments that help participants identify possible career paths and transferrable skills
b. help participants write an appealing resume that builds on the individual's strengths
c. use activities, videos, and mock interviews/role-plays to help clients communicate effectively in employment contexts (e.g., answer specific questions related to jobs and ex-offender status)

In order to help participants develop skills to establish, build, and maintain healthy relationships that enhance the quality of their social support, they will

  a. watch a video highlighting principles for developing positive relation-ships—particularly focusing on fostering positive interactions with non-criminal associates
  b. explore examples in participants' own lives and role-play scenarios to gain confidence in utilizing the skills they will learn
  c. discuss skills needed to build, maintain, and strengthen relationships (e.g., conflict resolution)
  d. on post-release, will be paired with a peer mentor and will also be expected to participate in community-building events/activities

Toward reducing recidivism rates with increased attention to psychological and social factors by helping participants to discover, anticipate, and cope with systemic and self-imposed career-related barriers, GREW service providers will

  a. administer a survey about different barriers to successful reentry
  b. utilize video presentations that highlight other ex-offenders' self-imposed barriers
  c. engage in group discussions regarding video/written content

In order to help participants increase their community and personal functioning, GREW service providers will

  a. help them get connected to appropriate community resources (e.g., counseling services, Alcoholics Anonymous) in order to address underlying mental health and substance use concerns
  b. use video materials and discussion to help participants learn how to recognize old behavior patterns, triggers, and toxic attitudes that influence the likelihood of turning back to illicit ways of earning income
  c. review knowledge and necessary skills for daily living (e.g., budgeting, health, social services resources)

RESOURCES NEEDED

An intervention of this magnitude will need the appropriate resources to launch and succeed.

1. Partnerships with prisons: Permission from the prisons to recruit clients prior to release.
2. Budget: Funding for staff, space, promotion materials, training materials, events, video equipment, computers, and miscellaneous expenditures.
3. Staff: Administrators, secretarial and clinical staff, a GREW Services coordinator, and peer support staff will be hired. Clinical staff is needed to facilitate groups and serve as supervisors. They will have a graduate degree in a mental health–related field (e.g., mental health counseling, social work, psychology) and experience working with individuals with substance abuse concerns. Professional experience relevant to the criminal justice system and vocational counseling would also be helpful. The GREW Services coordinator is needed to plan the program with clinical staff, build connections with governmental agencies, and evaluate program efficacy. This individual will be expected to have the credentials of the clinical staff plus qualifications in program development and evaluation (see tables 13.1 and 13.2 for relevant competencies in career counseling and social justice advocacy; Lewis, Arnold, House, & Toporek, 2003; National Career Development Association, 1997, 2009). Secretarial staff and administrators will be expected to have general office work, organizational, technological, and strong communication skills. Additionally, administrators will be required to have managerial experience.
4. Time: Staff will need time to prepare materials for group seminars (e.g., handouts) and receive training.
5. Space: Needed for offices, group rooms, and events.
6. Training materials: The program will need training materials as an anchor to many of the activities offered. There are a variety of materials available that combine video presentations with written materials to address criminogenic needs domains. For example, the Impact Publications toolkits (http://www.impactpublications.com/) include "Psychology of Incarceration," "From the Inside Out Curriculum: Taking Personal Responsibility for the Relationships in Your Life," and "Ex-Offenders CAN Ace the Interview" DVD sets.

Table 13.1. Relevance to Career Counseling Competencies

Career Counseling Competency	Addressed by Career Intervention	Relevance to Corresponding Competency
1. Career Development Theory	X	Incorporates Johnson's (2013) self-determination cognitive career theory (SDCCT) which is based on self-determination theory (SDT; Ryan & Deci, 2008) and social cognitive career theory (SCCT; Lent, Brown, & Hackett, 1994).
2. Individual and Group Counseling Skills	X	Facilitators engage participants in group discussion and workshops regarding career goals, barriers, and criminogenic needs domains.
3. Individual/Group Assessment	X	Assesses participants' vocational identity, job training, written materials, and interviewing skills.
4. Information/ Resources/ Technology	X	Fosters partnerships with law enforcement and social services agencies.
5. Program Promotion, Management, and Implementation	—	—
6. Coaching, Consultation, and Performance Improvement	—	—
7. Diverse Populations	X	Services are being provided to the underserved ex-offender population which often includes low-income people and men of color.
8. Supervision	—	—
9. Ethical/Legal Issues	X	Individuals providing services should understand institutional barriers (pre-release) and prisoner-specific requirements (post-release) that may unduly influence ex-offender participation. Those involved in the program should also: (1) know their professional responsibilities and (2) maintain awareness of their personal mores, ethical values, and related perceptions/biases, which may influence their own ethical frame of reference.
10. Research/ Evaluation	X	Demonstrates the evaluation of a career intervention, using feedback from participants, staff, and partnering agencies in order to enact change.

Source: NCDA, 1997, 2009.

Table 13.2.   Relevance to Advocacy Competencies

Advocacy Competency	Addressed by Career Intervention	Relevance to Corresponding Competency
1. Client/Student Empowerment	X	Helps participants identify transferrable skills and other important career development skills (e.g., interviewing skills that address questions regarding ex-offender status), as well as addresses social and psychological issues that impact their reintegration into society.
2. Client/Student Advocacy	X	Connects participants with social services resources that they can use to self-advocate.
3. Community Collaboration	X	Develops partnerships with law enforcement and social services agencies to serve as resources for clients. Connects participants with their community (via community events and peer mentorship) as a reintegration strategy.
4. Systems Advocacy	—	—
5. Public Information	—	—
6. Social/Political Advocacy	X	If evidence for this intervention's efficacy is supported, it may be used to advance advocacy efforts in policies, laws, and funding for re-integrating ex-offenders into the workforce.

Source: Lewis et al., 2003.

METHODS OF EVALUATION

Evaluation of the intervention will occur by those internally involved as members of the program and external agencies that collaborate with this program. Internally, program participants, professional staff, and peer staff will be given an opportunity to provide mixed-method evaluations about the program and their experiences. These evaluations serve as an effort to determine what, if any, changes should be made from their perspective. In particular, participants' feedback about whether their personal goals have been met will be important to consider. Relevant evaluation measures, such as the one used by the *Serious and Violent Offender Reentry Initiative Multi-Site Impact Evaluation* (Lattimore & Visher, 2013) may be adapted to fit this intervention. Evaluative open- and closed-ended questions should assess whether

participants felt that program objectives were met, including information regarding: participants' ability to maintain steady employment for longer than
six months, various ways they may be supporting themselves financially,
whether they have been admitted into a jail or prison since beginning the
program, barriers they encountered, whether they felt adequately prepared
to handle these barriers based on training received, relationships with others,
utilization of public services, addressing mental health and substance-use
concerns, participants' current living situation, and participants' overall self-
efficacy. Additionally, on a smaller scale, feedback should be elicited about
factors such as the physical space used, materials used, professional staff,
and topics they feel should be included, emphasized, or expanded upon.

Externally, it will be important to receive feedback from collaborating
law enforcement (police, parole officers, etc.) and social service agencies
(social workers, one-stop employees, etc.) about ways in which these relationships can continue to be improved and trends these stakeholders may
notice in the participant. The intervention should be evaluated every two
years to determine its overall effectiveness in achieving its long-term goals
and expected outcomes.

PLAN FOR REVISION

As the program aims to efficiently and successfully achieve its objectives,
it is important to evaluate the program and consider revisions to be implemented. Revisions made to the program will occur in both major and minor
ways. Changes will be made possible due to informal and formal feedback
elicited from the participants, professional staff, peer staff, and other stakeholders. Changes will be considered major when they encompass modifica-
tion to the structure, policies, and practices of the program. It is expected that
this evaluation will occur on a two-year basis. Minor changes will occur on a
more continuous level. To decide whether changes are major or minor, they
will be evaluated hierarchically.

A hierarchical flowchart should be established in order to provide guidelines to all involved with the program about who/how they should convey
concerns, suggestions, and other feedback. Program participants (level 1)
will report concerns to peer mentors and/or group facilitators (level 2) as
applicable. These concerns can then be escalated to program supervisors
or, depending on the nature of the concern, a revisions committee (level 3).

A revisions committee comprised of representatives of participants, peer mentors, group facilitators, and supervisors should be formed so that all perspectives are considered in decision-making. Members will join the committee on a voluntary basis and incentives for participation will be offered. Lastly, administration (level 4) will address multifaceted, systemic concerns. Individuals on each level will be made aware of the authority they have to enact change and whether feedback they receive will need to be addressed by someone in a higher position. For example, if program participants collectively feel that the group meeting time is inconvenient, the group facilitator will have the authority to change the time. However, the group facilitator will not have the authority to change the location of the group meetings without approval from a supervisor.

ETHICAL CONSIDERATIONS

It is important to be cognizant of the possible ethical and legal issues when developing a program. Similar to considerations for those conducting research with other special populations (e.g., minors and pregnant women), individuals providing services to ex-offenders should understand institutional barriers, participants' cognitive or communicative issues, participants' medical concerns, and economic incentives offered that may unduly influence ex-offender participation (Rogers & Lange, 2013). Bonner & Vandecreek (2006) specifically outline the ethical dilemmas that mental health providers may encounter within a correctional setting. After reviewing multiple codes of ethics, the authors found that many "commonalities emerge with regard to the ethical practice of mental health care: striving to benefit the welfare of the client, maintaining confidentiality, being cautious with dual relationships and avoiding boundary violations, obtaining informed consent, maintaining competence, and social responsibility" (p. 545).

Individuals facilitating group sessions with program participants should anticipate dealing with ambiguous situations. A participant may disclose information about issues going on within his or her life that may be illegal and/or unethical. For example, a participant may disclose violence within the home involving a minor or specific information about illegal means used to obtain money. These issues may especially become apparent during the sections of the program where relationships and jobs are discussed. Those involved in the program should know their professional responsibilities (e.g., counselors' status as a mandated reporter). Additionally, they should maintain awareness of their personal mores, ethical values, and related perceptions/biases, which may influence their own ethical frame of reference.

REFLECTIONS ON COUNSELOR SELF-AWARENESS OF POTENTIAL RESOURCES AND BIASES FROM PRIVILEGED AND MARGINALIZED IDENTITIES

Allyson K. Regis

Having parents who worked in law enforcement for over twenty years, I grew up always hearing stories about prisoners and ex-offenders reporting for probation/pre-trial services. Many times, these stories would involve newly released prisoners returning to the prison after being arrested for committing a crime shortly after their release. During the time that they were incarcerated, many of these ex-offenders had lost their homes, contact with their families, and/or jobs so they did not have much to return to. In addition, many individuals had been in prison for so long that they were not accustomed to functioning in "normal" society. For the newly released prisoners that tried to return to their former life, it was difficult to vocationally and socially reintegrate. This thought provided the inspiration for a career development intervention that would help ex-offenders reenter the work force—particularly focusing on addressing societal barriers and community engagement.

Gary L. Dillon Jr.

As a young, Black male of African American descent, I have always been very aware of the way I look and the way society and law enforcement have often viewed me. As a boy, I grew up knowing people in my personal life who had been ex-offenders—some of whom contributed to the stereotype of the criminalized Black man, and some who challenged it. Throughout my life, I have been racially profiled, which only further led me to understand the connection between the way I look and the negative assumptions ascribed to me. I've usually been made out to be a criminal. One example that comes to mind is being pulled over while in a car with four friends—three other men of color and a White female. I vividly remember the officers circling the car and then asking my female friend to step out of the car. I later found out that she was asked if she was "okay" or if she needed to say something that she could not have said in front of "them." This was one of many experiences that contributed to my interest in the incarceration of men of color and the discrimination they face before going in and after coming out of jail or prison.

Prior to obtaining my doctorate and becoming a counseling psychologist, I was a trainee in the Masters for Mental Health and Wellness at New York University. As part of my training, I completed clinical training at Riker's Island Correctional Facility, where I worked in a punitive segregation unit with adult male inmates—most of whom were men of color. As a counselor to these inmates, I would often speak to them about their journey and what led them not only to (allegedly) commit a crime, but also to be a repeat offender (at times). Hearing the narratives of these men gave me an understanding of their experience, what many of them would call "a stacked deck." These men—most of whom could acknowledge their role in their circumstances— could not overlook the way society, the job market, and the justice system seemed to further complicate their lives and discriminate against them, which often made it difficult to avoid recidivism post-release. As a psychologist, these experiences are ones that I have learned to leverage in a therapeutic alliance as a way to connect to and gain understanding of my clients. Conversely, as a researcher, I work to limit the ways in which these experiences bias me and my work—even if they are in part what ground my interest and curiosity.

CONCLUSION

There is much potential value in the GREW intervention, since it provides services that, according to a review of the literature, have been either neglected or minimally examined with this population. While many ex-offenders have received advisement while incarcerated, this intervention utilizes Johnson's (2013) self-determination cognitive career theory (SDCCT) to highlight the importance of both pre- and post-release learning. There are many barriers that this population faces, so this intervention will provide a space where they can be examined that will aid in informing realistic expectations and decisions when clients attempt to look for or begin a job. In addition, focusing on the social aspect of building healthy relationships will serve the dual purpose of providing support to the clients, which in turn may reduce the likelihood of their return to prison.

APPENDIX 13.1

Sample Program Outline

The following course outline was adapted from Chartrand and Rose (1996):

Unit 1: Orientation: Getting the Most Out of the Program
- *Week 1:* Introduction to Group and Process
  - Clients will be asked about their expectations of this course. Syllabus will be handed out and feelings on being in their current position (e.g., taking this course and being part of this program) will be shared and processed. In addition, course expectations of students will be addressed.

Unit 2: Gathering Information and Overcoming Barriers
- *Week 2:* Self-Imposed Limitations
  - Students will first take the Barriers to Career/Work Choices Survey. They will then watch the first DVD from the Psychology of Incarceration series and process their reactions to the video and survey.

Utilizing the rest of the Psychology of Incarceration DVDs, the criminogenic needs domains will be explored:
- *Week 3:* Employment/Education—Work and the role of work in one's life; attachment
- *Week 4:* Marital/Family Relations—Family members and the support one derives from them; love
- *Week 5:* Association/Social Interaction—Non-criminal associates and the opportunity for positive interaction; friendship
- *Week 6:* Substance Abuse—Living without reliance on alcohol and/or drugs; intimacy
- *Week 7:* Community Functioning—Knowledge and necessary skills for daily living; it includes residence, health, personal budgeting, leisure activities and the use of social services; gregariousness
- *Week 8:* Personal/Emotional Orientation—Control of one's life; it includes decision-making, coping with stress, and mental health; cooperation
- *Week 9:* Attitude—Living in law-abiding ways; trust

Unit 3: Job Search Strategies: Planning for What I Want

- *Week 10:* Communicating Effectively in Employment Interviews
  This session will utilize the Ex-Offenders CAN Ace the Interview
  DVD. According to the information about the DVD, clients will:
  - Receive an understanding of offender-specific interview barriers
  - Identify the strengths and weaknesses of the offender's interview
    skills
  - Identify and develop strategies for addressing interview barriers
  - Increase trainer's ability to advise and counsel trainees on their in-
    terview skills

Unit 4: Taking Responsibility for My Life: Adjusting to Work/Home

These sessions will utilize the From the Inside Out Curriculum: Taking Personal Responsibility for the Relationships in Your Life DVDs.

- *Weeks 11–12:* Taking Personal Responsibility
  Clients will explore principles for developing positive relationships and
  share some of the loving relationships in their lives through sharing
  stories and role-play scenarios.
- *Weeks 13–14:* Recognizing Old Behavior Patterns
  Clients will be presented with examples of toxic attitudes that people
  bring to relationships. They will explore: (a) how they can take steps
  to change and (b) the importance of being trustworthy in a relationship
  (which leads into Weeks 15–16).
- *Weeks 15–16:* Being Trustworthy
  Clients observe and discuss the connection between trust, communication, and a healthy relationship. Topics that will also be covered
  include: conflict resolution, the importance of choices, and potential
  consequences of actions.

Unit 5: Preparation for Program's Next (Post-Release) Phase

- *Week 17:* Discussion and processing phase 1
  Clients will take a course evaluation survey. Additionally, an informal
  discussion about benefits, what was learned, what could be improved,
  and so on will be facilitated.
- *Week 18:* Introduction to and discussion about phase 2
- *Week 19:* Guest Speaker from Phase 2
- *Week 20:* Wrap Up and Phase 1 "Graduation"

REFERENCES

Bonner, R., & Vandecreek, L. D. (2006). Ethical decision making for correctional mental health providers. *Criminal Justice and Behavior, 33*(4), 542–564. doi: 10.1177/0093854806287352.

Carson, E. A., & Anderson, E. (2016). *Prisoners in 2015* (NJC No. 250229). Retrieved from Bureau of Justice Statistics website: https://www.bjs.gov/content/pub/pdf/p15.pdf.

Chartrand, J. M., & Rose, M. L. (1996). Career interventions for at-risk populations: Incorporating social cognitive influences. *Career Development Quarterly, 44*, 341–354. doi: 10.1002/j.2161-0045.1996.tb00450.x.

Durose, M. R., Cooper, A. D., & Snyder, H. N. (2014). *Recidivism of prisoners released in 30 states in 2005: Patterns from 2005 to 2010* (NJC No. 244205). Retrieved from Bureau of Justice Statistics website: https://www.bjs.gov/content/pub/pdf/rprts05p0510.pdf.

Glaze, L. E., & Kaeble, D. (2014). *Correctional populations in the United States, 2013* (NCJ No. 248479). Retrieved from Bureau of Justice Statistics website: https://www.bjs.gov/content/pub/pdf/cpus13.pdf.

Goodwill Industries International (2011). *Road to reintegration: Ensuring successful community re-entry for people who are former offenders.* Retrieved from: https://www.goodwill.org/wp-content/uploads/2011/01/Road_to_ReIntegration_Exec_Summary.pdf.

Johnson, K. F. (2013). Preparing ex-offenders for work: Applying the self-determination theory to social cognitive career counseling. *Journal of Employment Counseling, 50*(2), 83–93. doi: 10.1002/j.2161-1920.2013.00027.x.

Kling, J. (2006). Incarceration length, employment, and earnings. *American Economic Review, 96*(3), 863–876. doi: 10.1257/aer.96.3.863.

Lattimore, P. K., & Visher, C. A. (2013). *Serious and violent offender reentry initiative (SVORI) multi-site impact evaluation, 2004–2011 [United States]* (ICPSR 27101-v1). Retrieved from: https://doi.org/10.3886/ICPSR27101.v1.

Lent, R. W., Brown, S. D., & Hackett, G. (1994). Toward a unifying social cognitive theory of career and academic interest, choice, and performance [Monograph]. *Journal of Vocational Behavior, 45*(1), 79–122. doi: 10.1006/jvbe.1994.1027.

Lewis, J., Arnold, M. S., House, R., & Toporek, R. L. (2003). *Advocacy competencies.* Endorsed by the American Counseling Association Governing Council. Retrieved from https://www.counseling.org/Resources/Competencies/Advocacy_Competencies.pdf.

National Career Development Association. (1997). *Career counseling competencies.* Broken Arrow, OK: Author.

———. (2009). *Minimum competencies for multicultural career counseling and development.* Broken Arrow, OK: Author. Retrieved from https://www.ncda.org/aws/NCDA/pt/fli/12508/false.

Pew Center on the States. (2011). *State of recidivism: The revolving door of America's prisons.* Washington, DC: The Pew Charitable Trusts. Retrieved from Pew Center on the States: http://www.pewcenteronthestates.org/uploadedFiles/Pew_State_of_Recidivism.pdf.

Rogers, W., & Lange, M. M. (2013). Rethinking the vulnerability of minority populations in research. *American Journal of Public Health, 103*(12), 2141–2146. doi: 10.2105/AJPH.2012.301200.

Ryan, R., & Deci, E. (2008). Self-determination theory approach to psychotherapy: The motivational basis for effective change. *Canadian Psychology, 49*(3), 186–193. doi: 10.1037/a0012753.

Schinkel, M., & Whyte, B. (2012). Routes out of prison using life coaches to assist resettlement. *The Howard Journal of Crime and Justice, 51*(4), 359–371. doi:10.1111/j.1468-2311.2012.00724.x.

Scholl, M. B., Perry, J., Calhoun, B., & Robinson, H. (2016). Career support workshop series: Promoting the resilience of community ex-offenders. *Career Planning and Adult Development, 32*, 169–178. Retrieved from: http://www.careernetwork.org/Journals.cfm.

Thompson, M. N., & Cummings, D. L. (2010). Enhancing the career development of individuals who have criminal records. *The Career Development Quarterly, 58*(3), 209–218. doi: 10.1002/j.2161-0045.2010.tb00187.x.

Uggen, C., & Shannon, S. K. S. (2014). Productive addicts and harm reduction: How work reduces crime—but not drug use. *Social Problems, 61*(1), 105–130. doi: 10.1525/sp.2013.11225.

U.S. Census Bureau (2011). *Overview of race and Hispanic origin: 2010.* Retrieved from http://www.census.gov/prod/cen2010/briefs/c2010br-02.pdf.

Varghese, F. P., & Cummings, D. L. (2012). Introduction: Why apply vocational psychology to criminal justice populations? *The Counseling Psychologist, 41*(7), 961–989. doi: 10.1177/0011000012459363.

Visher, C., Debus, S., & Yahner, J. (2008). *Employment after prison: A longitudinal study of releasees in three states.* Retrieved from: https://www.urban.org/research/publication/employment-after-prison-longitudinal-study-releasees-three-states.

Yang, C. S. (2017). Local labor markets and criminal recidivism. *Journal of Public Economics, 147*, 16–29. doi: 10.1016/j.jpubeco.2016.12.003.

14

Developing Managers' Skills for Countering Racial Color Blindness and Constructively Addressing Racial Microaggressions in the Workplace

Christine S. Romano

This career development intervention describes a psychoeducational program focused on helping individuals in a managerial or supervisory role develop the skills necessary to recognize and constructively address racial microaggressions in the workplace. Empirical evidence brings attention to the harmful impact of subtle expressions of discrimination by managers toward associates, specifically with regard to working relationships and productivity. By increasing awareness of unconscious bias, managers will be better able to understand and constructively respond to racial microaggressions experienced by people of color in their workplace community, promoting a positive work environment for employees and improving business.

SOCIAL JUSTICE NEEDS AND RATIONALE FOR THE CAREER DEVELOPMENT INTERVENTION

Racial color blindness, or expressions of unintentional subtle racism such as microaggressions, have been shown to negatively impact individuals of color and the dynamics of a relationship between the perpetrator and target (Sue et al., 2007). A study by Sue et al. supports the urgent need to spread awareness and understanding of microaggressions and their manifestations in society through psychoeducational training (Sue et al., 2007). Through this intervention, individuals will learn how to address and limit racial biases in the workplace. By developing skills to tolerate discomfort and vulnerability, participants are challenged to explore their racial identities and feelings about other racial groups (Sue et al., 2007). To foster multicultural self-awareness, an important component of cultural competence, activities are structured to support participants in exploring the personal meaning of diversity and understanding how their thoughts and values have formed. Undergoing a process of learning and critical self-examination of racism is a first step to understanding the impact of racial microaggressions on one's own life as well as the lives of others (Sue et al., 2007).

This career development intervention is designed to promote these critically important skills in multicultural competence with individuals who are supervisors or managers in increasingly diverse workplace settings. The United States Bureau of Labor Statistics 2016 Household Data Annual Averages reports that there were 7.5 percent Black or African American, 6.1 percent Asian, and 9.9 percent Hispanic or Latino employed persons in management occupations (United States Bureau of Labor Statistics, 2017). In a total of 17,418 management occupations, about 13,324 or 76.5 percent were occupied by White employees. Further, according to the U.S. Department of Labor, Bureau of Labor Statistics, 25 million people or 16.1 percent of the United States workforce are foreign-born workers who are finding it difficult to adapt to workplace settings and practices because of the native cultural and professional socialization status in the United States, which fosters stereotypical portrayals or general biases about immigrant professionals and discriminates against their accents and physical characteristics, thus rendering a hostile, ambiguous work environment (Shenoy-Packer, 2015). As the workforce become more diverse, unfair treatment of workers increases, especially toward those of racial and ethnic groups who are subject to the negative effects of microaggressions (King et al., 2011).

Since the implementation of legislative interventions that have deemed discrimination in the workplace to be illegal, contemporary methods of discrimination have more often come in subtle forms. A vastly referenced research study by Sue and colleagues (2007) explains that

> although the face of racism has changed, overt forms of racism have decreased while covert forms of racism like "aversive racism" or "implicit bias" have become more popular. . . . [These subtle forms of racism are] difficult to identify, quantify, and rectify because of their subtle, nebulous and unnamed nature. (p. 272)

These forms of racism have been defined as *racial microaggressions*; "Commonplace verbal or behavioral indignities, whether intentional or unintentional, which communicate hostile, derogatory, or negative racial slights and insults" that are directed toward people of color, often unconsciously or automatically (Sue et al., 2007, p. 278).

Color blindness is one example of a microaggression (a type of *micro-invalidation*) that has been found to be more prevalent in professional settings. Individuals, including those in power (e.g., managers) who have color blind attitudes, may "ignore unique cultural experiences, discount the value of diversity, culturally influence perspectives and threaten inclusion by denying the continuing prejudice facing people from minority back-grounds" (Offermann et al., 2014, p. 2). Microaggressions, including color blind attitudes, have been found to be associated with detrimental effects on the psychological and emotional well-being of non-White individu-als, and research shows that ethnic and racial discrimination significantly affects their health (Forrest-Bank & Jenson, 2015). Microinvalidations, which are "communications that exclude, negate, or nullify the psychologi-cal thoughts, feelings, or experiential reality of a person of color," can be experienced in the workplace; for example, when a person of color is com-plimented for speaking English well or asked where they were born so as to highlight differences from the "norm of Whiteness" and "negate their US American heritage and to convey that they are perpetual foreigners" (Sue et al., 2007, p. 274). As a result, such targeted individuals in a workplace may feel confused about the nature of the interaction or blame themselves for the act, questioning if they are overly sensitive. These reactions can, in turn, affect their self-esteem, which can impact work performance, work relationships, and perceptions of hostility toward their manager or supervi-sor (as cited in Sue et al., 2007). Forrest-Bank and Jenson (2015) state that "understanding the specific mechanisms by which microaggressions are perpetrated and examining the impact of such acts is critical to developing preventive interventions and policies necessary to reduce discrimination and service barriers for non-White people" (p. 142).

The career development intervention described in this chapter helps managers or supervisors to recognize the effects of workplace microag-gressions and build the skills necessary to prevent them (Forrest-Bank & Jenson, 2015). Statistics and research findings support educating all man-agers, considering their various identity roles and demographic character-istics, on racial color blindness and microaggressions as a way to explore their own biases and develop the skills necessary to counter stereotyping and prejudice in the workplace. Ultimately, managers might begin to acknowledge unconscious acts of racism, identify their behaviors, and understand the negative impact of discrimination in the workplace as a collective effort (Toporek, Sapigao, & Rojas-Arauz, 2017).

It is critical to foster healthy interpersonal dynamics in the workplace, especially between managers and their staff, to achieve maximum productivity and attain company goals (Society for Human Resource Management, 2016). "Toxic relationships can quickly lead to disgruntled employees, waning effectiveness levels and other negative consequences; positive relationships based on a foundation of mutual trust and understanding have the potential to enhance productivity and organizational success" (Society for Human Resource Management, 2016, p. 27). Moreover, by fostering positive relationships and encouraging a constructive dialogue, a bond of trust between managers and staff will be strengthened and "employees may be more likely to work through and stay committed during difficult times, reducing the chances of voluntary turnover and associated costs" (Society for Human Resource Management, 2016, p. 28).

CAREER DEVELOPMENT THEORETICAL
FRAMEWORK FOR THE INTERVENTION

The career development intervention described in this chapter builds on the framework of the theory of work adjustment (TWA; Dawis, 2005). According to TWA, as work plays a crucial role in an individual's life, it is important for people to "achieve and maintain a sense of correspondence with their work environments" (Jackson & Verdino, 2012, p. 1162). TWA proposes that job satisfaction and retention can be predicted by the level of correspondence or match between employees' values "(e.g., safety, comfort, altruism, autonomy, status, and achievement)" and the rewards or reinforcers of the work environment "(e.g., job security, compensation, working conditions, opportunities for advancement or to provide service)" (Jackson & Verdino, 2012, p. 1162).

A TWA framework can be used in training managers to assess employees' abilities, values, and work requirements to correspond with work environments as well as explore strategies for work adjustment related to experiences of racial microaggressions in the workplace. Finding a balance between meeting the needs of the individual worker and the demands of the work environment is ideal. However, this balance can be altered when racial microaggressions occur, creating disequilibrium for employees of color and for the work environment as a whole. The level of satisfaction for employees of color may decrease when microaggressions prompt them to wonder if their abilities may not meet the needs of the work environment, then triggering adjustment responses such as becoming less productive or being pushed to leave for another job. However, if managers and workers learn how to productively address racial microaggressions, then the work environment may be improved for all. The career development intervention described in this chapter may be adapted, from a TWA perspective, to help restore the equilibrium of the correspondence between employees' needs and values and the rewards provided by the job and work environment. By developing managers' skills for countering racial color blindness and constructively addressing microaggressions in the workplace, this intervention may also be used to inform social policy that promotes diversity training for improved communication and equity.

MEASURABLE OBJECTIVES AND EXPECTED OUTCOMES

At the end of this program, managers will be able to:

1. Report the benefits of working with a diverse group of people in the workplace
2. Report the negative impact of racial microaggressions in the workplace
3. Describe their racial biases and personal values to increase self-awareness
4. Identify racial microaggression experiences involving themselves (i.e., attitude, communication style) toward others in the workplace
5. Acquire skills to address issues or conflicts between them and their staff (i.e., microaggressions)
6. Develop an action plan to implement conflict resolution appropriately and prohibit any form of discrimination in the workplace
7. Promote a positive work environment with their employees

Empirical evidence supports the measurable objectives emphasizing the idea that education and training will aid managers in achieving the following: "(a) [an] increase [in] their ability to identify racial microaggressions in general and in themselves in particular; (b) understand how racial microaggressions, including their own, detrimentally impact clients of color; and (c) accept responsibility for taking corrective actions to overcome racial biases" (Sue et al., 2007, p. 283). This career development intervention is designed to increase awareness of microaggressions and their impact while supporting management professionals in navigating personal biases and taking action for changing supervisory behavior. Thus, the expected outcomes of this intervention include:

1. increased awareness of racial microaggressions
2. improved relationships between managers and associates
3. increased employee workplace satisfaction and engagement
4. enhanced workplace productivity and organizational success

PLAN FOR PROMOTING SERVICES

A team of consultants who specialize in diversity training will use their foundational intervention program and alter it as necessary to cater to the needs of the target population by obtaining information from Human Resources and current leadership about bias incidents that have occurred in the workplace. Anticipated intervention challenges will be identified when implemented in a corporate setting, and it will be altered as necessary. Outreach to corporations through their human resources representatives will help initiate the idea, and marketing will proceed from there.

Permission from corporate leaders and human resources partners will be obtained before implementing the intervention. A free consultation that highlights parts of the training that may benefit the business will be offered. Human resources representatives will be asked to partner with staff at each location of the company to help with marketing the services. Brochures will be designed and distributed to managers, and flyers will be posted in the workplace in common places for managers to see. There will also be a posting in the company newsletter as well as an email sent to all individuals whose participation is mandatory. An attendance list can then be generated and reminder emails sent to confirm the date, time, and location of the training. After workshop completion, program materials will be available on the company intranet. Once all the existing managers are trained and the pilot program has been evaluated, organizations may consider implementing the Developing Managers' Skills for Countering Racial Color Blindness and

Constructively Addressing Microaggressions in the Workplace intervention as a part of the orientation for newly hired managers.

PLAN FOR DELIVERING SERVICES

The lead consultant who will manage the delivery of services must have a masters or doctoral level of education in counseling or psychology; graduate program curriculum should include multicultural competency training. These qualifications are necessary to effectively prepare for facilitation of services and market the intervention plan to job sites (see tables 14.1 and 14.2 for relevant competencies in career counseling and social justice advocacy; Lewis, Arnold, House, & Toporek, 2003; National Career Development Association, 1997, 2009). Outreach via phone to human resources professionals, leadership, and development directors or the individuals facilitating the training for managers will explain the program and its beneficial outcomes for employees and the business. If communication is via email, the company representatives will be sent the program information including the executive summary, brochure, and the program agenda. In person, they will be shown a brief presentation of the negative effects of racial microaggressions in the workplace and the benefits of addressing it not only for the people of the workplace but also to benefit the workplace goals. The program will consist of two three-hour trainings, which are best provided on two consecutive days.

Table 14.1.   Relevance to Career Counseling Competencies

Career Counseling Competency	Addressed by Career Intervention	Relevance to Corresponding Competency
1. Career Development Theory	X	The intervention builds on the framework of the theory of work adjustment (Dawis, 2005) relevant to racial microaggressions (Sue et al., 2007) and human resource development in workplaces.
2. Individual and Group Counseling Skills	X	Counselors will have the opportunity to work individually and in a group setting with participants to help them set personal and professional goals to address microaggressive events.
3. Individual/Group Assessment	X	Counselors will develop skills to administer, score, and report evaluation findings. Counselors will also collect data from employee engagement surveys to assess employee satisfaction in the workplace.

(continued)

Table 14.1. *Continued*

Career Counseling Competency	Addressed by Career Intervention	Relevance to Corresponding Competency
4. Information/ Resources/ Technology	X	Counselors will demonstrate knowledge in researching resources and skills for clients to utilize in their personal and professional development. Research will identify employment trends and labor market information to help individuals realize the impact of turnover rates on profitability.
5. Program Promotion, Management, and Implementation	X	Counselors will develop, plan, implement, and manage this program and all its elements in any workplace environment. Counselors will develop leadership skills to create a needs assessment and evaluation of services, learning methods of forecasting, budgeting, planning, costing, resource allocation, and quality control.
6. Coaching, Consultation, and Performance Improvement	X	Counselors will help individuals with conflict resolution through this intervention as well as analyze the current culture in the workplace and level of employee's skills.
7. Diverse Populations	X	Counselors will assist leaders of the workplace by helping them to better understand the needs and characteristics of multicultural populations.
8. Supervision	—	—
9. Ethical/Legal Issues	X	Counselors must show adherence to ethical codes and standards as well as adhere to autonomy, nonmaleficence, beneficence, justice, and fidelity with participants, as their goal is to help them constructively address discrimination. (Niles & Harris-Bowlsbey, 2013). Informed consent and confidentiality are important ethical standards to consider.
10. Research/ Evaluation	X	Counselors will acquire competency in proposal writing to tailor intervention goals to the population served. Counselors will also gain competency in collecting and analyzing data from the measurable outcomes.

Source: NCDA, 1997, 2009.

Table 14.2. Relevance to Advocacy Competencies

Advocacy Competency	Addressed by Career Intervention	Relevance to Corresponding Competency
1. Client/Student Empowerment	X	This career intervention will help participants recognize their own cognitions and behaviors that reflect responses to systemic and internalized oppression.
2. Client/Student Advocacy	X	Counselors will help managers develop and implement a plan of action for confronting their barriers to address racial biases and stereotypes, help participants identify allies, and motivate them to put their plan into action.
3. Community Collaboration	—	—
4. Systems Advocacy	X	Counselors will gain competency in researching and educating participants on the empirical evidence that emphasizes the value of addressing discrimination in the workplace.
5. Public Information	X	Counselors will gain competency in recognizing racial microaggressions and the oppressive impact on their subordinates as a barrier for healthy development.
6. Social/Political Advocacy	—	—

Source: Lewis et al., 2003.

INTERVENTION PROGRAM CONTENT

The training will be held in corporate offices, conference rooms, or training rooms that provide a private space. Workshop facilitators, who in addition to the lead consultant, must have a master's- or doctoral-level education in counseling or psychology, will ensure that each participant has read and signed a copy of an informed consent and will discuss limitations to confidentiality. Facilitators will show adherence to ethical codes and standards as well as adhere to autonomy, nonmaleficence, beneficence, justice, and fidelity with participants (Niles & Harris-Bowlsbey, 2013). As the program's overarching goal is to help participants constructively address discrimination, multicultural awareness will also be important to consider in exploring the role of identity, power, privilege, and intersectionality in the impact of microaggressions. This workshop has been designed for all management staff, of diverse demographic characteristics, to resolve issues of bias in the workplace in a collective and consistent effort for maximum impact. One workshop facilitator will train one class of thirty to fifty managers at a time.

A crucial step in this training is to seek feedback from participants between the first and second day to assess participants' reflections on their thoughts, opinions, reactions, and personal values. Participants will be asked to consider social and environmental influences in their lives, in the past and present, between trainings. Initial trainings may be hosted nationwide in the form of a pilot to implement the program at various organizational sites, depending on the company's size. Program techniques will be taught to the onboarding educators in the company so they can train new managers going forward. Any new manager hired will be required to attend this training as part of their onboarding process. The program will be consistently held every six months.

The first day of training will include an overview of the research and statistics about the negative effects of racial microaggressions in the workplace (appendix 14.1). The facilitator will define microaggressions and the common types of microassaults, microinsults, and microinvalidations (Sue et al., 2007). Then, examples of common racial microaggressions will be reviewed (appendix 14.2). Once participants have been oriented to relevant terms and supporting research, participants will engage in "A Brief Experiential Exercise for Coming to Understand and More Constructively Respond to Racial Microaggressions" (see chapter 7 in this book). Facilitators may find it helpful to adapt this exercise to include examples that are specific to the particular workplace setting and the participant needs. When the exercise is completed, participants will be invited to process their responses and name some of the ways racial discrimination may have been felt by their employees. Then, group discussion about racial biases and personal values will take place. Finally, to emphasize the importance of exploring one's own thoughts and biases, participants will be assigned as homework a written reflection task to list influences of racial bias and cultural values in their life that have shaped their view of others and work with diverse individuals.

The second day of training will help participants develop strategies to address microaggressions to better reap the benefits of working in a diverse environment. The homework assignment will be discussed to allow for participants to share their discoveries and process their honest thoughts about unconscious racial biases and stereotypes. Next, participants will review examples of racial microaggressions occurring in the workplace (e.g., Nadal, 2011). Volunteers will be asked to share personal life events where they have observed or enacted racial microaggressions. The group will then be asked to break up into smaller groups and participate in role-play exercises to become more fully immersed in the experience. As a large group, thoughts and feelings from the role-playing activity will be explored, identifying possible plans for addressing the experiences of microaggressions previously explored. Participants will be taught various skills and strategies to helpfully address microaggressions to mend the situation and restore their relationship with their associate (appendix 14.3). It is the responsibility of the managers to rectify situations by educating themselves and their associates about microaggressions and to explain their actual thoughts and intentions (Sue et al., 2007). Next, participants will be asked to complete a written action plan that explains their commitment to being more self-aware about microaggressive behaviors, promoting a positive work environment, and preventing discrimination (appendix 14.4). Finally, the facilitator will review a list of services and resources in addition to this program that can be used to increase awareness of microaggressions and reduce discriminatory behaviors in the workplace in the future. The content of this list will vary and be tailored to employees of that particular company and context of the community.

RESOURCES NEEDED

The following resources are needed to deliver the program effectively:

1. Support from human resources partners to coordinate and invite managers and supervisors in the corporation to come to the workshop during company time (Niles & Harris-Bowlsbey, 2013).
2. Authorization from corporate senior executives to publicize and promote the workshop through internal newsletters, flyers, and email invitations (Niles & Harris-Bowlsbey, 2013).
3. A budget for materials including: folders for program information and resources, pads, pens, and light refreshments.
4. Audio visual equipment such as laptops, projectors, and technology support; to be determined depending on the setting and the resources accessible.

5. The use of printing facilities to make copies of program materials and follow-up materials.
6. Cost of program services will be paid to the lead consultant as well as the workshop facilitators who will be facilitating the workshop for services rendered.
7. Permission to do a follow-up evaluation with participants after ninety days.
8. Cost of evaluation services will be paid to the lead consultant and consulting team who will be conducting the evaluation portion of the program.

METHODS OF EVALUATION

Two methods to evaluate results of the program are proposed, based on the author's professional experience in human resources management. One evaluation method is to implement a partner program for the company and the managers to ensure long-term effectiveness beyond workshop training (appendix 14.5). During the second day of the program, the partner program will be explained and partners will be assigned. The idea of the partner program is to implement a monthly check-in to measure progress of the effects of the program. Partners will meet one day per month for one hour to discuss outstanding thoughts or concerns. During this session, they are required to discuss a real or fictional example of a microaggression in the workplace. They will discuss what they would do in that scenario and an action plan to continue promoting a positive work environment by decreasing discrimination in the workplace.

The other evaluation method is to conduct a follow-up study after ninety days by which the lead consultant and facilitators gather data to measure effectiveness and inform development of future workshops (appendix 14.5). The facilitator and their team will also conduct a follow-up evaluation ninety days after the program where they will contact those who participated either by phone, email, or in person for an interview to collect open-ended follow-up responses about the participants' thoughts, comments, and suggestions for improvement. As responses are collected from initial participants, the consulting team will design a specific evaluative tool to better organize and evaluate feedback from future participants. The aim in obtaining this information is to see if the program met the measurable objectives and expected outcomes. After a year of implementing the program into the work setting, data will be collected from employee engagement surveys, and the results of employee satisfaction in the workplace will be analyzed.

PLAN FOR REVISION

After the data are collected and the results are analyzed, there will be a better idea of how the program can be revised to best fit the needs of the corporation. The length of the training might be adjusted, and adjustment to the methods of evaluation might also be implemented. Expansion of the intervention to a variety of workplace settings can help others understand the importance of identifying and addressing racial microaggressions in the workplace. Finally, it will be important to consider program needs with multicultural awareness and identity roles in mind.

Corporations and companies will assess the feasibility of how frequently they are able to pay for a team of psychologists to implement a career development intervention training such as this one. Yet more and more corporations are putting increasing efforts and focus on training and coaching their leadership teams to implement strategies to retain their trained employees and reduce turnover expenses. For example, Starbucks held a training similar to this career development intervention "on race, bias and the building of a diverse welcoming company" to improve their customer service and promote a healthy work environment for their staff (Starbucks Newsroom, 2018, para. 1). Starbucks executive vice president, U.S. Retail, Rossann Williams, stated that this *"isn't a solution, it's a first step. . . . By educating ourselves on understanding bias and how it affects our lives and the lives of the people we encounter and serve, we renew our commitment to making the third place welcoming and safe for everyone"* (Starbucks Newsroom, 2018, para. 3). As an internationally recognized corporation, Starbucks took the initiative to set a foundation providing a preliminary training on understanding racial bias and plans to implement a long-term solution by conducting future trainings that address all aspects of bias and experiences and promote antibias, diversity, equity, and inclusion effort. Similar to the career development intervention proposed in this chapter, implementing a preliminary training from a team of facilitators and future trainings by a company's human resources department evolving from evaluation data will likely be more effective in promoting long-term solutions.

REFLECTIONS ON COUNSELOR SELF-AWARENESS OF POTENTIAL RESOURCES AND BIASES FROM PRIVILEGED AND MARGINALIZED IDENTITIES

I grew up in a middle-class neighborhood in the suburbs of New York City and was born to a third-generation Italian American father and a first-generation Jordanian and Palestinian mother. Despite each of my parents' vastly different upbringings, they both emphasized the importance of receiving an education and always provided encouraging words and support for my career path. Hard work, dedication, and passion were values that helped foster my growth and development in the field of counseling and became the foundation for my motivation for the work I do currently as a licensed mental health counselor. Personal experiences and academic and career opportunities aided in helping me gain insight into my own personal values and culturally diverse environment. While working with underserved adolescents in both the juvenile justice system and suburban high schools as a counselor, I started to recognize my privilege, how it impacted those I served, and how I could make personal changes to address social justice issues. I furthered my passion for working with marginalized populations through research experiences including involvement on a research team that assessed the development of mental disorders from childhood to adulthood in a Latino subgroup and contribution to a research service team that focused on career development for low-income and culturally diverse urban youth. Working in settings such as these and providing direct services to underserved populations has allowed me to not only become more self-aware but to also learn how to have conversations about social injustice on a micro and macro level. It was not until my experience working in the human resources profession that I realized that many of these issues were not being addressed in the workplace; I directly observed how bias and subtle forms of discrimination impacted my employees and coworkers. In my experience in human resources, both in a corporate setting and a nonprofit, I realized that these conversations were ignored due to the unexamined belief of it being a liability to expose social injustices. It was then that I recognized the importance of my role as a counselor and the need for addressing systemic oppression in the workplace.

Currently, I work for an outpatient mental health clinic providing counseling and therapy services to adults with severe mental illness. I now strive to recognize my privilege as a counselor to maintain awareness of the impact of my personal values and racial biases on the counseling experience. I feel that I have strengthened my multicultural competency by utilizing advocacy interventions with my clients and empowering them to process their internalized oppression and address the social injustices they experience on an intrapersonal and interpersonal level. By better understanding my clients, the social injustices they have faced on an institutional and community level, and their worldviews, our therapeutic relationship has strengthened and we have collaborated on promoting social justice advocacy together.

CONCLUSION

Corporations are understandably focused on business tactics, customer service, and profits; however, the importance of manager-employee relationships is undeniable. Addressing diversity through the lens of the Developing Managers' Skills for Countering Racial Color Blindness and Constructively Addressing Microaggressions in the Workplace program, managers can foster a positive work environment and support productivity, ultimately benefiting organizational culture and business goals. By implementing this program and educating leaders, individuals may become more knowledgeable about subtle forms of discrimination and the negative impact on people and businesses. With qualified facilitators, this program helps managers to explore their own personal unconscious biases and prejudices in a relatively safe space. This may allow managers to recognize the benefits of diversity in the workplace, more meaningfully value their working relationships, and increase job satisfaction. Motivated employees may drive productive business efforts and increase profits. Therefore, corporations may be more inclined to take initiative and promote efforts that value diversity.

APPENDIX 14.1

Overview of Research and Statistics on Racial Microaggressions in the Workplace

- The United States Bureau of Labor Statistics 2016 Household Data Annual Averages reports that there were 7.5 percent Black or African American, 6.1 percent Asian, and 9.9 percent Hispanic or Latino employed persons in management occupations (United States Bureau of Labor Statistics, 2017).

- In a total of 17,418 management occupations, about 13,324 or 76.5 percent were occupied by White employees (United States Bureau of Labor Statistics, 2017).
- According to the U.S. Department of Labor, Bureau of Labor Statistics, 25 million people or 16.1 percent of the United States workforce are foreign-born workers who are finding it difficult to adapt to workplace settings and practices because of the native cultural and professional socialization status in the United States (Shenoy-Packer, 2015). This fosters stereotypical portrayals or general biases about immigrant professionals and discriminates against their accents and physical characteristics, thus rendering a hostile, ambiguous work environment (Shenoy-Packer, 2015).
- Microaggressions can influence the standard of living and quality of life for underserved and marginalized populations like women and persons of color (Sue, 2012). Statistics support the fact that White American males constitute only 33 percent of the population. Yet they occupy approximately
  - 80 percent of tenured positions in higher education
  - 80 percent of the House of Representatives
  - 80–85 percent of the U.S. Senate
  - 92 percent of Forbes 400 executive CEO-level positions
  - 90 percent of public school superintendents
  - 99.9 percent of athletic team owners
  - 97.7 percent of U.S. presidents
- After the forty-fourth presidential inauguration, only 26 percent of Americans believed that racism was a major social problem (as cited in Wong et al., 2014), while 77 percent of Americans believed the current state of race relations were good (as cited in Wong et al., 2014)
- Negative effects of racial microaggressions in the workplace (Wong et al., 2014)
  - Physical health issues (e.g., higher blood pressure, cardiovascular conditions, respiratory conditions, and pain conditions)
  - Mental health issues (e.g., anxiety and anxious symptoms, depression, and depressed symptoms)
  - Decreased psychological well-being (e.g., low self-esteem, diminished self-efficacy, lower self-regard etc.)
  - Lower quality of life, including self-rated health, days of limited activity, and unhealthy days

APPENDIX 14.2

Examples of Common Racial Microaggressions
(quoted from Sue, 2010, 2012)

- When a White couple (man and woman) passes a Black man on the sidewalk, the woman automatically clutches her purse more tightly, while the White man checks for his wallet in the back pocket. (Hidden Message: Blacks are prone to crime and up to no good.) (Sue, 2010, para. 5)
- A third-generation Asian American is complimented by a taxi cab driver for speaking such good English. (Hidden Message: Asian Americans are perceived as perpetual aliens in their own country and not "real Americans.") (Sue, 2010, para. 6)
- A Black couple is seated at a table in the restaurant next to the kitchen despite there being other empty and more desirable tables located at the front. (Hidden message: You are a second-class citizen and undeserving of first-class treatment.) (Sue, 2012, para. 4)
- Police stop a Latino male driver for no apparent reason but to subtly check his driver's license to determine immigration status. (Hidden message: Latinas/os are illegal aliens.) (Sue, 2010, para. 7)
- American Indian students at the University of Illinois see Native American symbols and mascots—exemplified by Chief Illiniwek dancing and whooping fiercely during football games. (Hidden Message: American Indians are blood-thirsty savages, and their culture and traditions are demeaned.) (Sue, 2010, para. 8)

APPENDIX 14.3

Overview of Skills and Strategies Taught

Within this career development intervention, participants will be taught various skills and strategies for countering racial color blindness and constructively addressing microaggressions in the workplace.

1. Participants will learn about the benefits of working with a diverse group of people in the workplace, including these examples (as cited in Reynolds, 2017):

a. Inspiring creativity and driving innovation: Offering new perspectives that inspire colleagues to expand how they see the workplace, solving problems, meeting customer needs, various voices, perspectives and personalities can offer open exchange of ideas. Example: "[C]osmetic giant L'Oréal attributes much of its impressive success in emerging markets to its multicultural product development teams" (para. 7).

b. More competitive and more profitable business: Local connections, native language skills, and cultural understanding can boost international business development. Example: "Recent research from McKinsey also underscores the fact that diversity is good for a business's bottom line. . . . Ethnically diverse companies were shown to be 35 percent more likely to have financial returns above the national industry median" (para. 10).

c. Attract and retain the best talent: Standing out to candidates, broadens talent pool of prospective employees, improves retention and reduces the costs associated with employee turnover; employees are more loyal when they feel valued for unique contribution, promotes an inclusive atmosphere. Example: "According to a Glassdoor survey, two-thirds of job hunters indicated that diversity was important to them when evaluating companies and job offers" (para. 15).

d. Higher productivity and better performance: Increase problem-solving capacity, greater productivity, healthy competition, optimization of company processes for greater efficiency. Example: "[S]tudies have shown organizations with a culture of diversity and inclusion are both happier and more productive" (para. 21).

e. Opportunity for personal and professional growth: Learning about perspectives and traditions of other cultures, abandoning prejudices or an ethnocentric worldview allows exposure to new skills and approaches to work.

2. Participants will learn about examples of the negative impact of racial microaggressions in the workplace:

a. Employees experiencing racial microaggressions may feel unsafe and uncomfortable at work, decreasing correspondence between their values and the work environment, and causing reduced performance (as predicted by the theory of work adjustment; Dawis, 2005).

b. Foreign-born workers report finding it difficult to adapt to workplace settings and practices because of the native cultural and professional socialization status in the United States that fosters stereotypical portrayals or general biases about immigrant professionals and discriminates against their accents and physical characteristics, thus, rendering a hostile, ambiguous work environment (Shenoy-Packer, 2015).

c. Reactions from experiencing microaggressions can affect one's self-esteem which can impact work performance, work relationships, and perceptions of hostility toward their manager or supervisor (as cited in Sue et al., 2007).

d. "Toxic relationships can quickly lead to disgruntled employees, waning effectiveness levels and other negative consequences" (Society for Human Resource Management, 2016, p. 27).

e. See appendix 14.1 for the negative effects of racial microaggressions in the workplace (Wong et al., 2014).

3. Participants will learn how to describe their own racial biases and personal values that they discovered about themselves, which has further contributed to their self-awareness through the homework assignment (appendix 14.3).

4. Participants will learn about examples of common racial microaggressions (appendix 14.2) Three forms of microaggressions are as follows: microassaults which include "explicit racial derogation characterized primarily by a verbal or nonverbal attack meant to hurt the intended victim through name-calling, avoidant behavior, or purposeful discriminatory actions"; microinsults, which are "communications that convey rudeness and insensitivity and demean a person's racial heritage or identity"; and microinvalidations, which are "communications that exclude, negate, or nullify the psychological thoughts, feelings, or experiential reality of a person of color" (Sue et al., 2007, p. 274).

5. Participants will learn about examples of racial microaggressions in the workplace (Nadal, 2011) and be able to provide an example of a situation where they identified racial microaggression experiences involving themselves toward others in the workplace.

6. Participants will acquire necessary skills to address issues or conflicts between themselves and their staff; e.g., by using I-statements as part of the first day of training through the activity "A Brief Experiential Exercise for Coming to Understand and More Constructively Respond to Racial Microaggressions" (see chapter 7 in this book). By developing skills to tolerate discomfort and vulnerability, participants are challenged

to explore their racial identities and feelings about other racial groups (Sue et al., 2007). To foster multicultural self-awareness, an important component of cultural competence, activities are structured to support participants in exploring the personal meaning of diversity and understanding how their thoughts and values have formed. Undergoing a process of learning and critical self-examination of racism is a first step to understanding the impact on one's own life as well as the lives of others (Sue et al., 2007).

7. Participants will be taught how to develop an action plan to implement conflict resolution appropriately as a way to prohibit any form of discrimination in the workplace including highlighting specific preventative behaviors such as altering attitudes or communication styles (recognizing accents and physical characteristics and refraining from stereotyping as if that individual is not equal) to ensure they are being more culturally conscious and aware (appendix 14.5).

8. Participants will acquire behaviors or skills to use to promote a positive work environment for all employees as evidenced by measurable objectives above (numbers 1–6) for expected outcomes of recognizing the benefits of working with a diverse group of people in the workplace (number 1) and decreasing the negative impact of racial microaggressions in the workplace (number 2) and ultimately "enhance productivity and organizational success" (Society for Human Resource Management, 2016, p. 27).

APPENDIX 14.4

Sample Document of Plan for Addressing Racial Microaggressions

All professionals are expected to adhere to policies and procedures as it relates to social justice issues in the workplace. (Company Name) is committed to the development of all employees at all levels, and our leadership team is committed to seek every opportunity to address expectations when they are not met. This is not a reminder but a formal statement that changes need to be made in order to promote a positive and equal work environment.

Table A14.1.

Employee Name (Last) (First)	Date:

Expectation(s):

- Explain the event and specific behavior(s) that did not meet the expectation as it relates to the racial microaggressions and why this expectation is important.

Manager Comments on the Expectation Above:

- Ask individual to state their agreements, disagreements, understanding, and concerns.
- After listening to the individual, acknowledge agreements and disagreements.

Associate Comments on the Expectation Above:

- Ask individual to state their agreements, disagreements, understanding, and concerns.
- After listening to the individual, acknowledge agreements and disagreements.

Action Plan: To remain part of the team, you must meet all of (Company's Name)'s expectation(s) as it relates to social justice issues in the workplace. Therefore, it is essential that you provide a written action plan below as your commitment to address the expectation stated above.

- Write an action plan, highlighting specific preventative behaviors.
  - Example: I, (employee name), will make sure to think before I speak or act to ensure I am being culturally conscious and aware. . . .

Within thirty days, improvement to expectation must be shown, and this action plan assumes demonstration of full commitment to improve. If you do not improve, this process may result in additional formal statement(s) or you may be asked to decide if you'd like to continue your employment at (Company Name).

- Both sign document and agree on follow-up schedule in thirty days.

Table A14.2.

Manager Name (print)	Manager Signature	Date
Associate Name (print)	Associate Signature	Date
Date of Follow-Up Meeting (30 days following today's date):	Manager Initials (Acknowledging Completion of Follow-Up Meeting):	Associate Initials (Acknowledging Completion of Follow-Up Meeting):

Manager and/or Associate Comments during the Follow-Up Meeting

_____

_____

_____

APPENDIX 14.5

Evaluations

Evaluation of Phase 1: Partner Program

1. With your assigned partner, add monthly appointments to your calendar that last one hour in duration.
2. During each month's meeting, discuss with your assigned partner outstanding thoughts and concerns about personal racial biases and cultural values.
3. Discuss or role-play a real or fictional example of a racial microaggression in the workplace.
4. Using the real or fictional example of a racial microaggression in the workplace, each partner will discuss or act out how they would address the scenario in the moment.
5. Discuss an action plan or use the *Document of Plan for Addressing Racial Microaggressions* exercise template using learned skills and behaviors for constructively addressing racial microaggressions.

Evaluation of Phase 2: Follow-Up Survey Questions

1. What have you learned and/or experienced regarding the benefits of working with a diverse group of people in the workplace?

2. What have you learned and/or experienced regarding the negative impact of racial microaggressions in the workplace?

3. Describe the racial biases and personal values that you discovered about yourself that have further contributed to your self-awareness and explain why you feel this is important to recognize and acknowledge.

4. Provide an example of a situation where you identified an experience where racial microaggressions occurred, in any context, involving yourself (i.e., attitude, communication style) toward others in the workplace.

5. What skills did you acquire to address issues or conflicts between you and your staff (i.e., microaggressions)?

6. Please provide an example of a developed action plan used to implement conflict resolution appropriately.

7. What behaviors or skills have you acquired to use to promote a positive work environment for all employees?

8. We welcome feedback! Do you have any further thoughts, comments, or suggestions?

REFERENCES

Dawis, R. (2005). The Minnesota theory of work adjustment. In S. D. Brown & R. W. Lent (Eds.), *Career development and counseling: Putting theory and research to work* (pp. 3–23). New York: Wiley.

Forrest-Bank, S., & Jenson, J. M. (2015). Differences in experiences of racial and ethnic microaggression among Asian, Latino/Hispanic, Black, and White young adults. *Journal of Sociology and Social Welfare, 42*(1), 141–161. doi: 10.1037/t07335-000.

Jackson, M. A., & Verdino, J. (2012). Vocational psychology. In R. W. Rieber (Ed.), *Encyclopedia of the history of psychological theories* (pp. 1157–1170). New York, NY: Springer. doi: 10.1007/978-1-4419-0463-8.

King, E. B., Dunleavy, D. G., Dunleavy, E. M., Jaffer, S., Morgan, W. B., Elder, K., & Graebner, R. (2011). Discrimination in the 21st century: Are science and the law aligned? *Psychology, Public Policy, and Law, 17*(1), 54–75. doi:10.1037/a0021673.

Lewis, J., Arnold, M. S., House, R., & Toporek, R. L. (2003). *Advocacy competencies.* Endorsed by the American Counseling Association Governing Council. Retrieved from https://www.counseling.org/Resources/Competencies/Advocacy_Competencies.pdf.

Nadal, K. L. Y. (2011). Responding to racial, gender, and sexual orientation microaggressions in the workplace. In M. A. Paludi, C. A. Paludi Jr., & E. R. DeSouza (Eds.), *Praeger handbook on understanding and preventing workplace discrimination* (pp. 23–32). Santa Barbara, CA: Praeger.

National Career Development Association. (1997). *Career counseling competencies.* Broken Arrow, OK: Author.

———. (2009). *Minimum competencies for multicultural career counseling and development.* Broken Arrow, OK: Author. Retrieved from https://www.ncda.org/aws/NCDA/pt/fli/12508/false.

Niles, S. G., & Harris-Bowlsbey, J. E. (2013). *Career development interventions in the 21st century* (4th ed.). Upper Saddle River, NJ: Pearson Education.

Offermann, L. R., Basford, T. E., Graebner, R., Jaffer, S., De Graaf, S. B., & Kaminsky, S. E. (2014). See no evil: Color blindness and perceptions of subtle racial discrimination in the workplace. *Cultural Diversity and Ethnic Minority Psychology, 20*(4), 499–507. doi:10.1037/a0037237.

Reynolds, K. (2017, June 26). 13 benefits and challenges of cultural diversity in the workplace. [Blog post]. *Hult Blogs.* Retrieved from http://www.hult.edu/blog/benefits-challenges-cultural-diversity-workplace/.

Shenoy-Packer, S. (2015). Immigrant professionals, microaggressions, and critical sense-making in the U.S. workplace. *Management Communication Quarterly, 29*(2), 257–275. doi:10.1177/0893318914562069.

Society for Human Resource Management. (2016). *2016 employee job satisfaction and engagement: Revitalizing a changing workforce.* Retrieved from https://www.shrm.org/hr-today/trends-and-forecasting/research-and-surveys/Documents/2016-Employee-Job-Satisfaction-and-Engagement-Report.pdf.

Starbucks Newsroom. (2018, May 23). A preview of the May 29 curriculum for 175,000 Starbucks partners across the country. Retrieved from https://news.starbucks.com/news/starbucks-curriculum-preview-for-may-29.

Sue, D. W. (2010, October 05). Racial microaggressions in everyday life: Is subtle bias harmless? [Blog post]. *Psychology Today.* Retrieved from https://www.psychologytoday.com/us/blog/microaggressions-in-everyday-life/201010/racial-microaggressions-in-everyday-life.

———. (2012, November 17). Microaggressions: More than just race. Can microaggressions be directed at women and gay people? [Blog post]. *Psychology Today.* Retrieved from https://www.psychologytoday.com/us/blog/microaggressions-in-everyday-life/201011/microaggressions-more-just-race.

Sue, D. W., Capodilupo, C. M., Torino, G. C., Bucceri, J. M., Holder, A. B., Nadal, K. L., & Esquilin, M. (2007). Racial microaggressions in everyday life: Implications for clinical practice. *American Psychologist, 62*(4), 271–286. doi:10.1037/0003-066X.62.4.271.

Toporek, R. L., Sapigao, W., & Rojas-Arauz, B. O. (2017). Fostering the development of a social justice perspective and action: Finding a social justice voice. In J. M. Casas, L. A. Suzuki, C. M. Alexander, & M. A. Jackson (Eds.), *Handbook of multicultural counseling* (4th ed., pp. 17–30). Thousand Oaks, CA: Sage.

United States Bureau of Labor Statistics. (2017). *2016 household data annual averages: Employed persons by detailed industry, sex, race, and Hispanic or Latino ethnicity.* Retrieved from https://www.bls.gov/cps/cpsaat18.pdf.

Wong, G., Derthick, A. O., David, E. J. R., Saw, A., & Okazaki, S. (2014). The *what,* the *why,* and the *how:* A review of racial microaggressions research in psychology. *Race and Social Problems, 6*(2), 181–200. http://doi.org/10.1007/s12552-013-9107-9.

VIII

CAREER DEVELOPMENT INTERVENTIONS FOR
SOCIAL JUSTICE NEEDS IN COMMUNITY
AND EMPLOYMENT CONTEXTS WITH
UNDERSERVED OLDER ADULTS

15

Booming through Retirement

Optimizing Psychosocial Resources for
Retirement Success in Baby Boomers

Ashley E. Selkirk

Older adults are often victims of ageism, and they may incorporate ageist stereotypes into their self-concept. As the baby boom generation retires, the risks of succumbing to these stereotypes and prematurely foreclosing on the potential for continued growth and meaning making throughout the life span become real. On the other hand, baby boomers represent the largest cohort to ever reach old age and as a result are expected to redefine concepts of retirement, just as they have caused significant changes to each life stage they have occupied so far. A voluntary one-day, three-part workshop on optimizing psychosocial resources for retirement success is proposed for retirement community–dwelling baby boomers. Conducted by volunteer mental health professionals, the program is designed to promote understanding of resources that impact retirement adjustment using psychoeducation and a values-based approach to wellness. An opportunity is also provided to connect baby boomers with community resources via a "post-career" fair in order to enhance goal-directed activity and meaning making.

SOCIAL JUSTICE NEEDS AND RATIONALE FOR
THE CAREER DEVELOPMENT INTERVENTION

The oldest baby boomers began turning age sixty-five in 2011, and as of this time, ten thousand people per day will turn sixty-five (Pruchno, 2012). It is expected that older adults will comprise 20 percent of the United States' population by 2030, creating the largest cohort ever of older adults

(Alzheimer's Association, 2012). As a population, older adults are historically underserved in multiple societal arenas, including mental health. Startlingly, in a survey of psychologists, only 4.2 percent stated that older adults were the primary focus of their work (American Psychological Association, Center for Workforce Studies, 2008). Clearly there will be a dire need for increased services, mental health providers, and other professionals who specifically cater to the needs of older adults. Yet this is no easy task as older adults are an extremely diverse group, with research noting there is more heterogeneity within this group than in younger age groups (American Psychological Association, 2014). Consequently, interventions with older adults require an understanding of the complex interplay of multiple factors including developmental issues, generational perspectives and beliefs, culture, and mental and physical health (APA, 2014).

Ageist beliefs have also been demonstrated in developmental theory. For example, the disengagement theory, one of the first formal theories of aging, posited that as a person ages, there is a decreased interaction between the individual and his or her environment, resulting in the aged person turning inward and away from the external world (Cummings & Henry, 1961). Despite several decades of research to the contrary, this view of aging remains in the popular consciousness resulting in many negative stereotypes about the functioning, needs, desires, and identity of older adults. This systemic stereotyping often leads to discrimination against older people. These stereotypes are typically internalized at a young age and continue to solidify over time (Jackson, 2013; Jackson, 2017). Older adults who internalize more ageist stereotypes may be prone to more physical and cognitive difficulties and a decreased lifespan (Jackson, 2017). Black and Gregory (2011) found older adults felt ageism challenged one's sense of dignity and self-identity. Older adults have noted the experience of ageism contributes to a sense of invisibility. This invisibility and internalization of stereotypes may very well limit the older adult from seeking out new roles, new partners, and new activities (Schlossberg, 2017). A large public health study conducted by Harvard School of Public Health and Metropolitan Life Foundation (2004) concluded that in order to fight against ageism, the public and baby boomers themselves need to develop a new language and new stories to redefine the role and value of older adults in society. The following intervention applies career and developmental psychology theory and research to help baby boomers redefine themselves in retirement by taking a critical look at how psychosocial resources can be optimized in order to find satisfaction in the retirement years.

Nadler, Damis, and Richardson (1997) describe retirement as "an event, a status, and a process" (p. 46). Retirement, as an event, occurs at a particular time, usually the seventh decade of life when one ceases to work. Retirement is a status that is often viewed as an achievement, a marker that one has ended their role as a worker in society. Finally, retirement is a process, a transition from employment to non-employment and from adulthood into old age. A number of theories have attempted to describe retirement and its impact on the individual. Super (1990) discusses retirement adjustment as related to role adjustment. He states that satisfactory role adjustment "depend[s] on establishment in . . . a way of life in which one can play the kind of role that growth and exploratory experiences have led one to consider congenial and appropriate" (Super, 1990, p. 125). Building on Super's idea of continuing growth, Chen (2011) describes the stage of life-career reengagement, a time in later adulthood aimed at pursuing creativity and meaning, and engaging in activities that foster fulfillment. Social cognitive career theory (SCCT), based on Bandura's social cognitive theory, emphasizes self-efficacy as key to optimal adjustment (Lent, Brown, & Hackett, 2000). Bandura argues that one's sense of self-efficacy affects what activities a person pursues and how persistent a person is in the activity. In retirement, self-efficacy beliefs created during working years likely affect people's opinion of themselves after retirement and what activities are pursued in retirement. Conversely, it may also occur that a person whose entire sense of self-efficacy is based on work roles and identity may feel lost and unable to successfully engage in other activities during retirement. Other theories stress adaptation and balance. The theory of selection, optimization, and compensation (SOC) emphasizes the maximization of gains and minimization of losses in order to create "efficacious functioning of the individual in an identified system (biological, social, psychological), domain (sports, leisure, job, family) or task (self-actualization, cognitive performance, social integration)" (Baltes & Carstensen, 2003, p. 87). Retirement could be seen as a gain (e.g., eagerly awaited event) or a loss (e.g., forced to retired due to health or dismissal).

More recently, Wang, Henkens, and van Solinge (2011) proposed the resource-based dynamic theory of retirement, which attempted to streamline various theories to predict retirement adjustment. Similar to SOC, Wang, Henkens, and van Solinge viewed retirement adjustment as a process with continuously changing gains and losses of various resources. Within the resource model, many concepts from previous theories can fall neatly into a resource category. Resources include physical resources (e.g., good health);

cognitive resources (e.g., intact memory); financial resources (e.g., pension); social resources (e.g., social network, marital support); emotional resources (e.g., overall positive mood/affect); and finally, motivational resources (e.g., self-efficacy, sense of purpose/meaning, autonomy). Empirical research on individual resources has shown support for this model (Asebedo & Seay, 2014; Hershey and Henkens, 2013; Noone, Stephens & Alpass, 2009); however, much of the previous research on retirement was conducted using participants from the "mature generation," the parents of the baby boomers. Baby boomers, as a generation, have a drastically different worldview than their parents. The matures were characterized as the "work to live" generation and typically were conservative, disciplined, hard-working, and conforming, and they adhered to traditional family values (Beutell & Wittig-Berman, 2008). The baby boomers were influenced by periods of immense social change, civil rights struggles, and increased diversity, and they brought a tremendous amount of energy and dedication to the workforce as they reached adulthood. They adhered less to traditional family values and put a large value on success and achievement, creating a "live to work" mentality. Due to these generational differences, a recent study by Selkirk (2017) investigated resource impact on retirement satisfaction in baby boomers specifically. Selkirk found pre-retirement physical health and financial status were significant predictors of retirement satisfaction, but physical health, emotional health, and retirement choice (a motivational resource) were significant post-retirement predictors of retirement satisfaction. Retirement choice, defined as one's ability to voluntarily choose to retire versus being forced by the employer to retire, had the largest individual impact on retirement satisfaction, suggesting that motivational resources may have a greater impact on one's retirement experience than other resources. This is consistent with many of the theories of aging and retirement in the literature which discuss the importance of meaning-making, self-concept, perceived mastery, sense of purpose in life, self-efficacy, self-fulfillment, and self-realization (Asebedo & Seay, 2014; Chen, 2011; Super, 1990; Wang et al., 2011). In particular, Schlossberg (2004) asserts that adults approaching retirement carefully weigh the positives and negatives of current life versus imagined life after retirement to assist with decision-making. Schlossberg contends that each retirement path will be unique to the individual, and she emphasizes understanding, optimizing, and expanding one's psychological portfolio. Similar to the resource model presented above, Schlossberg's view is that this is a process that involves pursuing questions about the creation of a life and identity post-work that optimizes one's emotional and motivational resources.

Baby boomers have had huge societal, political, and economic impacts on every life stage they have inhabited. The impact they will have on old age and perceptions of life after retirement are yet to be definitively seen; however, it is clear from the empirical literature that their needs will likely be different from their predecessors. Career counselors can play a unique role in helping this population navigate this new life stage by recognizing that career development does not cease with the formal event of retirement. Given their unique worldview and immense diversity, the following are the specific needs of retired baby boomers that can be addressed by career development interventions:

a. Learn about and understand the impact of ageism on one's identity as an older person
b. Learn about the various psychosocial resources that can affect retirement adjustment
c. Assess emotional resources
d. Explore motivational resources
e. Relate motivational resources to self-concept and values in order to create achievable goals
f. Understand barriers to obtaining goals and develop plan for navigating these barriers
g. Learn about community resources that may facilitate the development of additional psychosocial resources

Given the outlined needs, the intervention detailed below is grounded in the resource-based dynamic theory of retirement (Wang et al., 2011).

MEASURABLE OBJECTIVES AND EXPECTED OUTCOMES

At the conclusion of Booming through Retirement, baby boomers who participate in all aspects of the intervention will be able to

a. Describe psychosocial resources that impact retirement adjustment
b. Complete and score two brief mental health measures to assess emotional resources
c. Name two value areas that they would like to pursue in order to increase motivational resources such as meaning making
d. Create one specific, measurable, and achievable goal that would allow them to live in accordance with one of the previously identified values

e. List barriers and strengths that could promote or hinder this goal
f. Gather informational pamphlets and/or contact information for community resources that can help increase psychosocial resources

PLAN FOR PROMOTING SERVICES

To begin the process of planning this intervention, a small selection of baby boomers who are regular members of a local community center, community center staff, and several independent community mental health practitioners (e.g., psychologists, social workers, and mental health counselors) will be invited to a brief presentation describing the Booming through Retirement program. Feedback will be solicited and discussed. Agreed-upon changes will be incorporated. The final program will be presented to community center program management for approval and scheduling.

PLAN FOR DELIVERING SERVICES

Booming through Retirement will be delivered by licensed mental health professionals assisted by paraprofessionals (e.g., graduate students) who are under the supervision of the aforementioned mental health professionals. All mental health professionals and paraprofessionals will be familiar with foundations in career development with older adults and trained to lead the small-group activities, facilitate discussion, and gather resources relevant to this intervention (see tables 15.1 and 15.2 for relevant competencies in career counseling and social justice advocacy; Lewis, Arnold, House, & Toporek, 2003; National Career Development Association, 1997, 2009). Participants will be self-selected baby boomers, who through self-report identify as retired or soon-to-be retired. Participants will be invited to participate through targeted community advertisement campaigns (e.g., flyers at the community center and other locales that may be frequented by baby boomers) and word of mouth from professionals who serve this population, not limited to mental health professionals, but also including financial planners, primary care doctors, and so on. The intervention will be held at a local community center consistent with APA's (2014) Guidelines for Psychological Practice with Older Adults (hereafter referred to as the Guidelines), which suggest that psychological services be provided to older adults in settings where older adults are typically located, such as community or senior centers. Each participant will engage in a one-day three-part workshop at a local community center consisting of a psycho-educational seminar, small-group activity and discussion, and finally a "post-career" fair.

Table 15.1. Relevance to Career Counseling Competencies

Career Counseling Competency	Addressed by Career Intervention	Relevance to Corresponding Competency
1. Career Development Theory	X	Booming through Retirement utilizes concepts from several theories (Lent et al., 2000; Richardson, 2012; Super, 1990) but emphasizes resource-based dynamic theory of retirement (Wang et al., 2011).
2. Individual and Group Counseling Skills	X	Counselors facilitate small-groups that utilize ACT interventions (Petkus & Wetherell, 2013).
3. Individual/Group Assessment	X	Assessments specified for use with older adults are utilized.
4. Information/ Resources/ Technology	X	A psychoeducational component and the "post-career" fair provide multidisciplinary information and resources. Resources may be needed for vision, hearing, and physical access accommodations.
5. Program Promotion, Management, and Implementation	X	The chapter discusses the needs, objectives, plan for promoting services, plan for delivering services, and content for the proposed career development program.
6. Coaching, Consultation, and Performance Improvement	X	The results of the evaluation, and feedback from baby boomers, mental health professionals, and staff, and are used to revise the program and prepare for future interventions.
7. Diverse Populations	X	Retirement adjustment for the growing number of baby boomer older adults is hindered by ageism and promoted by this intervention. By using a community center setting, the intervention may reach a greater diversity of this population.
8. Supervision	X	The intervention includes supervision and training for small-group leaders.
9. Ethical/Legal Issues	X	The chapter includes a summary of ethical considerations.
10. Research/ Evaluation	X	Evaluation of the intervention's effectiveness is utilized via a self-report questionnaire.

Source: NCDA, 1997, 2009.

Table 15.2.   Relevance to Advocacy Competencies

Advocacy Competency	Addressed by Career Intervention	Relevance to Corresponding Competency
1. Client/Student Empowerment	X	Mental health professionals assist a growing cohort of older adults facing ageism, baby boomers, in understanding how to best use their positive resources to make goals to better live in accordance with their values.
2. Client/Student Advocacy	X	Via the "post-career" fair, resources are presented to the participants.
3. Community Collaboration	X	Intervention organizers use community center staff to help plan programming and included community organizations in the "post-career" fair.
4. Systems Advocacy	X	Identify ageism as potentially hindering development post-retirement and how building psychological resources can promote retirement adjustment and health.
5. Public Information	—	—
6. Social/Political Advocacy	—	—

Source: Lewis et al., 2003.

INTERVENTION PROGRAM CONTENT

This one-day career development intervention will promote understanding of various resources that can affect retirement in order to optimize retirement satisfaction by providing psychoeducation regarding resources, promoting exploration of values to increase meaning making, and finally exposing participants to available community agencies that could assist in attainment of additional resources.

Psychoeducational Seminar

The initial component of the intervention will be a ninety-minute psychoeducational seminar. This is an attempt to adhere to the Guidelines suggestion that psychologists should play a larger role in health-promoting psychoeducational programs. In general, older adults respond to psychological interventions as well as their younger counterparts (APA, 2014). Furthermore, it has been found that psychoeducation specifically, even in a single session, can cause a significant impact on behavior (Azrin &

Teichner, 1998). Alvidrez, Areán, and Stewart (2005) found that a brief psychoeducational intervention tailored to older African Americans resulted in increased participation in psychological interventions at a later date suggesting that psychoeducational interventions may be particularly important for engaging older adults of color.

The seminar will provide information regarding retirement as an event, process, and status. Presenters will utilize audience members' sense of generational cohort identity to discuss how baby boomers are unique due to their generational worldview and how this may affect their lives after retirement (e.g., "How may retirement be different for you than for your parents? What may be some benefits and challenges during your retirement years?"). Using the elicited answers as examples, presenters will describe the resource model as described by Wang, Henkens, and van Solinge (2011). Presenters will also describe in colloquial language relevant research investigating which resources have been found to have a particular impact on retirement satisfaction with a baby boomer population. To address emotional resources in particular, myths about mental health and stereotypes about aging will be presented. To honor and explore the diversity of baby boomers, participants will also be asked to reflect on how race, gender, SES/class, nationality, or other identities might impact the myths or stereotypes of aging that are perpetuated in their families or communities. Common warning signs of depression and anxiety will also be described in order to increase mental health literacy. The next component of a small group activity will be described, followed by a brief refreshment break. At the end of the workshop, participants will be offered the option of an additional thirty-minute extension to complete, in private with one of the intervention leaders, two brief depression and anxiety screeners, the Geriatric Depression Scale—Short Form (Sheikh & Yesavage, 1986; GDS-SF) and the Geriatric Anxiety Inventory—Short Form (Byrne & Pachana, 2011; GAI-SF) for scoring, interpretation, questions, and referrals as needed.

Small Group Activity and Discussion

The second component of the intervention will focus solely on emotional and motivational resources, consistent with research by Selkirk (2017) that found these two resources were particularly impactful on retirement satisfaction for baby boomers. Participants will be divided into small groups of six to eight participants led by one mental health professional. The first segment of this intervention will focus on a brief discussion of the mental health measures, emphasizing that the results from these measures are for the participants' personal use and do not need to be shared. Group leaders will provide each participant with a list of community mental health organizations in order for participants to reach out for mental health support at their own discretion.

The remainder of the intervention will utilize concepts from acceptance and commitment therapy (ACT) that correspond nicely to the emphasis in the resource model and SOC of understanding gains and losses. ACT is an evidenced-based treatment that emphasizes acceptance of unchangeable losses and action-oriented behavior that connects with one's values (Petkus & Wetherell, 2013). Petkus and Wetherell argue that for older adults, value-driven interventions might be especially relevant in retirement if one has fused the value of making a meaningful contribution to society with the action of work and career. ACT may help defuse this belief and help older adults explore how else they may contribute to society. An acceptance approach will be presented in which participants will be challenged to focus on their remaining resources in order to reconnect with values that bring meaning to their lives. Participants will be provided with the Valued Living Questionnaire (VLQ; Wilson, Sandoz, Kitchens, & Roberts, 2010; https://contextualscience.org/node/2633). The VLQ lists ten valued domains of life and asks respondents to rate each domain's level of importance in their life and how consistently they have lived in accordance with this value within the past week. The aim of this questionnaire is to help identify which value areas are important to the participants and which values participants could aim to move toward. The results from the VLQ will help guide participants to choose one value area and identify a goal that will bring them closer to living in accordance with the chosen value. Participants will be encouraged to develop specific, measurable, and obtainable goals and brainstorm potential challenges (see Value-Driven Goals Worksheet in appendix 15.1). Finally, group leaders will describe the final component of the intervention, the "post-career" fair. Group leaders will briefly discuss how organizations represented at the fair may help participants increase their resources and work toward their goals and values. Lunch would be served in order to allow for social connection among participants and setup of the fair.

"Post-Career" Fair

According to Richardson (2012), the goal of vocational psychology is to "[help] people construct lives through work and relationships" (p. 191).

Richardson proposes a social constructivist perspective, based on feminist and social justice values, to broaden the field's definition of work and to redefine the value assigned to different types of work. Richardson defines work as "instrumental and purposive activity that produces goods, services, or social relations that have economic or social value" (p. 202). With this definition, work goes well beyond traditional paid work. At the proposed "post-career" fair, various community organizations will be present in order to expose participants to various forms of activity that could help add meaning to their lives or assist in the optimization of resources. This intervention is in accordance with APA's (2014) Guidelines that suggest mental health professionals should operate as advocates for a multidisciplinary approach to elder care. Community organizations could include representatives from mental health clinics, social work agencies, volunteer organizations, senior centers, AARP, and local colleges that offer learning opportunities for older adults (including financial planning workshops). As with the previous intervention components, the mental health professionals involved in intervention delivery will be available for assistance and questions.

RESOURCES NEEDED

In order to effectively implement Booming through Retirement, the following resources are needed:

1. qualified volunteer community mental health professionals
2. two to three hours of meetings arranged to assist in program development, planning, and approval within the community
3. two hours to provide intervention-specific ACT training to mental health professionals who will lead small groups with older adults
4. commercial use license of GAI-SF
5. large-print copies (for vision accommodations) of publicly available worksheets utilized in the intervention and of screening measures for depression and anxiety administered by the professionals
6. access to large event space with a projector in community center and various small rooms for small groups, with attention to hearing, vision, and physical access accommodations for facilities, materials, and interactions

METHODS OF EVALUATION

Anonymous self-report questionnaires will be administered at the end of the "post-career" fair to evaluate the objectives of the intervention. Specifically, participants will be asked to rate their overall satisfaction with each workshop component. Participants will also be asked multiple-choice questions regarding psychoeducation content to address Objective A. Participants will be asked if obtaining a score on the GDS-SF and GAS-SF provided new information regarding their emotional health and if they plan on seeking mental health care as a result of the screening. Participants will be asked to describe their ability to satisfy each objective for Objectives C and D. Finally, to evaluate Objective F, participants will be asked if they gathered contact information from various organizations at the "Post-Career" fair and to rate the likelihood of future contact. An open-ended comment section will also be provided for general feedback not addressed in any other question.

PLAN FOR REVISION

In the month following the intervention, the intervention developers, mental health professionals, community center staff, and a selection of intervention participants will meet to review the feedback from the self-report questionnaires and discuss the success of the intervention. Feedback will be elicited regarding future implementation of this intervention, including content areas covered, effectiveness of psychoeducational presentation and small-group activities, and the inclusion/exclusion of organizations present at the "post-career" fair. Revisions to the intervention will be made as needed.

ETHICAL CONSIDERATIONS

The APA (2002) provides ethical principles and a code of conduct expected of all psychologists. An area stressed within this code is working within the boundaries of one's professional competence. All mental health professionals included in this intervention will have had supervised experience and training in working with older adults, including how to ethically obtain informed consent to administer, score, and interpret the depression and anxiety screening measures (GDS-SF and GAI-SF) and (if needed) implement a referral process. ACT training specific to the intervention will be provided by the intervention planner, a licensed psychologist who is qualified to train and supervise the intervention providers. In accordance with the APA (2002) code of conduct, informed consent for all intervention activities will be provided to participants throughout to explain that their participation in all parts of the intervention is completely voluntary, confidentiality within each small group will be stressed, and confidentiality of their assessment results will be protected with limits specified.

Finally, the guiding ethical principle of respect for people's rights and dignity (APA, 2002) is honored in every aspect of the intervention with special attention paid to language used to describe the target population, and with the emphasis on participants' autonomy and strengths. Age is specifically included within this principle's description as a difference that must be consciously acknowledged. Given Western society's tendency toward ageist stereotypes, older adults must be treated with the same respect as younger persons and given the same assumption of personal agency.

CONCLUSION

Baby boomers will soon comprise the largest cohort of older adults ever and are expected to change the face of retirement. Western society is tasked with confronting previously held stereotypes of aging as this new generation of older adult brings the same energy and achievement-orientation to retirement as they previously brought to the workforce. Mental health professionals will be challenged with meeting the needs of the baby boomer generation, taking into consideration that their unique worldview and diversity will necessitate specialized and flexible interventions that promote healthy aging. The career development intervention presented above represents an attempt to use the traditional and current theory and research on career and lifespan development to provide baby boomers with the opportunity to enhance their knowledge of what impacts retirement adjustment in order to optimize their psychosocial resources. In particular, the intervention is modeled on the resource-based dynamic theory of retirement (Wang et al., 2011). As a strength-based career development intervention likely to counter ageist stereotypes for a growing cohort of older adults, Booming through Retirement stresses emotional and motivational resources to increase the likelihood of meaning making and living in accordance with one's values.

REFLECTIONS ON COUNSELOR SELF-AWARENESS OF POTENTIAL RESOURCES AND BIASES FROM PRIVILEGED AND MARGINALIZED IDENTITIES

I am a young adult, age thirty, who has committed my academic and professional life to serving older adults and intimately understanding their worldview. I was raised in a small rural community that emphasized traditional family values, including respect for one's elders. My grandfather was and remains the patriarch of my family, and what he says goes. He is the source of all wisdom. I had a front-row seat to his transition from a dedicated and overworked small-business owner to a retiree with time to fill in his schedule. I witnessed him shift his energy to other activities including becoming more active within community organizations, picking up new hobbies, and writing brief stories of his childhood. Now, I am witnessing my father, a baby boomer, make a similar but slower transition to retirement. He is leading a more phased-retirement, as is popular with his generation (i.e., a slow transition out of the workforce). I have noticed, too, other differences between my father and grandfather. My grandfather refuses to wear hearing aids due to the idea that it is a sign of weakness. My father thinks this is ridiculous and sees it as impeding his ability to enjoy his old age. This is a concrete value difference. What is clear is that among the three generations in my family, we all have drastically different generational worldviews, and just as my grandfather and father are taking different approaches to retirement, I likely will too when I reach that time in my life. From the privileged position of the young, I have witnessed aging and retirement, but I have not experienced it personally, which puts me at a disadvantage of understanding the population I serve.

As Jackson (2013) states, no one is immune to ageist bias. Despite my immense respect for my elders, I include myself in that category. I have been known to feel more paternalistic toward my older adult patients (and family members), especially those who present as less physically healthy. I have often assumed, incorrectly, that older adults have poor mental health literacy. Over time I have strived to become more consciously aware of my tendency to overexplain mental health symptomatology or offer physical help when it is not solicited. Oftentimes, I think this comes across as excitement and caring, but it could also be demeaning. When developing the intervention for this book chapter, I tried to consciously make myself aware of the language I used to describe older adults, and how the proposed interventions could respect the dignity of all persons while delivering something that could be easily digested and understood. I wanted to emphasize that self-discovery and feelings of achievement can continue at all life stages while understanding that losses are an inevitable part of aging.

APPENDIX 15.1

Booming through Retirement: Value-Driven Goals

Step 1: Utilizing the VLQ, what is one value area that is important to me that I would like to strive toward?

Value: _____

(Example—Community)

Step 2: How can I practice or promote this value?

Practice: _____

(Example—Become engaged in a volunteer organization)

Step 3: Turn this intention to practice into an obtainable goal:

Step 3a: Specify Goal—What exactly will you accomplish?

Goal: _____

(Example—Make initial contact with volunteer organization)

Step 3b: Obtainable/Measurable—Is this goal realistic for me? How will I know when this goal is achieved?

Obtainable/Measurable: _____

(Example—Call and obtain response from one volunteer organization and receive materials to discuss how to become a volunteer)

Step 3c: Time Line—When can I expect to complete my goal?

Time Line: _____

(Example—Within 2 weeks)

Step 4: Are there potential barriers/obstacles to my goal?

Barriers/Obstacles: _____

_____

(Example—I can only volunteer on Tuesdays; it is hard for me to stand for long periods of time)

Step 4: How can I work around these barriers/obstacles?

Ideas: _____

_____

(Example—Look for volunteer organizations that provide flexible scheduling; ask questions regarding physical responsibilities.)

REFERENCES

Alvidrez, J., Areán, P. A., & Stewart, A. L. (2005). Psychoeducation to increase psychotherapy entry for older African Americans. *American Journal of Geriatric Psychiatry, 13*(7), 554–561. doi: 10.1097/00019442-200507000-00003.

Alzheimer's Association. (2012). Alzheimer's disease facts and figures. *Alzheimer's and Dementia: The Journal of the Alzheimer's Association.* Retrieved from http://www .alz.org/downloads/facts_figures_2012.pdf.

American Psychological Association. (2002). Ethical principles of psychologists and code of conduct. *American Psychologist, 57*(12), 1060–1073. doi: 10.1037/0003-066X.57.12.1060.

———. (2014). Guidelines for psychological practice with older adults. *American Psychologist, 69*(1), 34–65. doi:10.1037/a0035063.

American Psychological Association, Center for Workforce Studies. (2008). *2008 APA survey of psychology health service providers.* Retrieved from http://www.apa.org/workforce/publications/08-hsp/ index.aspx.

Asebedo, S. D., & Seay, M. C. (2014). Positive psychological attributes and retirement satisfaction. *Journal of Financial Counseling and Planning, 25*(2), 161–173. doi: 10.2469/dig .v45.n6.1.

Azrin, N. H., & Teichner, G. (1998). Evaluation of an instructional program for improving medication compliance for chronically mentally ill outpatients. *Behaviour Research and Therapy, 36*(9), 849–861. doi:10.1016/S0005-7967(98)00036-9.

Baltes, M. M., & Carstensen, L. L. (2003). The process of successful aging: Selection, optimization and compensation. In U. M. Staudinger, U. Lindenberger (Eds.), *Understanding human behavior* (pp. 81–104). Dordrecht, Netherlands: Kluwer Academic Publishers. doi: 10.1007/978-1-4615-0357-6_5.

Beutell, N. J., & Wittig-Berman, U. (2008). Work-family conflict and work-family synergy for generation X, baby boomers, and matures: Generational differences, predictors, and satisfaction outcomes. *Journal of Managerial Psychology, 23*(5), 507–523. doi:10.1108/02683940810884513.

Black, K., & Gregory, S. (2011). *Aging with dignity and independence initiative: Actionable themes: Issues and opportunities.* Sarasota: University of South Florida.

Byrne, G. J., & Pachana, N. A. (2011). Development and validation of a short form of the Geriatric Anxiety Inventory—the GAI-SF. *International Psychogeriatrics, 23*(1), 125–131. doi:10.1017/S1041610210001237.

Chen, C. P. (2011). Life-career re-engagement: A new conceptual framework for counseling people in retirement transition. *Australian Journal of Career Development, 20*(2), 25–29. Retrieved from: https://www.acer.edu.au/press/ajcd/contents.

Cummings, E., & Henry, W. H. (1961). *Growing old: The process of disengagement.* New York: Basic Books.

Harvard School of Public Health & Metropolitan Life Foundation (2004). *Reinventing aging: Baby boomers and civic engagement.* Retrieved from the AARP website: http:// assets.aarp .org/rgcenter/ general/boomers_engagement.pdf.

Hershey, D. A., & Henkens, K. (2013). Impact of different types of retirement transitions on perceived satisfaction with life. *Gerontologist, 54*(2), 232–244. doi:10.1093/geront/gnt006.

Jackson, M. A. (2013). Counseling older workers confronting ageist stereotypes and discrimination. In P. Brownell & J. J. Kelly (Eds.), *Ageism and mistreatment of older workers: Current reality, future solutions* (pp. 135–144). New York: Springer.

———. (2017). Ageism. In K. L. Nadal (Ed.), *The Sage encyclopedia of psychology and gender* (pp. 38–40). Thousand Oaks, CA: Sage.

Lent, R. W., Brown, S. D., & Hackett, G. (2000). Contextual supports and barriers to career choice: A social cognitive analysis. *Journal of Counseling Psychology, 47,* 36–49. doi: 10.1037//0022-0167.47.1.3.

Lewis, J., Arnold, M. S., House, R., & Toporek, R. L. (2003). *Advocacy competencies.* Endorsed by the American Counseling Association Governing Council. Retrieved from https://www.counseling.org/Resources/Competencies/Advocacy_Competencies.pdf.

Nadler, J. D., Damis, L. F., & Richardson, E. D. (1997). Psychosocial aspects of aging. In P. Nussbuam (Ed.), *Handbook of Neuropsychology and Aging* (pp. 44–59). New York: Springer US. doi:10.1007/978-1-4899-1857-4_5.

National Career Development Association. (1997). *Career counseling competencies.* Broken Arrow, OK: Author.

———. (2009). *Minimum competencies for multicultural career counseling and development.* Broken Arrow, OK: Author. Retrieved from https://www.ncda.org/aws/NCDA/pt/ fli/12508/false.

Noone, J. H., Stephens, C., & Alpass, F. M. (2009). Preretirement planning and well-being in later life: A prospective study. *Research on Aging, 31*(3), 295–317. doi:10.1177/ 0164027508330718.

Petkus, A. J., & Wetherell, J. L. (2013). Acceptance and commitment therapy with older adults: Rationale and considerations. *Cognitive and Behavioral Practice, 20*(1), 47–56. doi:10.1016/j.cbpra.2011.07.004.

Pruchno, R. (2012). Not your mother's old age: Baby boomers at age 65. *Gerontologist, 52*(2), 149. doi:10.1093/geront/gns038.

Richardson, M. S. (2012). Counseling for work and relationship. *Counseling Psychologist, 40*(2), 190–242. doi: 10.1177/0011000011406452.

Schlossberg, N. K. (2004). *Retired smart, retire happy: Finding your true path in life.* Washington, DC: American Psychological Association.

———. (2017). *Too young to be old: Love, learn, work, and play as you age.* Washington, DC: American Psychological Association.

Selkirk, A. S. (2017). A longitudinal study of retirement satisfaction in baby boomers and Vietnam-era veterans (Unpublished doctoral dissertation). Fordham University, New York, NY.

Sheikh, J. I., & Yesavage, J. A. (1986). Geriatric Depression Scale: Recent evidence and development of a shorter version. *Clinical Gerontologist, 5,* 165–173. doi:10.1300/J018v05n01_09.

Super, D. E. (1990). A life-span, life-space approach to career development. In D. Brown & L. Brooks (Eds.), *Career choice and development: Applying contemporary theories to practice* (2nd ed., pp. 197–261). San Francisco, CA: Jossey-Bass.

Wang, M., Henkens, K., & van Solinge, H. (2011). Retirement adjustment: A review of theoretical and empirical advancements. *American Psychologist, 66*(3), 204–213. doi:10.1037/a0022414.

Wilson, K. G., Sandoz, E. K., Kitchens, J., & Roberts, M. E. (2010). The Valued Living Questionnaire: Defining and measuring valued action within a behavioral framework. *The Psychological Record, 60,* 249–272. doi: 10.1007/BF03395706.

Appendix A: Career Counseling Competencies

Career counseling is defined as the process of assisting individuals in the development of a life-career with focus on the definition of the worker role and how that role interacts with other life roles. NCDA's Career Counseling Competencies are intended to represent minimum competencies for professionals practicing in, or training for practice in, this specialty at or above the master's degree level of education, including adherence to professional ethical responsibilities. In 2009, NCDA updated the Career Counseling Competencies to include multicultural competencies, affirming that professionals practice in ways to promote the career development and functioning of individuals of all backgrounds. In order to work as a professional engaged in career counseling, the individual must demonstrate minimum competencies in ten designated areas, briefly defined as follows.

1. Career Development Theory

- Understands the strengths and limitations of career theory and utilizes theories that are appropriate for the population being served.

2. Individual and Group Counseling Skills

- Is aware of his/her own cultural beliefs and assumptions and incorporates that awareness into his/her decision-making about interactions with clients/students and other career professionals.

- Continues to develop his/her individual and group counseling skills in order to enhance his/her ability to respond appropriately to individuals from diverse populations.
- Is cognizant of the group demographics when working with groups and monitors these to ensure appropriate respect and confidentiality is maintained.

3. Individual/Group Assessment

- Understands the psychometric properties of the assessments he/she is using in order to effectively select and administer assessments, and interpret and use results with the appropriate limitations and cautions.

4. Information, Resources, and Technology

- Regularly evaluates the information, resources, and use of technology to determine that these tools are sensitive to the needs of diverse populations amending and/or individualizing for each client as required.
- Provides resources in multiple formats to ensure that clients/students are able to benefit from needed information.
- Provides targeted and sensitive support for clients/students in using the information, resources, and technology.

5. Program Promotion, Management and Implementation

- Incorporates appropriate guidelines, research, and experience in developing, implementing, and managing programs and services for diverse populations.
- Utilizes the principles of program evaluation to design and obtain feedback from relevant stakeholders in the continuous improvement of programs and services, paying special attention to feedback regarding specific needs of the population being served.
- Applies his/her knowledge of multicultural issues in dealings with other professionals and trainees to ensure the creation of a culturally sensitive environment for all clients.

6. Coaching, Consultation, and Performance Improvement

- Engages in coaching, consultation, and performance improvement activities with appropriate training and incorporates knowledge of multicultural attitudes, beliefs, skills, and values.
- Seeks awareness and understanding about how to best match diverse clients/students with suitably culturally sensitive employers.

7. Diverse Populations

- Applies multicultural knowledge and skills in providing career counseling and development services specific to the needs of the individuals served.

8. Supervision

- Gains knowledge of and engages in evidence-based supervision, pursues educational and training activities on a regular and ongoing basis inclusive of both counseling and supervision topics. Further, is aware of his/her limitations, cultural biases, and personal values and seeks professional consultative assistance as necessary.
- Infuses multicultural/diversity contexts into his/her training and supervision practices, makes supervisees aware of the ethical standards and responsibilities of the profession, and trains supervisees to develop relevant multicultural knowledge and skills.

9. Ethical/Legal Issues

- Continuously updates his/her knowledge of multicultural and diversity issues and research and applies new knowledge as required.
- Employs his/her knowledge and experience of multicultural ethical and legal issues within a professional framework to enhance the functioning of his/her organization and the image of the profession.
- Uses supervision and professional consultations effectively when faced with an ethical or legal issue related to diversity to ensure he/she provides high-quality services for every client/student.

10. Research/Evaluation

- Designs and implements culturally appropriate research studies with regard to research design, instrument selection, and other pertinent population-specific issues.

Adapted abbreviated excerpts from the full documents "Career Counseling Competencies" and "Minimum Competencies for Multicultural Career Counseling and Development" of the National Career Development Association (1997 and 2009, respectively), Broken Arrow, OK. Adapted with permission.

Note: In using this document, we recommend the inclusion of pronouns "his/her/their" to acknowledge nonbinary gender identities.

Appendix B: Advocacy Competencies

Advocacy Competency Domains

ADVOCACY COMPETENCIES

Client/Student Empowerment

- An advocacy orientation involves not only systems change interventions but also the implementation of empowerment strategies in direct counseling.

- Advocacy-oriented counselors recognize the impact of social, political, economic, and cultural factors on human development.
- They also help their clients and students understand their own lives in context. This lays the groundwork for self-advocacy.

Empowerment Counselor Competencies

In direct interventions, the counselor is able to:

1. Identify strengths and resources of clients and students.
2. Identify the social, political, economic, and cultural factors that affect the client/student.
3. Recognize the signs indicating that an individual's behaviors and concerns reflect responses to systemic or internalized oppression.
4. At an appropriate development level, help the individual identify the external barriers that affect his or her development.
5. Train students and clients in self-advocacy skills.
6. Help students and clients develop self-advocacy action plans.
7. Assist students and clients in carrying out action plans.

Client/Student Advocacy

- When counselors become aware of external factors that act as barriers to an individual's development, they may choose to respond through advocacy.
- The client/student advocate role is especially significant when individuals or vulnerable groups lack access to needed services.

Client/Student Advocacy Counselor Competencies

In environmental interventions on behalf of clients and students, the counselor is able to:

1. Negotiate relevant services and education systems on behalf of clients and students.
2. Help clients and students gain access to needed resources.
3. Identify barriers to the well-being of individuals and vulnerable groups.
4. Develop an initial plan of action for confronting these barriers.

5. Identify potential allies for confronting the barriers.
6. Carry out the plan of action.

Community Collaboration

- Their ongoing work with people gives counselors a unique awareness of recurring themes. Counselors are often among the first to become aware of specific difficulties in the environment.
- Advocacy-oriented counselors often choose to respond to such challenges by alerting existing organizations that are already working for change and that might have an interest in the issue at hand.
- In these situations, the counselor's primary role is as an ally. Counselors can also be helpful to organizations by making available to them our particular skills: interpersonal relations, communications, training, and research.

Community Collaboration Counselor Competencies

1. Identify environmental factors that impinge upon students' and clients' development.
2. Alert community or school groups with common concerns related to the issue.
3. Develop alliances with groups working for change.
4. Use effective listening skills to gain understanding of the group's goals.
5. Identify the strengths and resources that the group members bring to the process of systemic change.
6. Communicate recognition of and respect for these strengths and resources.
7. Identify and offer the skills that the counselor can bring to the collaboration.
8. Assess the effect of counselor's interaction with the community.

Systems Advocacy

- When counselors identify systemic factors that act as barriers to their students' or clients' development, they often wish that they could change the environment and prevent some of the problems that they see every day.

- Regardless of the specific target of change, the processes for altering the status quo have common qualities. Change is a process that requires vision, persistence, leadership, collaboration, systems analysis, and strong data. In many situations, a counselor is the right person to take leadership.

Systems Advocacy Counselor Competencies

In exerting systems-change leadership at the school or community level, the advocacy-oriented counselor is able to:

1. Identify environmental factors impinging on students' or clients' development.
2. Provide and interpret data to show the urgency for change.
3. In collaboration with other stakeholders, develop a vision to guide change.
4. Analyze the sources of political power and social influence within the system.
5. Develop a step-by-step plan for implementing the change process.
6. Develop a plan for dealing with probable responses to change.
7. Recognize and deal with resistance.
8. Assess the effect of counselor's advocacy efforts on the system and constituents.

Public Information

- Across settings, specialties, and theoretical perspectives, professional counselors share knowledge of human development and expertise in communication.
- These qualities make it possible for advocacy-oriented counselors to awaken the general public to macro-systemic issues regarding human dignity.

Public Information Counselor Competencies

In informing the public about the role of environmental factors in human development, the advocacy-oriented counselor is able to:

1. Recognize the impact of oppression and other barriers to healthy development.
2. Identify environmental factors that are protective of healthy development.
3. Prepare written and multi-media materials that provide clear explanations of the role of specific environmental factors in human development.
4. Communicate information in ways that are ethical and appropriate for the target population.
5. Disseminate information through a variety of media.
6. Identify and collaborate with other professionals who are involved in disseminating public information.
7. Assess the influence of public information efforts undertaken by the counselor.

Social/Political Advocacy

- Counselors regularly act as change agents in the systems that affect their own students and clients most directly. This experience often leads toward the recognition that some of the concerns they have addressed affected people in a much larger arena.
- When this happens, counselors use their skills to carry out social/political advocacy.

Social/Political Advocacy Counselor Competencies

In influencing public policy in a large, public arena, the advocacy-oriented counselor is able to:

1. Distinguish those problems that can best be resolved through social/political action.
2. Identify the appropriate mechanisms and avenues for addressing these problems.
3. Seek out and join with potential allies.
4. Support existing alliances for change.
5. With allies, prepare convincing data and rationales for change.
6. With allies, lobby legislators and other policy makers.

7. Maintain open dialogue with communities and clients to ensure that the social/political advocacy is consistent with the initial goals.

Reprinted from "Advocacy Competencies" by J. Lewis, M. S. Arnold, R. House, & R. L. Toporek, 2003. Endorsed by the American Counseling Association Governing Council. Retrieved from https://counseling.org/Resources/Competencies/Advocacy_Competencies.pdf. Reprinted with permission.

Note: In using this document, we recommend the inclusion of pronouns "his/her/their" to acknowledge nonbinary gender identities.

Index

About the Editors and Contributors

Margo A. Jackson, PhD, is a professor of counseling psychology in the Graduate School of Education at Fordham University, Lincoln Center. Her scholarship and mentoring are grounded in values of social justice awareness and advocacy; multicultural and interdisciplinary perspectives; and scientist-practitioner approaches to training and practice that are holistic, strength-based, developmental, and focused on facilitating healthy human relationships. Her research, teaching, and service focus on methods to assess and constructively address hidden biases and strengths of counselors, psychologists, educators, and other leaders; career development across the life span; and ethical training and supervision in multicultural counseling and psychology. Dr. Jackson can be reached at mjackson@fordham.edu.

Allyson K. Regis, PhD, is a licensed psychologist who received her doctorate in counseling psychology from Fordham University. Dr. Regis has worked in a variety of clinical settings and particularly enjoys working with college students who have difficulty adjusting to/navigating the college environment. Her research, teaching, and leadership experiences have focused on multicultural considerations in clinical work, strength-based approaches to wellness, and career development theory. Dr. Regis can be reached at allyson.regis@gmail.com.

Kourtney Bennett, PhD, is a licensed psychologist at the Loyola University Maryland Counseling Center. She completed her doctoral studies in counseling psychology at Fordham University. Her clinical experiences include supporting youth and adults in community mental health, college counseling, and career development center settings. Her research and service interests include multicultural and intersectional identity; vocational development among adolescents and emerging adults; and social justice and advocacy. Dr. Bennett can be reached at kbennett@loyola.edu.

∼

Victoria Broems holds a BA in Psychology from Marist College and is currently studying to earn her PhD in school psychology at Fordham University in New York City. At Fordham, she serves as a board member of the Fordham Student Association of School Psychologists (SASP) and studies awareness of white racial privilege among school psychology graduate students. Victoria's research interests include White racial identity development, stereotype reversal training, and the psychological impacts of racial microaggressions, as well as other social justice issues related to school psychology.

Gary L. Dillon Jr., PhD, is a clinical psychologist with the Mental Health Service Corps (MHSC) under the ThriveNYC initiative. Dr. Dillon's current worksite is at Queens College (CUNY) where he conducts individual and group psychotherapy and academic and career counseling with students from diverse backgrounds. He obtained his BA and MA from New York University (NYU) in Applied Psychology and Mental Health Counseling respectively, and his PhD in counseling psychology from Fordham University, where his research focused on racial and ethnic microaggressions. His clinical work involved working largely with marginalized populations from a multiculturally informed approach.

Kathleen Hahn, MEd, is a clinical case manager at Mental Health Association of New York City, supporting the Adolescent Skills Center in Bronx, New York. In that role, she provides emotional, educational, and vocational services, as well as case management support for at-risk youth in an alternative school setting. Prior to this role, she worked for many years as a finance executive in an international firm.

Jill Huang, PhD, is a licensed psychologist in Ventura County in Southern California. In her private practice, she specializes in working with ethnic minorities, survivors of trauma, and lesbian, gay, bisexual, and transgender populations. She received her EdM and MA from Teachers College, Columbia University and PhD from Fordham University in counseling psychology. Some of her interests include expanding multicultural sensitivity and awareness by investigating the intersection of race, ethnicity, and sexual orientation.

Fanny Kuang holds an MSEd in mental health counseling from Fordham University. She has conducted research in the areas of neuropsychology, anxiety disorders, and career counseling.

Shannon O'Neill is a doctoral candidate within Fordham University's counseling psychology PhD program and is currently completing her internship at the Phoenix VA Healthcare System. She has dedicated research to aid in diminishing the urban-rural imbalance and to give recognition to the society, identity, and well-being of rural culture. Areas of professional interest include health psychology, behavioral medicine, anxiety-related disorders, and rural mental health.

Elizabeth Quiñones is the cofounder and CEO of Lil' Eggheads, an education company aimed at preparing children ages three to seven emotionally, socially, and academically for the NYC classroom. Her formal career counseling experience includes applying a narrative approach to working with middle school students and with adults who have suffered from a traumatic brain injury (TBI). She received her MSEd in mental health counseling from Fordham University in 2017.

Christine S. Romano, LMHC, is a licensed mental health counselor with a certification in sex and sexuality therapy and a background in human resources and law. She holds a BA in applied psychology from Bryant University and a MSEd in mental health counseling from Fordham University; she currently works as a clinician at a community mental health organization and in human resources for a major retail corporation. Her academic research interests and experiences include multicultural counseling, racial and gender microaggressions, interpersonal relationships, sexual behavioral health, mental illness and substance use, career development, and global business.

Ashley E. Selkirk holds a BA from University of Notre Dame, an EdM in mental health counseling from Teachers College at Columbia University, and a PhD from Fordham University in Counseling Psychology. Throughout her professional career, Ashley has maintained a special interest in clinical work with older adult populations, with an emphasis on tailoring short-term dynamic and existential therapies to suit the needs of this demographic. Research interests include the impact of a generational cohort on normative life transitions, adjustment to late-life illness, and caregiver stress.

Lauren Ann Sonnabend, LMSW, MA, is a doctoral student in the Counseling Psychology PhD Program at Fordham University. She has extensive experience as a researcher and therapist with underserved adolescents and their families in hospital and school settings. Her research interests include improving mental health and education outcomes for underserved adolescents through mindfulness-based interventions and community-based participatory research.

Ariel Sorensen, MHC-LP, is a mental illness and chemical addiction specialist in the CAMBA women's homeless shelter system. Prior to this, she was a counselor at Lehman College, where she provided individual and group counseling to a population of largely minority and first-generation college students. Her research interests are in outreach for traditionally therapy-avoidant populations.

Adia Tucker is a licensed mental health counselor who works in both higher education and private practice. She assists clients with career exploration and change, vocational assessment, and workplace challenges, paying particular attention to the intersection of career and personal wellness. Adia possesses a bachelor's degree in literature from Harvard University and a master's degree in mental health counseling from Fordham University.

Printed in Great Britain
by Amazon

65530904R00201